Enrico Michelini

The Role of Sport in Health-Related Promotion of Physical Activity

The Perspective of the Health System

Springer VS

Enrico Michelini
Dortmund, Germany

Dissertation Eberhard Karls Universität Tübingen, Germany, 2013

ISBN 978-3-658-08187-4 ISBN 978-3-658-08188-1 (eBook)
DOI 10.1007/978-3-658-08188-1

Library of Congress Control Number: 2014955156

Springer VS

Printed on acid-free paper

Springer VS is a brand of Springer Fachmedien Wiesbaden
Springer Fachmedien Wiesbaden is part of Springer Science+Business Media
(www.springer.com)

The Role of Sport in Health-Related Promotion of Physical Activity

Table of Contents

1. Introduction **13**

2. Literature Review **19**

2.1 The Acceptance of Sport in the Health System 20
2.1.1 Health and Sport in Systems Theory 21
2.1.2 Expansion of the Health System 23
2.1.3 Positive Acceptance of Sport as a Health-Medium 25
2.1.4 The Role of Sport within Health-Strategies 28

2.2 Summary of the Literature Review, Desiderata, Next Steps 33

3. Theoretical Framework **35**

3.1 Defining Health, Physical Activity, Sport and Their Relationship 35
3.1.1 Health 36
3.1.2 Physical Activity 38
3.1.3 Sport 39
3.1.4 Physical Exercise 41
3.1.5 Physical Inactivity 42
3.1.6 Fitness 43
3.1.7 'Double Ambiguity' in the Relationship between Physical Activity and Health 43

3.2 Preliminary Theoretical Choices 45
3.2.1 Constructivism as an Epistemological Position 46
3.2.2 Systems Theory as a Theoretical Framework 48
3.2.3 The Relationship between Theory and Empiricism 50

3.3 Health and Sport Systems 51
3.3.1 Function Systems in Systems Theory 51
3.3.2 Health and Sport as Function Systems 55
3.3.3 Characteristics of Function Systems 56
3.3.4 Functions of Health and Sport Systems 57
3.3.5 Binary Codes of Health and Sport Systems 59

3.3.6 Programmes of Health and Sport Systems 61
3.3.7 Organisations of Health and Sport Systems 63
3.3.8 Roles in Health and Sport Systems 66

3.4 Relationships between Sport and Health Systems 67
3.4.1 Relationships between Systems in the Systems Theory 67
3.4.2 Different Relationships between the Sport and the Health Systems 71
3.4.2.1 Qualification of Sport in the Health System's Communications 71
3.4.2.2 Disqualification of Sport in the Health System's Communication 75

3.5 Governance in the Promotion of Physical Activity 80
3.5.1 Governance in Systems Theory 80
3.5.2 Problems and Chances of Governance 83
3.5.3 Super-Experts as a Premise of Governance 86
3.5.3.1 The WHO as a Super-Expert in the Promotion of Physical Activity 87

3.6 Summary of the Theoretical Framework, First Results, Next Steps 91

4. Methodology 95

4.1 Comparison and Sampling 95
4.1.1 Objective and Logic of Comparison 97
4.1.2 Number of Case Studies 98
4.1.3 Framework and Sampling of the Case Studies 100

4.2 Choice of the Documents 103
4.2.1 Logic Behind the Choice of the Documents 103
4.2.2 List and Description of the Documents per Case Study 105
4.2.3 French Documents 106
4.2.4 German Documents 107
4.2.5 Italian Documents 108

4.3 Document Analysis 110
4.3.1 Mixed Methods 110
4.3.2 Integration of the Methods 112
4.3.3 Mixed Methods in Content Analysis 114
4.3.4 Quantitative Content Analysis 116
4.3.5 Strategies to Ensure the Rigour in Quantitative Content Analysis 118
4.3.6 Qualitative Content Analysis 118
4.3.7 Strategies to Ensure the Rigour in Qualitative Content Analysis 120
4.3.8 Step by Step Explanation of Content Analysis Proceedings 122

4.4 Test of the Design ... 125
4.4.1 The 'Global Strategy on Diet, Physical Activity and Health' ... 126
4.4.2 Analysis of the 'Global Strategy on Diet, Physical Activity and Health' ... 128

4.5 Summary of the Methodology and Next Steps ... 132

5. Empirical Analysis of the Case Studies ... 137

5.1 'What is the Recommended Dose of PA?' ... 138
5.1.1 Distribution of the Recording Units ... 140
5.1.2 Results per Population Segment ... 141
5.1.3 Results per Characteristic of PA ... 142
5.1.4 Reflection on the Results ... 143

5.2 'What Role Do the Sport Organisations Have?' ... 144
5.2.1 Distribution of the Recording Units ... 145
5.2.2 Results of the Analysis ... 146
5.2.3 Reflections on the Results ... 148

5.3 'For Which Reasons is Sport Delegitimised as a Medium of Health?' ... 149
5.3.1 Distribution of the Recording Units ... 150
5.3.2 Results of the Analysis ... 151
5.3.3 Reflection on the Results ... 153

5.4 'How Sound are the Key Concepts?' ... 154
5.4.1 Definitions and Uses of Key Concepts ... 155
5.4.2 Ambiguity Related to the Dose of PA ... 156
5.4.3 Reflections on the Results ... 160

5.5 Comparison of the Case Studies ... 161
5.5.1 Results of the analysis ... 162
5.5.2 Reflections on the Results ... 168

5.6 Summary of the Empirical Results and Discussion ... 170

6. Concluding Remarks ... 173

Bibliography ... 181

List of Figures

Figure 1 Dimensions of Health Assessed in the Retrieved Items 31
Figure 2 Codes of the Health System 60
Figure 3 Codes of the Sport System 61
Figure 4 Features of Sport and Health Systems 92
Figure 5 Number of Countries and Abstraction of the Comparison (Landman, 2002, p. 4) 99
Figure 6 Typologies of Welfare States in Capitalist Economies (Esping-Andersen, 1990) 100
Figure 7 Results of the Web Search 104
Figure 8 French Documents 107
Figure 9 German Documents 108
Figure 10 Italian Documents 109
Figure 11 'Priority-Sequence Model' from Morgan (1998, p. 368) 113
Figure 12 List of Key Words 117
Figure 13 Steps of the Content Analysis (Modified version of Mayring, 2003, p. 89) 123
Figure 14 Key Words in the Case Studies 137
Figure 15 Distribution of Recommendations on the Dose of PA 140
Figure 16 Sport System's Organisations and Roles 145
Figure 17 Distribution of Sentences on the Role of Sport Organisations 146
Figure 18 Distribution of Functions of the Sport System 147
Figure 19 Distribution of the Deligitimisation of Sport 150
Figure 20 Distribution of Imprecise Quantification of PA 158
Figure 21 Distribution of Recommendations on the Dose of PA in the Documents 163
Figure 22 Distribution of Functions of the Sport System in French Documents 164
Figure 23 Distribution of Functions of the Sport System in German Documents 165
Figure 24 Distribution of Functions of the Sport System in Italian Documents 165
Figure 25 Distribution of Deligitimisations of the Sport System in the Case Studies 166
Figure 26 Distribution of Ambiguous Quantification of Sport in the Case Studies 167
Figure 27 Distribution of the Term 'Everyday' in the Case Studies 168

Abbreviations[1]

APA	Adapted Physical Activity
CONI	Comitato Olimpico Italiano
CP	Comparative Politics
EB	Executive Board
GHG	Global Health Governance
HEPA	Health-Enhancing Physical Activity
HG	Health Governance
HIIT	High-Intensity Interval Training
HRQoL	Health-Related Quality of Life
LWS	Lateral World System
MSSD	Most Similar Systems Design
MDSD	Most Different Systems Design
NCDs	Noncommunicable Chronic Diseases
NOC	National Olympic Committee
PA	Physical Activity
PI	Physical Inactivity
PNPAPS	Plan National de Prévention par l'Activité Physique ou Sportive
PNNS	Programme National Nutrition Santé
PSA	Physical and Sport Activity
PSN	Piano Sanitario Nazionale
SAQA	Summative Approach to Quantitative Analysis
SDPA	Global Strategy on Diet, Physical Activity and Health
UN	United Nations
WHA	World Health Assembly
WHO	World Health Organization

[1] During the dissertation, the above-mentioned words have been abbreviated only when their repetitions uselessly slow down the reading and do not add depth to the text.

1. Introduction

'Before starting an intense physical activity, it's a good idea to speak to your doctor'[2]
(Italian Ministry of Employment, Health and Social Policies, 2009, p. 5; translation EM)

One of the most pressing health challenges of the early 21st century is the promotion of physical activity (PA). Indubitably, the world's population is currently dealing with a decrease in PA. This reduction is provoked mostly by irreversible changes in ways of life connected to phenomena like urbanisation and an increase in technology (Astrand, 1994, p. 101). The lack of PA has proven to be one of the principal causes (Kohl et al., 2012, p. 294; WHO, 2006, p. 3) for the escalation of some noncommunicable chronic diseases (NCDs), which are leading causes of death for both men and women worldwide (Yach, Hawkes, Gould, & Hofman, 2004, p. 2616). For these reasons, the promotion of PA today is a priority for the health system, governments and other organisations (Biddle & Mutrie, 2008, p. 3). In particular, the health system has again started to participate in the promotion of PA after a period in which it has focused on other health issues and delegated this aim to the sport system. Since the end of the 20th century, the health system has gained a leading position in the promotion of PA and also emerged with a widely accepted coordinative position in this field. Particularly in the area of PA promotion, cooperation is considered by the health system itself as fundamental for the successful promotion of PA.

Sport alone does not seem to be the right solution to this problem. Indeed, the sport system is unable to combat sedentariness just by expanding the participation in sport activities and incapable of specifically involving those population segments which are more touched by NCDs in sport. However, sport active people logically do a greater amount of movement than sedentary people. Also, they generally display a lower prevalence in unhealthy behaviours that may interfere with sport performances (Diehl, Thiel, Zipfel, Mayer, & Schneider,

[2] Original quotation: '*Prima di intraprendere un'attività fisica impegnativa, è bene parlarne con il proprio medico*' (Italian Ministry of Employment, 2009, p. 5).

2012, p. 7; Lisha & Sussman, 2010, p. 7).[3] Furthermore, sport organisations are the point of reference for programmes of health promotion through physical activity.

For these reasons, among the many partners considered fundamental for the promotion of PA by the health system, the sport system still occupies theoretically a key position and sport activities and sport organisations are still constantly mentioned in the context of health promotion. However, the chances of cooperation between the health and the sport systems should not be taken for granted. Indeed, often the health system recommends generally to increase the level of PA which is broadly understood as 'any bodily movement produced by skeletal muscles that results in energy expenditure above resting level' (Bouchard & Shephard, 1994, p. 77). However, if compared to the ones from the 1990s, recent recommendations on physical activity progressively reduced the intensity and duration of PA (Blair, LaMonte, & Nichaman, 2004). In the modern the discussion on PA promotion, specific and concrete advice regards only PAs which are injury-proof and integrated into everyday life. These recommendations instead delegitimise the role of sport as a health-medium. In fact, sport is a subset of PA characterised for being recreational, governed by rules and orientated towards performance (modified definition of Heinemann, 2007, 56).[4] It is, at least in its traditional-competitive forms, not commensurable with the recommendations of the health system.

In other words, even if the health system shows the will to involve the sport system, the characteristics of PA that the health system advises the population to engage in differ clearly from the activities offered by the sport system. For example, the recommendation of 'at least 30 minutes of regular, moderate-intensity physical activity on most days' (WHO, 2004, 4) has become a kind of standard contained in many strategies for the promotion of PA. Of course, while engaging in sport does often require organisations and programmes of the sport organisations, engaging in brisk walking does not.

Against this background, the main research question assessed in this dissertation is: 'What role does sport play in the health-related promotion of PA?' At the side of this central question, the topic of health system's perspective on sport as a health-medium raises further interesting queries like: How healthy is traditional competitive sport considered by the health system? What about intensive PA? How should people combine sport and moderate PA? Which PAs

---

[3] Instead, the general idea that sport serves as a protective factor against involvement in deviant activities is still debated (Begg, Langley, Moffitt, & Marshall, 1996; Diehl, Thiel, Zipfel, Mayer, Litaker, et al., 2012; Eitle, Turner, & Eitle, 2003; Schafer, 1969).

[4] In the following discussion 'sport' is to be understood in its traditional-competitive form and does not comprehend broader forms of PA and exercise.

should people carry out in sport organisations for the best health-outcomes? How appropriate is the expertise of professionals in sport to counsel people about healthy PA?

To assess these questions, this dissertation analyses a selection of national[5] health-strategies[6] for the promotion of PA issued by the health ministries of Germany, Italy, and France. The chosen documents are only representative of the health system's point of view. This perspective is particularly interesting due to the prominent position of the health system in the promotion of PA and because of an on-going paradigmatic change of logic within the health system: it no longer follows a code based on the distinction between 'health/illness', but much more a code based on the distinction between 'hindering/promoting health' (Bauch, 1996). This change is deeply connected with the augmented interest of the health system for the promotion of PA and is particularly important for understanding the growth of the health system's social functions and responsibilities. The health ministries have been chosen as particularly relevant organisations of the health system at national level and for their direct connection with the World Health Organization (WHO) on an international level. This topic is particularly relevant because the tendency towards sedentariness and the (related) costs for medical care have both pejorative trajectories (Breedveld et al., 2003; Department for Culture & Strategy Unit, 2002; Powell & Blair, 1994; Weiss, 2000; Zheng, Ehrlich, & Amin, 2010). In fact, the problem of physical inactivity affects an increasingly large part of the global population, is common in developed countries, and is a growing problem in developing countries. The need for further research is underlined both within academia (particularly in the health sciences) and also in politics. In particular, the scientific community is already highly active in different areas, for example in seeking to understand which strategies are successful (best practice), how behavioural changes happen and which PAs lead to the healthiest outcomes. However, much less has been written about the cooperation between systems in the promotion of PA. This research could reveal important information useful for a deeper understanding of both the theoretical and the practical aspects of the problem.

Nevertheless, this dissertation has an explorative purpose and follows the guidelines and aims of classical sociological research (M. Weber, 1978). The sociological view implies that this research does not focus on the relationship between causes and effects nor does it aim to furnish advice or prescriptions for

---

[5] The regional level has been considered less relevant for the analysis because of the hierarchical organisation of national health systems and the direct communications between the World Health Organization and national health ministries.

[6] 'Health-strategy' is defined as every document published by a health organisation, which entails either a general or detailed plan of action for the promotion of health.

models of efficient cooperation between the sport and health systems. For instance, the discussion will not judge, nor will it speculate on the phenomenon outside of its social boundaries (Bette, Kühnle, & Thiel, 2012, p. 25).[7] Instead, it aims to observe a social phenomenon under the surface, to put in question its social acceptance and to rethink it in the light of a different theoretical perspective (Bette & Schimank, 2006, p. 20). To meet this aim, the sociological analysis of this dissertation relies on a constructivist paradigm. Along with sociology, theories borrowed from political and sport sciences will also play an important role in this doctoral thesis. In fact, this inquiry has been carried out in an interdisciplinary situation and has been influenced by different scientific fields.[8] For these reasons the dissertation is in its core a sociological analysis but relies with regards to some aspects upon different disciplinary bases. These different perspectives will be integrated through the use of a unitary theoretical perspective and a common language based on Luhmann's systems theory. A thorough review of the existing literature, the use of a sociological perspective and empirical research are expected to furnish important steps further in both the empirical and theoretical knowledge of the topic.

The following research is composed of six chapters:

- The first chapter introduces and outlines the central problem of the dissertation.
- The second chapter offers a review of the relevant literature on the topic, particularly within the sport and the health sciences. The desiderata identified in this chapter serve for further developing the research plan.
- The third chapter describes the theoretical framework. It starts with the definition of the central key terms of the doctoral thesis. After that it discusses the very fundamentals of systems theory and ends with the application of systems theory to the specific topic of this dissertation, particularly regarding the cooperation between systems.
- The fourth chapter contains theoretical reflections and practical explanations regarding the rationale for the sampling of documents analysed and the methodology of the empirical analysis. It also entails the test of the empirical instruments through the pilot document analysis on the WHO's 'Global Strategy on Diet, Physical Activity and Health' (2004).

[7] Of course, absolute objectivity is an ideal rather than a reality (Macionis, 2012, p. 32). For this reason, the readers may even consider the back ground of sport sociology of the author when interpreting the conclusions of this research. However, the best has been done for not letting conscious or unconscious biases distort the findings and for keeping a professional distance from the results.

[8] This is due both to (1) the background of the PhD dissertation which has been issued under a Cotutelle between Italy and Germany and (2) to the influence of the graduate school 'International and Comparative Research on Education and Education Policy in the Welfare State' being shaped particularly by the perspectives of political and education sciences.

- The fifth chapter assesses four queries regarding the role of sport in the health system's communication through the analysis of 15 health-strategies for the promotion of PA issued by the health ministries of France, Germany and Italy. The results of these analyses have been than compared between the case studies and interpreted in the perspective of systems theory.
- The dissertation's conclusions contain some reflections on the possible further developments of the inquiry and on the relevance of its results.

A final observation must be made here regarding the style of this doctoral thesis. It is well known that '[w]hen academics write about sports, they are capable of accomplishing the impossible: sucking all the pleasure and fun from the spectacle' (Foer, 2006, p. 86). This dissertation does not constitute an exception. However, the style of the following sections aims to make the contents palpable for non-expert readers and to lead them through the complexity of the discussion. For this reason, each chapter ends with a brief summary of the stand of the discussion, the definitions of the basic terms are repeated at the crucial points and the theoretical terms have been simplified.[9] This final action has been carried out very carefully, in order not to lose the precision and advantage given by the use of systems theory as a theoretical framework. From these efforts, the author hopes to have succeeded in composing an 'enjoyable' contribution on this socially relevant topic for the few people who will read the manuscript. Instead, 'if I succeed in boring you, believe me I didn't want to' (Manzoni, 1985, p. 746; translation EM).

[9] The complexity of Luhmann's systems theory especially regarding its semantic and abstraction, has been widely recognised and discussed among system theorists (for example Bette, 1999, pp. 75-84; Luhmann, 1982a, p. XIII; 1990c, p. 11; Willke, 2006b, pp. 12-14).

2. Literature Review

'[L]ike dwarves perched on the shoulders of giants'[10]
(Bernard of Chartres, Unknown; translated in Salisbury, 1955, p. 167)

For Hart (1999, p. 13), a classical literature review is '[t]he selection of available documents [...] on the topic, which contain information, ideas, data and evidence written from a particular standpoint to fulfil certain aims or express certain views on the nature of the topic and how it is to be investigated, and the effective evaluation of these documents in relation to the research being proposed.'

In general, the literature regarding the healthy benefits of sport on health has an extremely voluminous and old tradition (Waddington, Malcolm, & Green, 1997, p. 165)[11] and it is, at the same time, often contradictory (S. Becker, 2011, p. 31; Knoll, 1997, p. 24). Furthermore, the general discussion on this subject is highly fragmented and entails many different perspectives (S. Becker, 2011, p. 23). This does not constitute a problem *per se*, but the few attempts to organise these already voluminous theoretical and empirical discourses in a unique research programme are very partial and unstructured.

For overcoming these issues, the present chapter identifies as a first step the closest studies to the topic examined. Starting from this basis, the literature review will focus on different sub-topics which are necessary to understand and deepen the existing research on the role of sport in health-related promotion of PA. The entire discussion is based mostly on the perspectives of the health and the sport sciences. These are in turn the backgrounds of health-related communications containing PA as a health-medium that will be examined in the empirical analysis. Finally, the section critically places the dissertation in a wider academic context and analyses desiderata and weaknesses in the research.

[10] Original quotation: *'[N]anos, gigantum humeris insidentes'* (Bernard of Chartres, Unknown).
[11] In fact, the first written attempts to establish a connection between health and sport date back to the ancient Greek and Roman empires (Cachay & Thiel, 2000, pp. 65-66). Also during the Middle Ages and the Renaissance, PA was investigated and recommended as an integrative part of medicinal-orientated therapies (Cachay & Thiel, 2000, p. 66).

2.1 The Acceptance of Sport in the Health System

This section analyses the sociological literature regarding the acceptance of sport in health-related communications for the promotion of physical activity. This has been the first logical step for composing the present literature review. By giving a narrow focus to the specific research question of this dissertation, a lack of measuring sticks within the sociologies of sport and of health and illness has been detected. With the exception of few contributions produced by the author himself (Michelini, 2011; Michelini & Thiel, 2013), accurate research has shown that analyses focussed on the role of sport in health-related communication for the promotion of physical activity have never before been performed on either theoretical or empirical levels.

In fact, this specific topic has been repeatedly, but marginally, assessed only by Thiel and Cachay (1999a, 1999b, 2000; 2004). In these contributes they focused mostly on the opportunities available to sport students within health organizations in Germany.[12] For example, they acknowledged (Cachay & Thiel, 1999b, pp. 152-153): on the one hand, the progressive increase of diploma study courses in the sport science orientated toward the professional field of health; on the other hand, the limited chances for sport scientists to establish a stable professional position within health system's organisations. The problematic inclusion of sport students in the health system from the middle of the 1990s has been put by the two authors in relation with: struggles between different logics of the health system and a turn in the expectations of the political discussion (Cachay & Thiel, 1999b, p. 153; Thiel & Cachay, 2004, p. 115).

For explaining this phenomenon, Cachay and Thiel (1999b) acknowledge a firm orientation to illness in the take-off of this system, which needed to be modified in the second half of the 20th century as a reaction to internal and external critics. The criticisms developed within the health system regards (Cachay & Thiel, 1999b, pp. 150-151): the excessive reductionism of considering bodies as an ensemble of separated segments, the rising of subjects like aetiology and epidemiology within the health system, the change within the illness panorama and the augmenting interest towards the origin and maintenance of health. Instead the external critics came particularly from the economic and political systems which started to put in question the costs and the sustainability

[12] The topic of the acceptance of sport professionals in the education system has been the subject of some inquiries of the same authors (Cachay & Kastrup, 2006; Cachay, Thiel, & Kastrup, 2010). In this context, physical education teachers are formally fully integrated in schools but are still socially less valuated than the teachers of other subjects. For this reason they face the danger of a reduction of hours dedicated to the subject or of being substituted by other professional which, even if less trained, could be considered enough skilled for teaching physical education (Cachay & Kastrup, 2006, pp. 169-170).

of a model orientated mainly towards curative interventions. In turn, these positions developed in the demand for preventive and health orientated programme by the side of the health system (Cachay & Thiel, 1999b, pp. 151-152).

These internal and external critics rely at the basis of the change of the logic of the health system from a health/illness orientated code to a logic turned toward promoting/hindering health acknowledged by Bauch (1996, p. 111; 2004, p. 66). This change of logic permitted the expansion of the health system's functions to health-orientated programmes and determined the extension of the health system's tasks on PA promotion. However, the results of this programmes are mostly still evaluated by the health system through the illness-orientated logic (Bauch, 1996, p. 130). Because medicine still occupies the core position within the health system, there is a limited acceptance of programmes which are not evaluable with the logic 'health/illness', like those of health promotion and of sport.

The research programme presented above constitutes an already developed theoretical framework and in general a good starting point for the present research. However, this theoretical basis needs to be further developed for the inquiry at the hand. Indeed, these analyses are limited to the German situation and do not focus on the communication of the health and the sport system at the theoretical or the empirical levels.

2.1.1 *Health and Sport in Systems Theory*

The theoretical framework plays a key role in the present sociological analysis. The literature which lies at the basis of the model described above and the extensions used for the complete development of the theoretical framework of this doctoral thesis has been commented in the following.

Luhmann is considered to be 'Germany's most prominent and controversial social theorist' (Luhmann, 1995b, p. X) and his modern systems theory has 'emerged as one of the most widely discussed theories of society in a number of academic communities' (Albert, 2004, p. 22). During his lifetime, Luhmann was extremely productive and innovative, with a publication list of more than 70 books and almost 400 articles regarding numerous subjects (S. Fuchs, 1999, p. 118).[13] In particular, this dissertation's theoretical framework is based upon some Luhmann's original (Luhmann, 1970, 1971, 1975, 1981a, 1981b, 1983a, 1983b,

[13] Famous in this regard, is an anecdote about the beginning of his academic career as sociologist at the University of Bielefeld, during which, upon being asked about his research agenda, he answered that his project was to develop a theory of society, which would take him thirty years and would not cost anything (D. Lee, 2000, p. 320).

1984, 1985a, 1985b, 1986, 1990a, 1990d, 1994a, 1994b, 1997a, 1999, 2001, 2002a, 2006, 2008b, 2009) and translated (Luhmann, 1977, 1982a, 1982b, 1987, 1988, 1990b, 1990c, 1992, 1993, 1995a, 1995b, 1995d, 1997b, 2002b, 2003, 2008a) works. In addition, introductive literature on systems theory (for example Baraldi, Corsi, & Esposito, 1997a; Berghaus, 2004; Kneer & Nassehi, 1994; Krause, 2005; Luhmann, 2008b; Moeller, 2006; Reese-Schäfer, 1992; Willke, 2001b, 2005, 2006b) has been extensively used.

Because these are so comprehensive, the dissertation's theoretical discussion is based almost only on the original work of Niklas Luhmann. However, some extensions of his theories by other authors have been necessarily integrated for completing the theoretical framework. In fact, Luhmann's works do not cover two central topics of this doctoral thesis.

Firstly, Luhmann did not describe in depth the evolution of the sport and the health systems. In particular, the development of the sport system has been completely overlooked by Luhmann. This gap has been covered by the work of some other systems theorists. In particular, the differentiation of the sport system has been investigated by Cachay (1988); Cachay and Thiel (2000); Heinemann (2007); Schimank (1988); Stichweh (1990). Instead, the evolution of the health system has been marginally investigated by Luhmann in three scripts (1983a, 1983b, 1990d). This explanation has been integrated with the works of Cachay (1988), Bauch (1996, 1997, 2000, 2004) and Pelikan (2007; 1999; 2001).

Secondly, within his work on systems theory, Luhmann has been sceptical about the chances of steering systems, has left a gap regarding the theoretical functioning of cooperation between function systems (Krause, 2005, p. 65), has given no solid theoretical basis for the analysis of governance mechanisms (Wiesenthal, 2006, p. 68) and has even been accused of being imprecise in his reasoning regarding over mentioned topics (Krause, 2005, pp. 68-70). However, the consequences of the autopoietic turn regarding the relationships between systems have been often overestimated. Luhmann's concepts of integration and structural coupling (Luhmann, 1990a, 1994b, 2008b) instead have had an underestimated explanative power. In fact, these two concepts have been used as a theoretical basis sufficient to cover almost all the argumentations related to the topic of a system's interaction.

Instead, in order to theoretically explain governance[14] in the systems theory, the extension of Helmut Willke (1990, 1994, 2001a, 2001b, 2005, 2006a, 2007a, 2007b) has been necessary to cover the theoretical gap left by Luhmann. As an exception the topic of 'governance' has been theoretically assessed not only by the literature on systems theory, but also by general literature (Bevir, 2009;

[14] In this dissertation, governance is defined as: 'the activity of coordinating communications in order to achieve collective goals through collaboration' (Willke, 2007b, p. 10).

Hagen, 2000; Kjær, 2004; Lange, 2004; Offe, 2009; Rosenau, 1998; Wiesenthal, 2006) and particularly by the streams of actor-centred institutionalism (Mayntz, 2003; Mayntz, Rosewitz, Schimank, & Stichweh, 1988; Mayntz & Scharpf, 1995; Mayntz & Streeck, 2003; Scharpf, 2000; Schimank, 2000) and of multi-level governance (Benz, 2007; Benz & Eberlein, 1999; Benz, Lütz, Schimank, & Simonis, 2007). Beyond the aforementioned concepts of governance and structural coupling, frameworks for the description of social networks have also been recently adapted to systems theory for clarifying the functioning of social interactions. Even if the topic of social networks has been only superficially assessed by Luhmann (1995c), today the literature regarding this topic in the systems theory is quite abundant (Bommes & Tacke, 2006; Borggrefe, 2013; P. Fuchs, 1997; Fuhse, 2005, 2009; Tacke, 2000). These concepts have been used for some theoretical reflection on the interpretation of the empirical data.

In this way, the present dissertation not only extensively uses both the tools furnished by classical systems theory and by new extensions for the analysis of interaction between systems. Also desiderata, explanatory limits and possible extensions of the existing theoretical models will be considered.

2.1.2 Expansion of the Health System

The struggles between different logics and the expansion of the health system play key roles in determining the inclusion of sport as a medium of health. This topic has been widely explored in the sociology of health and illness. The discourse on the definition of health plays a relevant role for following this development, because it furnishes important information about the evolution of and discussion within this system (Baier, 1970). In particular the discussions concerning the meaning of 'health', (Göckenjahn, 1991; Hurrelmann, 2006; Jadad & O'Grady, 2008; Thiel, Seiberth, & Mayer, 2013; Üstün & Jakob, 2005; WHO, 1946) play a key role for both the theoretical and empirical analysis of this dissertation.

Within this discipline, various terms such as 'healthism' (Crawford, 1980; Rose, 1999; Skrabanek, 1994) and 'medicalization' (Conrad, 1992; Conrad & Schneider, 1980; Zola, 1991) emerged to describe this social phenomenon. Indicatively, both have a pejorative meaning: 'healthism' is an ideological construct concerning health and medicine, which places the problem of health and disease at the level of the individual (Crawford, 1980), or refers to governments imposing norms for a 'healthy lifestyle' through the use of propaganda and coercion (Skrabanek, 1994); 'medicalization' 'consists of defining a problem in medical terms, using medical language to describe a problem, adopting a medical framework to understand a problem, or using a medical intervention to “treat” it’ (Conrad, 1992, p. 211), as well as the process through which medical supervision dominates everyday life (Zola, 1983).

Skolbekken (2008) acknowledges a solid link between medicalization and the adoption by the health system of the risk factor model. In social-epidemiological research, the connections between individual, environmental and social factors and health consequences is called the Risk Factor Model (Hurrelmann, 2006, p. 126). In this model, risk factors are variables related to an increased or decreased risk of diseases and determinants are the variables associated with this fluctuation. In turn, these determine the statistical chance of a person becoming ill. Risk factors are related, and not causal to, illnesses. Indeed, this model only calculates a person’s exposure to risks over a certain timespan. If there are statistically relevant pathological differences between persons exposed to risk factors and those who are not exposed, then it is possible to speak about a risk factor (Pflanz, 1973, p. 13). This switched the health system’s interests to creating strategies which prevent illnesses and/or promote health. Medicalization relies in turn at the basis of the exponential growth of the health system since the beginning of the 20th century.

Also, some system theorists like Luhmann (1983a, 1983b, 1990d), Bauch (1996, 1997, 2000, 2004) and Pelikan (2007; 1999; 2001) have dedicated scripts to the expansion of the health system by means of a change of its logic. Indeed, by reviewing the literature, it can be stated that principally three different binary codes have been proposed. In order to understand which code is the most suited for this research, the core characteristic of each one will be summarised in the following paragraphs.

In his three papers on health, Luhmann assumes the emergence of a specific health related function system in modern societies, with ill/healthy as a binary code (Luhmann, 1990d, p. 186). This code orientates the system’s processes principally at the negative value ‘ill’, and not at the positive value ‘healthy’ (Luhmann, 1990d, pp. 187-188).

Bauch and Pelikan criticise the most that Luhmann, in this way, is not taking into account all the operations of the health system, considering cure and healing as the health system’s only operation. For example, Bauch (2004, p. 61) criticises Luhmann for not bearing more modern developments in the health system in mind and criticises Luhmann’s imprecision. Indeed, on the one hand, he refers only to the operation of illnesses’ healing, and, on the other hand, observes that the health system includes itself in many of society’s problems by medicalising them. Pelikan also criticises Luhmann’s imprecision for not distinguishing between ‘treatment of disease’, ‘treatment of ill person’ and ‘medicine’ (Pelikan, 2007, p. 88).

Hence, Pelikan (2007, p. 88) argues that for a certain period, the health system limited its operations to the management of illness and that in this time it was orientated toward the binary code presence/absence of illness and not the code health/illness. Instead, Pelikan (2007, p. 89) argues that in modern times the health system operates by means of two different binary codes:

- presence/absence of illness for ill physical health; and
- sub-optimal/optimal health for positive physical health.

In Bauch's opinion, the focus of the health system in modern societies has switched from infectious diseases to chronic diseases.[15] This phenomenon implies the development of new operations, which cannot be logically explained with Luhmann's code of health/illness (Bauch, 1996, p. 24). This is particularly evident in the case of health promotion, an operation which does not refer to illness and whose communications become the principal operation. For this reason, Bauch assumes that Luhmann's code is today only representative of a specific part of the operations of the health system (Bauch, 2004, p. 63). He proposes a new and wider binary code (Bauch, 1996, 1997, 2004), which is more appropriate to describe the new operations of the modern health system: promoting/hindering health (Bauch, 2004, p. 66).[16] Moreover, Bauch assumes that these two codes are concurrent. This happens because they tend towards exclusivity and because their logic is hard to join: for example, medicine is case-orientated and individualist, while illness prevention is population-orientated and generalist (Bauch, 2004, p. 75). The point of conjunction of these three authors is the common opinion about the expansion of the health system to new areas that were before considered external to health. Their discussions also involve the topic of the inclusion of prevention and health promotion as new programmes of the health system. In this way, the subject of the promotion of PA as a medium of health has been also superficially assessed by Pelikan (2007, 2009). However, an extensive exploration of the topic of the inclusion of sport as a health-medium by the health system is far to be completed and has been instead only set out.

2.1.3 Positive Acceptance of Sport as a Health-Medium

For enquiring the role of sport as a medium of health in the communication of the health system, it is necessary to assess the historical and social context of this

[15] This is a relevant point of fracture between Luhmann's and Bauch's discussions on health system, which otherwise could be seen as commensurable.

[16] In his early works, Bauch (1996, pp. 80-97) speaks in this regard to this code as a societal 'super-code' for the whole of society (*Gesellschaftlicher Leitcode*) and assumes a code orientated towards the code 'promoting/hindering life' (1996, p. 78). These positions appear in a mitigated form in later works of this author.

connection. Sport is traditionally associated with health at many different levels (Thiel et al., 2013, p. 105). For example, at the programme level this connection is detectable in sport organisations and, at least until the 1980s, also massively in programmes of health insurance politic, schools and health organisations. Also, the development of health-orientated programmes within of the sport system is a perfect example of this trend. For instance, health sports[17] have been developed as activities with the direct aim to promote, maintain or restore health (K Bös & W Brehm, 1998; Bös & Brehm, 2006; Brehm, 1998; Breuer & Wicker, 2008; A Woll & Bös, 2004). The background of these programmes is the idea that doing sport is healthy and that practicing sport for a lifetime protects from illnesses (Thiel et al., 2013, p. 105). The last section has argued that the evolution of the health system has been fundamental for understanding the roots of this social construct. For assessing the other side of the coin, this section reviews the standpoint of sport science, particularly of sports sociology, regarding the benefits of sport in a broad sense[18] as a medium of health.

As for many other function systems, systems theory has been applied to the analysis of the sport system. In contrast with Luhmann's reception in health sciences, systems theory has a great tradition in sport sociology (Schulze, 2005, p. 12). This had already began between the 1970s and 1980s with the works of Lüschen (1976), Rigauer (1982) and Bette (1984). On the basis of this tradition, this dissertation bases its analysis of the sport system on the descriptions furnished by Schimank (1988, 2008), Thiel (2000; 1997; 2009), Bette (1989, 1999), Stichweh (1990) and Heinemann (2003, 2007). In this context, many authors have focused on the central question of whether the sport system should be considered a function system (Bette, 1989; Cachay & Thiel, 2000; Schimank, 1988). Within the other topics discussed, the relationship between the health and the sport systems is one of the most recurrent subjects (Cachay, 1988; Cachay & Thiel, 2000; Heinemann, 2007; Schimank, 1988, 2005; Stichweh, 1990). Many of the aforementioned authors agree that the connection of the two systems is so strict that it even influences the evolution of their respective independent identities. However, their findings and arguments diverge greatly on other points; their research does not cover a common timespan and is particularly discordant in the discussions of recent developments. For these reasons the theoretical framework

[17] Thiel et al. (2013, p. 105) acknowledge the differentiation of 4 different typologies of health sports: health promotion through sport, prevention of illness through sport, therapy through sport and rehabilitation through sport.

[18] The extensive and differentiated definition of the terms related to PA and sport based on scientific literature (Bouchard & Shephard, 1994; Caspersen, Powell, & Christenson, 1985; Güldenpfennig, 2004; Haag & Haag, 2003; Heinemann, 1986; Pietilä, Hentinen, & Myhrman, 1995; Stichweh, 1990; Waddington et al., 1997) is contained in the chapter 'Defining Health, Physical Activity, Sport and Their Relationship.'

of this dissertation reviews and updates this discussion and the empirical data extend it, particularly with regards to the perspective of the health system on sport as a medium of health. With the exception of some critical voices (for example: S. Becker, 2011; Lüschen, Abel, Cockerham, & Kunz, 1993; Opper, Woll, & Minnebeck, 1993; Rütten, 1993), the majority of authors agree about the relevant role of sport in the area of health promotion and prevention of illnesses. For example, within this discussion, the sport system has even been identified as the 'health system' of modern society (Stichweh, 1990, p. 382) and the health system's need of sport for the enhancement of population's health as a validation of the sport system role in the society (Schimank, 2005, p. 23).

This tendency to positively evaluate the benefit of sport on health has also been detected in other humanistic disciplines[19] within the sport science. For example, in the area of sport psychology the topic of the beneficial influence of sport on psychological health has been intensively assessed since the beginning of the 1980s (R. Fuchs, 2003, p. 1).[20] This field has scientifically proven some of the benefits of sport on people's psychology. In many other cases reasonable presumption can simply be spoken about (R. Fuchs, 2003; Wagner, Singer, Woll, Tittlbach, & Bös, 2004). For example, it is scientifically proven that PA relieves symptoms of depression and anxiety and improves mood or, more generally, psychological well-being (Public Health Service. US office of the Surgeon General & President's Council on Physical Fitness and Sports, 1998, p. 8). Instead, its preventative effects on depression have not been scientifically proven (Public Health Service. US office of the Surgeon General & President's Council on Physical Fitness and Sports, 1998, p. 8).

Also in the politics of sport, the topic of health promotion through physical activity started to be studied in sport science around the 1990s (Rütten, Frahsa, & Abu-Omar, 2010, p. 18). This area fundamentally entails two different rationales: one is infrastructure/policy-orientated (Giles-Corti, Timperio, Bull, & Pikora, 2005; King et al., 1995; Kolb, 1995; Owen, Humpel, Leslie, Bauman, & Sallis, 2004; James F. Sallis, Bauman, & Pratt, 1998) and the other is activity orientated, for example through health-enhancing physical activity (Pate et al., 1995) and health sport (Bös & Brehm, 2006; Brehm, 1998). Alfred Rütten fo-

[19] The term 'humanistic disciplines' is used here to artificially distinguish the speculative-orientated area from the scientific-orientated area of sport science. This entails motor control and biomechanics, physiology, nutrition and diet, sport technology, anthropometry, kinanthropometry, computer science in sport and sport medicine.

[20] In sport psychology, many authors focused their entire research on the topic of the relationship between sport and health. For example, Wolfgang Schlicht (1994, 1995a, 1995b; 2007; 2003) and Reinhard Fuchs (1989, 1997, 2003, 2007, 2012) dedicated dozens of publications to the theme of sport and health. Other works on the subject relevant for this dissertation have been produced by: Abele, Brehm, and Gall (1991); Alfermann, Stoll, Wagner, and Wagner-Stoll (1995).

cused almost his entire scientific career on the topic of health and PA with circa 50 publications related to this topic. Of these publications, some also empirically compare national strategies for the promotion of PA (Abu-Omar, Rütten, & Lehtinen, 2004; Rütten, Abel, Kannas, von Lengerke, Lüschen, Diaz, Ståhl, et al., 2001; Rütten, Abel, Kannas, Von Lengerke, Lüschen, Diaz, Vinck, et al., 2001; Rütten & Abu-Omar, 2004a, 2004b; Rütten, Lüschen, et al., 2003; Rütten, Ziemainz, et al., 2003; Ståhl, Nutbeam, Kannas, & Rütten, 2002).[21] Also in sport politics, it is normally taken for granted that sport is fundamental for keeping people healthy.

Finally, many studies assess the role of physical education in public health (Brettschneider & Naul, 2004; Demetriou, 2012; Hardman, 2004, 2007, 2011; J.F. Sallis & McKenzie, 1991; J.F. Sallis et al., 2012; Trost & van der Mars, 2010; Trudeau, Laurencelle, Tremblay, Rajic, & Shephard, 1999; Waddington et al., 1997). The effect of PE upon lifestyle and upon health are often used as rationale against the reduction of PE (Trost & van der Mars, 2010). However, the objectives and effects of PE on health are still debated (Balz, 1992; Waddington et al., 1997).

In conclusion a review of the literature related to the research question in sport science demonstrates that the topic of the correlation between sport and health in different disciplines of sport science is widely assessed and mostly positively perceived. The critical, and especially sceptical, perspectives are exceptions in these disciplines.

2.1.4 The Role of Sport within Health-Strategies

The lack of research regarding the role of sport as a medium of health in the communication of the health system makes the literature review within sport science insufficient as basis for proceeding to the analysis of this dissertation. For this reason this section discusses further relevant background material and literature gathered by an analysis of the situation of the sociology of health and illness and the communications of the health system. This permits to understand which

[21] However, these studies are focused on environmental and political aspects of the topic and the theoretical framework plays a very small role. For this reason, Rütten's research programme is incommensurable with the present doctoral thesis. Other cross-country studies partially related to the doctoral thesis's topic have been performed by A. Woll, Tittlbach, Bös, and Opper (2003), by Sjöström, Oja, Hagströmer, Smith, and Bauman (2006) and by Daugbjerg et al. (2009). Also these are too different for being identified as predecessors of this dissertation.

scientific discussions rely on modern health-strategies[22] for the promotion of PA. In fact, by starting very close to the social phenomenon observed these sections piece together the logics contained in strategies for the promotion of PA. Starting from this point, an inquiry of the acceptance of sport as a health-medium within health sciences has been performed.

Since the end of the 20th century, health-strategies have become a tool for the prevention of noncommunicable chronic diseases, used by health ministries and other organisations in all developed countries. At the international level, the two strategies which have raised the most interest are the WHO's 'Global Strategy on Diet, Physical Activity and Health' (2004) and the European Commission's 'White Paper on Sport' (2007). At the national level, almost every developed country issued one or more strategies for the health-orientated promotion of PA. As an example, this dissertation entails a semi-standardised sampling of national strategies for the promotion of health-related PA issued by the French, German and Italian health ministries.[23]

The justification used by public administrations for the implementation of strategies for the health-orientated promotion of PA is based on cost–benefit analyses comparing the health-care expenses and costs for implementing strategies to enhance the population's level of PA (Breedveld et al., 2003; Department for Culture & Strategy Unit, 2002; Martin et al., 2001; Powell & Blair, 1994; Weiss, 2000; Zheng et al., 2010). Instead, the rationale of the recommendations on the dose of PA contained in these documents is founded on specific studies relating to the dose/response of PA (ACSM, 1981, 1990; ACSM & AHA, 2007; CDC & ACSM, 1995; Health and Human Services, 2008; WHO, 2010). These in turn rely on a mix of four different approaches:

- Public health for the evidence-based foundation of health monitoring and population-based interventions centred on the promotion of physical activity.
- Epidemiology for the identification of health risks and conditions of the health maintenance.
- Sport psychology and pedagogy for the promotion of an individual's stable patterns of action for the promotion of health and well-being
- (Sport) Medicine for the maximization of the physiological adaptation and minimalisation of health risks.

---

[22] In this dissertation the documents analysed are broadly identified as being health-strategies. 'Health-strategy' is defined as every document published by a health organisation, which entails either a general or detailed plan of action for the promotion of health.

[23] This catalogue of documents is representative for assessing the main topic, offers the chance to compare case studies and is suitable for answering the research question. The logic of this sampling is extensively assessed in the chapter 'choice of the documents.'

In fact, health-strategies must take into account not only the physiological effects of PA on health, but also issues related to the economical sustainability, the comprehensibility of the message and the population's attitude and acceptance. The perspective of the sport science on the function of sport as a medium of health has been already explored in the last section.

In the following paragraphs, the literature review focuses instead on the health system's perspective on the role of sport as a health-medium. For this aim, an exemplary examination of the existing reviews and meta-analyses on this topic within the health sciences has been performed. This search for literature was carried out in November 2012 in the database 'MedLine'. This bibliographical database has been chosen for its accessibility, its relevance and its extensive usage in biomedical research and for its compilation of articles from a wide range of disciplines within the life and biomedical sciences. The search was set by using the keywords: 'sport' AND 'health' AND 'physical activity' AND 'meta-analysis'. By using these key words and adding filters to exclude items without an available abstract, that were older than 10 years[24] or not written in English, 85 items were found. By excluding the items unrelated to the topic, this number has been reduced to 40. By analysing the dimensions of health assessed in these items the following distribution has been found:

[24] Previous relevant studies on this topic have been performed by: Berlin and Colditz (1990); Kujala, Kaprio, Sarna, and Koskenvuo (1998); Jeremy N. Morris and Crawford (1958); Paffenbarger Jr, Hyde, Wing, and Hsieh (1986); Paffenbarger and Hale (1975); Powell, Thompson, Caspersen, and Kendrick (1987). The sample represents a list of some of the most important studies on this topic. It is impossible to mention all the existing studies here.

Dimensions of Health	Articles
Physical	Ada, L., Dean, C. M., Vargas, J., & Ennis, S. (2010): Ashworth, N. L., Chad, K. E., Harrison, E. L., Reeder, B. A., & Marshall, S. C. (2005); Atlantis, E., Barnes, E. H., & Singh, M. A. (2006); Babatunde, O. O., Forsyth, J. J., & Gidlow, C. J. (2012); Busch, A. J., Barber, K. A., Overend, T. J., Peloso, P. M., & Schachter, C. L. (2007); Gourlan, M. J., Trouilloud, D. O., & Sarrazin, P. G. (2011); Hamer, M., & Chida, Y. (2008a); Hamer, M., & Chida, Y. (2008b); Harriss, D. J., Atkinson, G., Batterham, A., George, K., Cable, N. T., Reilly, T., . . . Renehan, A. G. (2009); Howe, T. E., Rochester, L., Neil, F., Skelton, D. A., & Ballinger, C. (2011); Howe, T. E., Shea, B., Dawson, L. J., Downie, F., Murray, A., Ross, C., . . . Creed, G. (2011); Ismail, I., Keating, S. E., Baker, M. K., & Johnson, N. A. (2012); Kelley, G. A., Kelley, K. S., & Tran, Z. V. (2005); Lee, C. D., Folsom, A. R., & Blair, S. N. (2003); Leung, D. P., Chan, C. K., Tsang, H. W., Tsang, W. W., & Jones, A. Y. (2011); Loew, L., Brosseau, L., Wells, G. A., Tugwell, P., Kenny, G. P., Reid, R., . . . Coyle, D. (2012); Martyn-St James, M., & Carroll, S. (2008); Marzolini, S., Oh, P. I., & Brooks, D. (2012); Pang, M. Y., Eng, J. J., Dawson, A. S., & Gylfadottir, S. (2006); Polidoulis, I., Beyene, J., & Cheung, A. M. (2012); Rand, D., Miller, W. C., Yiu, J., & Eng, J. J. (2011); Sadoghi, P., von Keudell, A., & Vavken, P. (2012); Saunders, D. H., Greig, C. A., Mead, G. E., & Young, A. (2009); Sherrington, C., Tiedemann, A., Fairhall, N., Close, J. C., & Lord, S. R. (2011); Snook, E. M., & Motl, R. W. (2009); Strasser, B., Siebert, U., & Schobersberger, W. (2010); Pang, M. Y., Eng, J. J., Dawson, A. S., & Gylfadottir, S. (2006); Polidoulis, I., Beyene, J., & Cheung, A. M. (2012); Rand, D., Miller, W. C., Yiu, J., & Eng, J. J. (2011); Sadoghi, P., von Keudell, A., & Vavken, P. (2012); Saunders, D. H., Greig, C. A., Mead, G. E., & Young, A. (2009); Sherrington, C., Tiedemann, A., Fairhall, N., Close, J. C., & Lord, S. R. (2011); Snook, E. M., & Motl, R. W. (2009); Strasser, B., Siebert, U., & Schobersberger, W. (2010); Minns Lowe, C. J., Barker, K. L., Dewey, M. E., & Sackley, C. M. (2009); Moseley, A. M., Stark, A., Cameron, I. D., & Pollock, A. (2005); Murphy, M. H., Nevill, A. M., Murtagh, E. M., & Holder, R. L. (2007); Strasser, B., Siebert, U., & Schobersberger, W. (2010); Zainuldin, R., Mackey, M. G., & Alison, J. A. (2011); Zheng, H., Orsini, N., Amin, J., Wolk, A., Nguyen, V. T., & Ehrlich, F. (2009)
Social, Psychological and Physical	Craft, L. L., Vaniterson, E. H., Helenowski, I. B., Rademaker, A. W., & Courneya, K. S. (2012); Daley, A., Jolly, K., & MacArthur, C. (2009); Mead, G. E., Morley, W., Campbell, P., Greig, C. A., McMurdo, M., & Lawlor, D. A. (2009); Netz, Y., Wu, M. J., Becker, B. J., & Tenenbaum, G. (2005); Wang, C., Bannuru, R., Ramel, J., Kupelnick, B., Scott, T., & Schmid, C. H. (2010)
Psychological	Andriolo, R. B., El Dib, R. P., & Ramos, L. R. (2005); Conn, V. S., Hafdahl, A. R., Porock, D. C., McDaniel, R., & Nielsen, P. J. (2006); Forbes, D., Forbes, S., Morgan, D. G., Markle-Reid, M., Wood, J., & Culum, I. (2008); Mishra, S. I., Scherer, R. W., Snyder, C., Geigle, P. M., Berlanstein, D. R., & Topaloglu, O. (2012); Mishra, S. I., Scherer, R. W., Snyder, C., Geigle, P. M., Berlanstein, D. R., & Topaloglu, O. (2012)

Figure 1 Dimensions of Health Assessed in the Retrieved Items

Of the 40 retrieved items: 31 studies only assess physical health and tend to involve very specific topics like the effect of a particular PA on illnesses; five only assess psychological health, specifically general psychological well-being[25] (three times) and depression (twice); and four studies involve a broader perspective on health by including socio-psychophysical aspects. None of these studies enquire into the influence of traditional-competitive sport on health. 'Sport' is instead mentioned as a sub-category of PA and often as a synonym of 'exercise'.[26] Furthermore, the four items (Andriolo et al., 2005; Conn et al., 2006; Forbes et al., 2008; Mishra et al., 2012b) also involving multiple dimensions of the relationship between PA and health involve very specific target groups: patients receiving cancer treatment (twice), people with dementia and adults with Down's syndrome. Three of these items (Conn et al., 2006; Forbes et al., 2008; Mishra et al., 2012b) involve the concept of 'quality of life' and of 'health-related quality of life' (HRQoL).[27] By further examining the scientific niche enquiring into the influence of PA on HRQoL, additional studies involving particular population segments (Abell, Hootman, Zack, Moriarty, & Helmick, 2005; Acree et al., 2006; Drewnowski & Evans, 2001; King et al., 2000; McAuley et al., 2006; Mishra et al., 2012a, 2012b; Painter, Krasnoff, Paul, & Ascher, 2003; Rejeski & Mihalko, 2001) and the population in general (Anokye, Trueman, Green, Pavey, & Taylor, 2012; Bize, Johnson, & Plotnikoff, 2007; Blacklock, Rhodes, & Brown, 2007; Brown et al., 2003; Brown et al., 2004; Klavestrand & Vingård, 2009 (Retracted); Rejeski, Brawley, & Shumaker, 1996; Vuillemin et al., 2005; Wendel-Vos, Schuit, Tijhuis, & Kromhout, 2004) have been found. Indeed, this scientific stream today produces the greatest quantity of efforts to assess the multidimensional effects of PA on health. However, the acceptance of these studies is still limited in the scientific community and they are highly influenced by their own strategy of questioning, because it focuses on the subjective perception of the individual or groups being studied.

This limited sample has been chosen to highlight the trend in research on the topic of the relationship between PA and health in health sciences:

- The research is highly fragmented and tends to explore very specific niche-topics.

[25] Well-being refers to 'people's emotional responses, domain satisfactions, and global judgments of life satisfaction' (Diener, Suh, Lucas, & Smith, 1999, p. 277).

[26] For Caspersen (1985, p. 126), 'exercise' is a subset of physical activity that is planned, structured, and repetitive and has as a final or an intermediate objective the improvement or maintenance of physical fitness'.

[27] The HRQoL is a concept which encompasses the overall quality of life that can affect physical or mental health, including health risks and conditions, functional status, social support and socioeconomic status (CDC, 2000, p. 6).

- The most attention and efforts are directed towards the physical dimension of health.
- If the effect of a specific form of PA on health is not involved, the characterisation of PA is very superficial.
- Traditional-competitive sport and team sport activities are not mentioned at all.
- The attempts to re-organise the existing knowledge in a broader theoretical framework are limited.

In conclusion, the health sciences' discussion on PA and sport as medium of health entails a high degree of ambiguity. In particular a fundamental vagueness of the basic terms, the over-specialisation and the exclusion of traditional sport have been detected. This is an initial result and implies a risk that this ambiguity also affects other discussions, like the ones on public health and on the role of sport as a health-medium.

2.2 Summary of the Literature Review, Desiderata, Next Steps

The topic of the relationship between physical activity and health is highly prevalent in different social dimensions: it is discussed within many scientific disciplines; it has been assessed in different policies from both the health and the political systems; and it is highly present in social discussions. However, these discussions are often characterised by scarce self-reflection, superficiality and ambiguity. On an abstract level, S. Becker (2011, pp. 31-41) acknowledges the general lack of theoretical models regarding the influence of sport on health with the exception of Antonovsky's salutogenetic model (1979, 1987, 1990, 1996, 1997), Elkeles and Mielck's model for explaining social and health inequalities (1993, 1997) and Bouchard and Shephard's model of the relationship between health and sport (Bouchard & Shephard, 1994; Bouchard, Shephard, & Stephens, 1994). Even literature providing solid scientific results is often limited to specific aspects of the topic and fails to situate itself in the broader scientific discussion.

This chapter reviewed in particular the literature of two different thematic areas, which play relevant roles in this dissertation, namely the relationship between sport, physical activity and health in the sport and in the health sciences. The main results of this analysis are resumed in the following:

- Within sport science, the topic of the correlation between physical activity, sport and health is mostly taken for granted and the topic of the progressive loss of relevance of sport as a medium of health in the area of health promotion is a blind spot within the discussion of sport science.

- Within the health sciences, the discussion on PA and sport as medium of health is highly developed and, at the same time, is unstructured, ambiguous and overlooks traditional sport as a medium of health.

Even at this point, the present dissertation enriches the scientific discourse regarding the promotion of health-related PA and performs a critical reflection on its status. The analysis of the scientific discussion on sport as a medium of health could surely be deepened and entail broader interesting issues. In particular, the ambiguity and fragmentation of the scientific discourse needs to be proven and acknowledged as a first step for its re-thinking and new systematisation. This would not only allow for a further step in the scientific discussion, but also could be an important task to prevent ambiguity in the scientific discourse from affecting the quality of the political and social discussion.

However, this research aims to cross the abstraction of to the scientific level and to analyse its concretisation in operative health-strategies. In fact, the change of health system's consideration of sport as a medium of health entails severe consequences, not only on an academic level but also on a social level and needs to be empirically analysed. In turn, an analysis of the rhetoric and argumentation contained in strategies for the promotion of PA regarding the role of sport as a medium of health could contribute to a critical self-reflection still lacking in the scientific literature.

To reach this aim, the dissertation firstly needs a theoretical framework as a structure that identifies and describes the major elements of the subject explored (Ennis, 1999, p. 129). In turn, this will permit the sharpening of the research focus, properly organise the research plan by meaning of precise research questions and, in a second period of time, to interpret and understand the results of the scientific research. This task will be assessed in the next chapter.

A theoretical framework also becomes necessary at this point for further developing the research plan. The main research question 'What role does sport play in the health-related promotion of PA?' is too complex to be assessed as a whole. To make it manageable, the following sub-question has been identified: 'Which central documents have been developed for the health-related promotion of physical activity?' In turn, this sub-question entails three further queries:

- Which organisations produce relevant communications on health-related promotion of PA?
- What logic relies at the basis of these organisations?
- Which are the relevant documents published by these health organisations?

These queries will be partly assessed in the theoretical framework through the use of primary and secondary literature and partly within the methodological chapter.

3. Theoretical Framework

'A theory of society; duration: 30 years; costs: none'[28]
(Luhmann, 1997a, p. 6; translation EM)

This chapter contains a detailed explanation of the entire theoretical model used to analyse the social phenomenon at hand. Its scope is to put forth a comprehensive theory that explains the function of communications between systems and that suits the particular case of the communication of the health system on the role of sport in health-related promotion of physical activity. Nonetheless, this allows in turn the theory-guided construction of instruments for concretising the research question, for choosing the methodological instruments and for interpreting the results of the empirical analysis. In particular, the health system's perspective on the role of sport as a health-medium will be discussed through a theoretical framework based on Luhmann's systems theory. The following sections address: the basis of the systems theory regarding the differentiation of function systems and their characteristics; the description of the sport and the health systems as function systems; the functioning of structural coupling and governance for the theoretical comprehension of the relationship and cooperation between the sport and health systems. Together, these sections constitute a framework, which has its strengths in the analysis of inter-systemic communications and will be used to analyse and interpret the communication of the health system regarding the role of sport in documents for the promotion of PA issued by the health ministries of France, Germany, and Italy.

3.1 Defining Health, Physical Activity, Sport and Their Relationship

By focusing on the role of sport in the health-related promotion of physical activity, definitions in general, and particularly those related to health, PA and sport, are relevant both for the theoretical discussions and for the empirical analysis of this sociological enquiry. Defining these terms is a hard task. In fact, 'health'

[28] Original quotation: '*Theorie der Gesellschaft; Laufzeit: 30 Jahre; Kosten: keine*' (Luhmann, 1997a, p. 6).

alone is a highly disputed concept (Hurrelmann, 2006, p. 117) and the use of terms related to PA is often ambiguous and imprecise within the scientific community as well as in social situations (Caspersen et al., 1985, p. 126).[29] For example, Caspersen (1985, p. 126) acknowledges that 'physical activity, exercise and physical fitness are terms that describe different concepts. However, they are often confused with one another, and the terms are sometimes used interchangeably'. Furthermore, the relationship between these notions is experiencing a turning point (Michelini & Thiel, 2013, p. 334). For these reasons, this section summarises the stand of the scientific discussion on these concepts and on their relationship to each other. This is essential to the scope of this thesis because it prevents ambiguity within the discourse from weakening the clarity of the sociological analysis and it sets boundaries for the empirical part of the dissertation based on content analysis. Given the complexity and vagueness of the current stand of this discussion, the attempt to sort the meanings attached to these terms and to understand their usage in the context of health-strategies is a highly ambitious task for this doctoral thesis.

3.1.1 Health

The word 'health' has Germanic origins and has been related to the concept of wholeness from its very beginnings (Oxford Dictionaries, 2012). In English, the concept of 'bad health' can apply to the subjective perspective (illness), objective perspective (disease) and societal perspective (sickness). There is no similar division for the concept of health (Siegrist, 2005, p. 32). However, defining 'health' is a difficult task because it is a multi-dimensional phenomenon and it has been investigated by many disciplines (Hurrelmann, 2006, p. 113).[30] Furthermore, health is a social construction that is constantly evolving and dependent on its temporal and cultural environment (Faltermaier, 2005; Thiel et al., 2013). For these reasons, many different definitions of health exist, but none is universally accepted (Waller, 2006, p. 9).

Göckenjahn (1991, pp. 15-18) classifies health's modern definitions[31] on the basis of their reference to the concepts of: delimitation, for example as the absence of illness; value, for example as 'state of complete physical, mental and

[29] Also interesting is that fact that Wikipedia's page for PA redirects the user to the page on physical exercise (Wikipedia, 2011) because of a disambiguation rule.
[30] In particular it has been discussed in the fields of medicine, psychology, sociology, and anthropology. The discussion is often fragmented within these disciplines and has had various turning points.
[31] Discipline-orientated definitions of health which do not connect the concepts of 'health' and 'illness' (Dubos, 1965; Alexa Franke, 1993; A Franke, 2006; Naidoo & Wills, 2003; V. Schneider, 1990; Seedhouse, 1986) have not been discussed here.

social well-being';[32] and functionality, for example as the capacity of fulfilling expected social functions.[33] Still, these definitions do not say when and from which perspective someone has to be classified as healthy or ill (Thiel et al., 2013, p. 108). To overcome this problem, this dissertation refers to three paradigms which have dominated the current discussion (Faltermaier, 2005):

- the biomedical disease model, which sees diseases as disorders of the organism that can be assessed by the classical medical practices of diagnosis and medical treatment;
- the bio-psychosocial disease model, which extends the component of health and illness over the physical components by adding social and psychological dimensions;
- and the model of salutogenesis,[34] which assesses the problem of human salutogenetic resources as a counterweight of pathogenic factors.

In the discussion of the meaning of health, a relevant role is occupied by the WHO's definition: 'Health is a state of complete physical, mental and social well-being and not merely the absence of disease or infirmity' (WHO, 1946, p. 1).[35] This definition has achieved a wide consensus and raised the broader animated discussions in the period following the Second World War (Hurrelmann, 2006, p. 116). It is characterised by (Hurrelmann, 2006, p. 117): the subjective perception of health; the ideal-utopian status of health; the multidimensionality of health; and the concepts of health and illness as poles between a continuum. Despite its success, this definition has been also criticised for (Hurrelmann, 2006, p. 118; Jadad & O'Grady, 2008, p. 1363; Üstün & Jakob, 2005): the subjective relativity of health; the unrealistic character of health as 'complete well-being'; the vagueness regarding the psychological and social dimensions of health; and the overlooking of the relationship between health and illness.[36] Even if the WHO demonstrated the desire to assess some of these critiques, its definition of health remained substantially unchanged. This makes this definition out-

[32] Diener et al. (1999, p. 277) consider subjective well-being as 'a broad category of phenomena that includes people's emotional responses, domain satisfactions, and global judgments of life satisfaction.'

[33] The work of the American sociologist Parsons (1989) on the concept of the 'sick role' played a fundamental role for this paradigm.

[34] The term *salutogenesis* has been coined by the American-Israeli sociologist Aaron Antonovsky (1979). The term is composed by the Latin word *salus* (health) and the Greek word *genesis* (origin). The term can be understood as the contrary of pathogenesis (Hurrelmann, 2006, p. 119).

[35] This definition is also the basis of WHO's Ottawa Charter (WHO, 1986). This document adds that health is 'seen as a resource for everyday life, not the objective of living' and that '[h]ealth is a positive concept emphasizing social and personal resources, as well as physical capacities' (WHO, 1986, p. 1). Nevertheless, the basic definition of health remains identical to the one of 1946 (WHO, p. 1).

[36] The dichotomous, bipolar, orthogonal and three-dimensional models of the relationship between health and illness assess exactly this desiderata (Thiel et al., 2013, pp. 111-115).

dated, at least for scientific purposes, because it doesn't take into account the most modern health theories. However, this definition remains a point of reference for the successive theories and definitions and the operational definition of health for the health system (Hurrelmann, 2006, p. 119). For these reasons it has been used in this dissertation to explain the health system's perspective on sport. In fact, the acknowledgment of the psychosocial dimensions[37] of health explains the health system's renewed interest in PA and sport.

3.1.2 Physical Activity

In this doctoral thesis, PA is defined as 'any bodily movement produced by skeletal muscles that results in energy expenditure above resting level' (Bouchard & Shephard, 1994, p. 77).[38] This wide definition suits the aim of this chapter, namely to bring order to the terms by categorising them and creating a rational schema. PA here is the basic set, which contains all the other concepts as if it were the largest in a set of Russian matryoshka dolls. In fact, this definition includes the whole range of possible human activities involving bodily movements like playing football, jogging, walking, cycling, dancing, gardening and house work (Cavill et al., 2006, p. 3).

In order to work analytically with such a scheme, it is necessary to further classify PA. Caspersen (1985, p. 126) suggests that one ought 'to segment physical activity on the basis of the identifiable portions of daily life during which the activity occurs' (Caspersen et al., 1985, p. 127). Through this distinction it is possible to differentiate the PA carried out, for example, while working or during leisure time. In this categorisation, leisure activities can be further categorised into 'occupational, sports, conditioning, household, or other activities' (Caspersen et al., 1985, p. 127). Other categories mentioned by Caspersen are ones which classify 'all physical activities into those that are of light, moderate, or heavy intensity; those that are wilful or compulsory; or those that are weekday or weekend activities' (Caspersen et al., 1985, p. 127).

These are all sound operational categorisations. However, this dissertation requires a more precise categorisation. Many authors (Ainsworth et al., 2000; Caspersen, Christenson, & Pollard, 1986; Dishman, Sallis, & Orenstein,

[37] In a later attempt, the WHO (1987) also added the spiritual and ecological dimensions, but these have never been permanently included in the definition.

[38] In the scientific literature, some authors (Cavill, Kahlmeier, & Racioppi, 2006, p. 2; Preece et al., 2009, p. 1; Stamatakis, 2006, p. 48; van Poppel, Chinapaw, Mokkink, van Mechelen, & Terwee, 2010, p. 567) confuse this quotation with the definition of PA by Caspersen at al. (1985, p. 126): 'any bodily movement produced by skeletal muscles'. This definition has been discarded as it is less specific.

1985; Evenson, Rosamond, Cai, Diez-Roux, & Brancati, 2002; Hagströmer, 2007; King, 2001) characterise PA through its mode, intensity, duration, frequency and continuity.[39] In this categorisation:

- *Mode* refers to the type of activity or to the circumstances under which the activity is performed.
- *Intensity* represents the energy expenditure (light, moderate, vigorous) while an activity is performed.[40]
- *Duration* is the measurement of time (normally given in hours or minutes) in which the activity is carried out.
- *Frequency* is the number of times (normally per week or month) in which the activity is executed.
- *Continuity* is the period of time during which the activity is performed.

This categorisation through mode, intensity, duration, frequency and continuity can be applied to the whole range of PAs (including sports) and permits their precise description and categorisation. For this reason it has been chosen for describing PA in the document analysis of this dissertation.

3.1.3 Sport

The etymology of the word 'sport',[41] short form of old French *desport*, indicates amusement and play (Haag & Haag, 2003, p. 472). The discussion on its definition has been historically carried out by philosophers (De Wachter, 1983; Guttmann, 1979; Kretchmar, 1994; Stygermeer, 1999; Suits, 2007) and sociolo-

[39] The names of these categories vary within each author but are very similar in their contents.

[40] Intensity needs to be further specified because it is less intuitive than the other categories. Energy expenditure can be measured through oxygen consumption. This also allows the calculation of energy expenditure consumption (kcal·min-1), expressed normally as multiple of resting metabolic rate (Hagströmer, 2007). To account for the differences in resting metabolic rates related to gender, age and body composition, the Metabolic Equivalent (MET) classification has been developed (Ainsworth et al., 1993; Ainsworth et al., 2000). Within this classification, light, moderate and vigorous PAs are calculated on the basis of the energy expenditure at the resting level, which has to be multiplied by 3 for moderate and by 6 for vigorous activities. When explained in even greater detail, PA is light if < 3 METs, moderate if between 3 and 6 METs and vigorous if > 6 METs (Ainsworth et al., 2000, p. 499). For example: a light activity is walking (2.0 mph, level, slow pace, firm surface), it increases the body's metabolism to 2.5 METs (Ainsworth et al., 2000, p. 500); a moderately-intense physical activity is raking the lawn, increasing the body's metabolism to 4.0 METs (Ainsworth et al., 2000, p. 500) by increasing the heart-beat and leaving the person feeling warm and slightly out of breath; vigorously-intense physical activities usually involve sports or exercise like running (8 METs by 5mph) or fast cycling (8 METs by 12-13, 9mph) (Ainsworth et al., 1993, pp. 74-79). They enable people to sweat and make them lose their breath.

[41] In this section, the word sport does not have quotation marks. Their excessive repetition would have slow down the reading and not add depth to the text.

gists (Bette, 1999; Cachay, 1988; Digel, 1995; Drexel, 2003; Güldenpfennig, 2004; Heinemann, 1998; Steinkamp, 1983) and is still highly animated.

In this dissertation, sport can (and will) be described from two different perspectives: as a social construct on the one hand (Heinemann, 1998, p. 53); on the other hand as a mode of PA. This section defines sport as a mode of PA with peculiar characteristics, which distinguish it from other forms of PAs. Even if 'sport is a highly ambiguous term having different meanings for various people' (Loy, 1968, p. 1), various authors agree, with slight differences, about the four fundamental characteristics of sport described in the following list (Heinemann, 2007, p. 56; Timpka & Lindqvist, 2001, p. 20):

1. It is a physical activity. This term has been defined above and needs no further explanation. Everything that concerns sport operations regards bodily PAs (Stichweh, 1990, p. 378).
2. It is performance-orientated.[42] For Stichweh (1990, p. 378), body-related operations in sport contexts are always connected to the skill of the hosting body.[43] Performances are the universal form of operationalisation of skills in sport (Stichweh, 1990, p. 378).[44]
3. It has its purpose in itself. This concept is often expressed in the literature with the term 'autotelic.' The operations of sport are disconnected from utilitarian aim and are therefore unproductive.[45]
4. It is governed by rules. For some authors (Güldenpfennig, 2004; Heinemann, 1986), rules are fundamental to sport because they form the distinction between play and sport. Sport rules can be formal (like specific rules of sport disciplines) or informal (like the concept of fair-play).

These represent *conditio sine qua non* to speak about sport. However, especially at the level of organisations through the phenomena of structural coupling, other systems like the economic or health systems influence sport and create cases in which one or more of these basic characteristics are respected. These borderline cases do not falsify the listed characteristics, but instead introduce one of the biggest impediments in the discourse on sport: The fact that sport has be-

---

[42] If referred to sport, the word 'performance' doesn't have the same meaning as it does for the operation of function systems. In fact, the performances of sport are not connected or connectable to the action of other systems (Stichweh, 1990, p. 379).

[43] Performance is also what distinguishes sport from games: while in sport, victories are connected with better skills, games are more influenced by chance.

[44] This concept is often substituted with the term 'competition.' While performance has a broader meaning, competition always involves an opponent. Performances in sport include, but are not limited to, competition against opponents. Better skills normally lead to a superior performance and consequentially to the opponents' defeat.

[45] For Stichweh, defining sport is not autotelic because the actions of sport consist in the communications on a specific topic, in this case performances of bodies, just as is the case when regarding other systems (Stichweh, 1990, p. 379).

come 'an ever present element of modern society' (McPherson, Curtis, & Loy, 1989, p. 2), but at the same time lacks precise boundaries in many social situations. For example, sport is sometimes used as a synonym for physical exercise or even for activities completely disconnected from sport, such as walking a dog. In particular, the word sport itself has been de-sportified (Bette, 1995; Cachay, 1990; Digel, 1990): it is currently often used in many contexts and with regards to many PAs which do not have the fundamental characteristics of sport.[46] Instead, whenever discussions of this doctoral thesis involve sport as an analytical sub-category of PA, the dissertation will attentively not transfer this ambiguity to the basis of the present sociological analysis. For this reason, whenever necessary, the discussion will be specified as referring to the broad usage of the term, or to the specific traditional-competitive meaning of sport.

3.1.4 Physical Exercise

For Caspersen (1985, p. 126), 'physical exercise' or just 'exercise' 'is a subset of physical activity that is planned, structured, and repetitive and has as a final or an intermediate objective the improvement or maintenance of physical fitness'. In greater detail, Haag and Haag (2003, p. 263) consider physical exercise to be the 'totality of all motor activities that are realized in motor learning, exercising (training) and sport competition'. They distinguish between exercise as a process and as a result: 'As a process, exercise is the repeated execution of predetermined movement sequences (exercising) with different levels of intensity; as a result, exercise is a part of a comprehensive motor performance or presentation' (Haag & Haag, 2003, p. 176).

It is important to clarify that '[p]hysical exercise is defined as exercise during leisure and not as, for example, during working' (Pietilä et al., 1995, p. 330) and that the purpose of exercise is the 'improvement or maintenance of one or more components of physical fitness' (Caspersen et al., 1985, p. 128). Interestingly, in 'Western countries (approx. since the 1970s) the term has been increasingly replaced by '"sport", which – despite a holistic meaning – bears the inherent danger of limiting the meaning of the term to high-performance sport and competition' (Haag & Haag, 2003, p. 264). The difference between sport and exercise is that '[...] if all sport involves physical exercise, it is not the case that all physical exercise involves sport, for what is usually considered a further nec-

[46] Generally people participate in sport actively or passively as spectators (Haag & Haag, 2003, p. 473). This dissertation refers only to active sport participation while spectators are not included in the discussion.

essary component of sport - the competitive element - is frequently more or less absent from many forms of physical exercise' (Waddington et al., 1997, p. 170).

3.1.5 *Physical Inactivity*

Physical inactivity, or lack of physical activity, can be roughly defined as the absence or insufficient occurrence of PA. Bergman & Norlander (2005, p. 796) define PI 'as the absence of voluntary exercise, low daily physical activity involved in hobbies, no physical activity involved in travel to and from work, or at work. In addition to those who are inactive, there are also those who engage in some, but not sufficient, physical activity'.[47] Although this concept seems to be relatively unproblematic, it is hard to quantify what is 'absent or insufficient PA'. The main reason for this difficulty is that in the greater part of this scientific discourse is strictly focussed on pathogenic outcomes (Bergman & Norlander, 2005, p. 796; Dishman, Washburn, & Heath, 2004; Haag & Haag, 2003, p. 364; Hagströmer, 2007, p. 2). For instance, together with other factors (such as smoking, inadequate diet and stress), physical inactivity has proven to be connected to the incidence of many chronic diseases, in particular those connected to the circulatory system, but also to some typologies of cancers, obesity, diabetes and osteoporosis (Haag & Haag, 2003, p. 364). In turn, the acceptance of the biopsychosocial disease model as well as the acknowledgment of the existence of salutogenetic resources are the theoretical basis for the implementation of PA as a medium of health in strategies based on the risk factor model (Michelini, 2011, p. 309). For these reasons, the problem to be solved when defining physical inactivity becomes: 'Under which dosage of PA do people endanger the maintenance of good health and the prevention of bad health?'

For Schoenborn (2004, p. 3) this is 'never engaging in any light, moderate, or vigorous leisure-time physical activity'. By referring to the Ainsworth's compendium, this is at least questionable because people without serious illnesses or other impediments perform at least light PA in their everyday life, both during work and leisure time. For their survey, Babey, Diamant, Brown, & Hastert (2005, p. 7) considered people as physically inactive who, dur-

[47] Strictly connected to PI is the concept of sedentary living (or lifestyle). Generally, '[p]ersons with no or irregular leisure-time activity' are defined as being sedentary (CDC, 1993). More precisely, these people carry out little or no moderate or vigorous activities in their daily lives and instead have for most of the time occupations which imply light energy expenditure like sitting, reading, watching television and working on the computer. Instead, active living (or an active lifestyle) is 'a way of life that integrates physical activity into daily routine' (Cavill et al., 2006, p. 3). Specifically, active living integrates at least half an hour of at least moderate PA into daily routines (Cavill et al., 2006, p. 3). Such a lifestyle is acknowledged as being protective of health.

ing the seven days preceding the survey, were involved in 'no vigorous activity (activity that made the respondent "sweat or breathe hard" for at least 20 minutes) and performed no light to moderate activity (such as walking or bicycling for at least 30 minutes).' Consequently physical inactivity indicates a lack of PA necessary for the maintenance of health and physical activity has to be at least moderate to enhance health (Cavill et al., 2006, p. 3) and this dissertation defines PI as: 'the absence or lack of moderate or vigorous bodily activity in everyday life of a subject'. For the WHO (2004, p. 4) this can be quantified with 'at least 30 minutes of walking every day.'

3.1.6 Fitness

The wide definition of health also involves the concepts of positive health and well-being and the capacities of enjoying life and overcoming challenges (Biddle & Mutrie, 2008, p. 10). 'Fitness' is surely connected with these concepts and generally with health (Caspersen et al., 1985, p. 126). Being physically fit indicates 'the ability to carry out daily tasks with vigour and alertness, without undue fatigue and with ample energy to enjoy leisure-time pursuits and to meet unforeseen emergencies' (President's Council on Physical Fitness and Sports, 1965, p. 5). Physical fitness is not an active action, but instead 'a set of attributes that people have or achieve' (Caspersen et al., 1985, p. 128). The set of attributes concerns a wide range of components like cardio-respiratory endurance, muscular endurance, muscular strength, body composition and flexibility (Caspersen et al., 1985, p. 128). In the International Consensus Statement of Physical Activity, Fitness and Health (Bouchard et al., 1994), this set is composed of morphologic factors, muscular performance, motor ability and cardio respiratory capacity (Morey, Pieper, & Cornoni-Huntley, 1998). Physical fitness is considered as being an outcome of habitual physical activity (Morey et al., 1998). From this perspective, independently of the social and psychic dimensions, which are difficult to attach to a general concept such as PA, it can be at least stated that PA can enhance people's fitness and in this way positively influences their health status.

3.1.7 'Double Ambiguity' in the Relationship between Physical Activity and Health

The previous considerations on the meaning of health and of the definitions of terms related to PA constitute the basis for discussing the relationship between health and PA. As a multidimensional concept, which does not limit to the absence of illness, 'health' includes at least physical, psychical and social dimensions. This wide definition also involves the concepts of positive health and well-being and the capacities of enjoying life and overcoming challenges (Biddle & Mutrie, 2008, p. 10). For these reasons, sport should theoretically be promoted both for the prevention of chronic diseases and for the improvement of positive health as a particular subset of PA. Instead, even if traditionally taken for granted, the relationship between positive health and sport has become increasingly contradictory in recent decades (Michelini, 2011, p. 319; Michelini & Thiel, 2013, p. 333; Thiel et al., 2013, p. 124). Even if the concept of sport is surely still semantically bended with the concept of health (Michelini & Thiel, 2013), a leading stream of the scientific community manifests open scepticism on the function of sport activities as a medium of health. Indeed, since the beginning of the 1980s, many studies (British Medical Association, 1992, p. 14; J.N. Morris, Everitt, Pollard, & Chave, 1980; Paffenbarger Jr et al., 1986; Smith & Jacobson, 1988, p. 126) have started to emphasise the beneficial effects of moderate and regular forms of physical activity (Waddington et al., 1997, pp. 168-169). The idea that 'daily physical activity of moderate intensity, e.g. brisk walking, is sufficient for health benefits in many sections of populations' (Oja, 2004, p. 169), also called the 'moderate-intensity' concept, has consolidated during the recent years in the scientific health-community. Indeed, the formula of 'at least 30 minutes of regular, moderate-intensity physical activity on most days' (WHO, 2004, p. 4) has become a type of standard of recommendation on the dosage of physical activity. Instead, when the discussion regards vigorous physical activity, the question of health benefits becomes more disputed. In fact, as Waddington et al. (1997, p. 169) point out that 'one cannot assume that the health benefits associated with moderate exercise will simply be duplicated -still less can one assume that they will be increased- by exercise which is more frequent, of longer duration and of greater intensity, for exercise of this kind, as we shall see later, may generate substantial health "costs" in terms of additional stresses or injuries'. In particular, various scientists (Haskell, 2004; Hootman et al., 2002; Oja, 2004; Rutherford & Schroeder, 1998) argue that the health benefits connected to PA stabilise or even decrease if the dose or the intensity of PA is high. In light of this reasoning, sport is excluded from the group of health enhancing physical activities (HEPA).[48] Indeed, particularly professional and traditional-competitive sport as well as partly amateur activities risk the health of the participants because of their orientation towards performance (Nixon, 1994). However, this reasoning tends to assess single aspects of health in a strictly disease-orientated

[48] HEPA is defined as 'any form of physical activity that benefits health and functional capacity without undue harm or risk' (Foster, 2000, p. 9). HEPA is orientated towards physical exercise and every day moderate PAs like walking, cycling, going up the stairs.

model perspective and does not evaluate overall physical health. Furthermore, the multi-dimensionality of health implies that 'regardless of the causal relationship between sport and the objective state of health, there is of course the matter of cultural interplay and lifestyle' (Lüschen, Cockerham, & Kunz, 1996, p. 199). This means that sport, in this case not a subset of PA but rather a social phenomenon, tends to have a positive (healthy) influence on the lifestyle of the practitioners and of the athletes. Considering only the implications of sport on the health of bodies does not acknowledge the socio-psychological implications of sport, which can have important beneficial influence on general well-being (R. Fuchs, 2003, p. 1). This reveals an outdated orientation towards illness, which does not assess the wider and unanimously accepted dimensions of health.

In conclusion, it can be stated that the discourse on the effect of PA on health is affected by a 'double ambiguity'. On the first level, the basic terms are ambiguous because:

- health has multiple dimensions, its meaning is still debated and the reference to its meanings and dimensions is often unclear;
- terms related to PA are often confusing and imprecise and they are used as synonyms or interchangeably.

On the second level, the vagueness of these concepts increases the ambiguity of the discourse on their relationship. For example, a sentence like 'sport is good (or not good) for health' can easily be misunderstood: it can refer to health as a holistic term, or to one or more of its dimensions and it can be referred to sport as a competitive PA or to physical exercise or to other forms of PA. Dealing with this double ambiguity represents one of the core problems of this dissertation. Indeed, the empirical enquiry aims to gain insight about how this problem in the scientific discourse affects the messages of strategies for the promotion of PA issued by the health ministries of France, Germany and Italy.

3.2 Preliminary Theoretical Choices

This chapter aims to explain the choices concerning the theoretical basis of this dissertation. These represent the very fundamentals of this research and therefore need to be explicit in order to respect the scientific criteria of rigor concerning openness, transparency and repeatability.

'There is nothing more practical than a good theory' writes Lewin in his 'Field theory in social science' (1952, p. 169). Vansteenkiste and Sheldon (2006, p. 63) suggest that Lewin's message has two meanings: on the one hand theorists should provide ideas for understanding or conceptualising social phenomena; on the other, applied researchers should provide theorists with key information and facts relevant to solving practical problems. This dissertation aspires to merge these positions by performing research, in which generation of theory and empirical analyses are in continuous and cyclical communication. Practically, the research's issue will be first observed as general phenomenon[49] and then observed through the perspective of a theoretical framework. These steps allow for the creation of a theoretical basis and of the categories useful for properly analysing the phenomenon of the acknowledgement of sport in health-orientated strategies for the promotion of PA at an empirical level. In the last step, the results of the empirical analysis will again be interpreted in the light of the chosen theory. In this way, (1) an advance in empirical data regarding the social phenomenon studied and (2) an extension of the theory by applying it to the specific topic of this doctoral thesis will be pursued. For explaining the theoretical choices which allow this process, the following sections assess in detail the following topics: first, the basic theoretical assumption which lays at the basis of this doctoral thesis; then, the specific theoretical framework for the research; and finally, the topic of the relationship between theory and empirical elements within this dissertation.

3.2.1 Constructivism as an Epistemological Position

An analysis of the role of sport within the health system's communication on PA's promotion has to start with a reflection upon how this phenomenon can be observed at all. Moreover, this reflection should also involve questions about how knowledge is possible in itself. This dissertation involves two distinct but connected subjective perspectives: the one of the scientist who composes this doctoral thesis on an observed phenomenon; which in turn establishes the second viewpoint, namely that of the health system on the role of sport in the health-orientated promotion of PA.

For this reason, constructivism has been preferred as a main epistemological perspective to structuralism, post-structuralism, existentialism, modernism and post-modernism. In fact, it involves the subjective-autopoietic perspective of the health system on the environment. In particular, the radical constructivist stream (Maturana, 2000; Maturana & Varela, 1980, 1987, 1992; Varela, 1997, 1999; Von Foerster, 1993) has been preferred to other streams of construc-

[49] That only means that the social phenomenon has been firstly observed without the 'glass' of the theoretical framework. Instead, it is not assumed that this first observation is more or less objective than the second observation.

tivism because it played a key role in the development of the systems theory that has been used as framework for this dissertation.[50]

The term 'constructivism' denotes a psychological-philosophical, epistemological perspective, which deals with the nature of knowledge, thought and judging. This perspective has historically been fiercely criticised in particular for leading to relativism (Fox, 2001; Phillips, 1995). Nevertheless, today it has generally gained broad acceptance, in particular in the social sciences, where it also appears more digestible on an intuitive level (Collin, 2008, p. 87). In opposition to positivism, the basic assumption of constructivism is that knowledge cannot be based on a correspondent external reality, but is instead always determined by a construction made by the observer (Esposito, 1997, p. 77). For this reason, scientific knowledge is also constructed by the scientist and not provided simply by reality. The concept of reality itself is only critically accepted by constructivists: without denying that reality does exist, constructivism is radically sceptical on the possibility of knowing it as such. From this perspective, the aim of knowledge is one of observing observations: a second-order observation orientated not to 'what' the first order observation is, but to what the first order observation 'is like'. In other words: it observes how an observer observes (Esposito, 1997, p. 78).

Furthermore, by having a framework based on Luhmann's systems theory, this doctoral thesis relies on a particular typology of constructivism, the one of systems theory. In his autopoietic turn, Luhmann has been largely influenced by radical constructivist theories, especially by Varela and Maturana's studies (in particular: 1987). The direct result of this influence is that social systems are, in Luhmann's eyes, operationally closed and experience the environment through their own subjective perspective (Collin, 2008, p. 105). Luhmann's constructivism has been called by Luhmann himself 'operational constructivism' because it does not focus on the distinction between subject/object, but on the distinction between operation/observation (Esposito, 1997, p. 79). From this perspective, a second-order observer who observes a distinction by basing his or her thoughts on a different distinction can also see: (1) what the first-order observer didn't see and (2) and that the first-order observer didn't see it. However, the second-order observation will also have blind spots, which can be observed by a new second-order observation (Bette & Schimank, 2006, p. 20; Esposito, 1997, p. 79). In the case of this dissertation, the enquiry observes how the health system observes the sport system specifically regarding PA's promotion. By observing the health system's observations, at least a part of what the health system could not see is

[50] Indeed, radical constructivism has influenced the Luhmann's systems theory's autopoietic turn and has been adapted by Luhmann himself (Luhmann, 1993) to his theoretical work (Esposito, 1997, p. 79; Vogd, 2005b, 2007).

thought to be seen by having a different perspective on the phenomenon. However, the whole discussion will be conducted with the complete awareness that also this observation will have blind spots.

3.2.2 Systems Theory as a Theoretical Framework

Within the theories established to study systems in general,[51] Niklas Luhmann's systems theory has been preferred to Bertalanffy's general systems theory (1968) and to the Talcott Parsons's action theory (1949, 2000). This theory has been already applied to the topic of this dissertation[52] and offers particularly explanatory advantages. For these reasons, it has been chosen for approaching the topic of the function of sport in health-related promotion of PA. For Luhmann (1982a, p. XIII), the ultimate goal of systems theory was 'to develop a conceptual vocabulary that is refined, variegated, and supple enough to capture what he sees as the unprecedented structural characteristics of modern society'.[53] This sociological theory can be described as a network of ideas, representations and definitions, which relies on shared theoretical fundamentals. For Willke (2006b, pp. 1-4), systems theory represents a notable turning point for the social sciences in general for three reasons:

1. It developed into a universal theory, which claims to be used as theoretical framework for all the possible questions of the social sciences.
2. It constitutes a universal interdisciplinary theoretical basis for the analysis of systems and it creates common points with neighbouring sciences.
3. It has developed a high capacity to deal with the problem of complexity.

In the particular case of this doctoral thesis, systems theory has been chosen because this developed contemporary theory allows:

– for the proper analysis of the communications of the health system on sport, as it implies a constructivist perspective and focuses on communication as the basic element of social systems (Seidl & Schoeneborn, 2010, pp. 7-8).
– For the use of a broad range of tools, which are useful for the analysis on both theoretical and empirical levels (Bette, 1999, p. 76).

---

[51] However, postmodern and poststructuralist theorisations of sport and health systems (see for example: Bunton, 1997; Caudwell, 2006; Evans, Davies, & Wright, 2004; McDermott, 2007; McDonald & Birrell, 1999; Osborne, 1997; Silk & Andrews, 2006; Wheatley, 2005) offer a developed and performative framework, which could be seen as a respectable alternative to systems theory.

[52] See the chapter 'literature review.'

[53] A couple of years later, Luhmann (1984, p. 19) referred to systems theory with the term *supertheory* (*Supertheorie*) for the description of the society, with the aim to stress the universal ambition of his theoretical framework.

- for the clear division between social systems and individual persons (Luhmann, 2001, p. 111) which represents a great heuristic reduction of complexity without the danger of illegitimate simplifications (Seven, 2008, p. 15).
- for the involvement of aspects of governance on different levels in the discussion of cooperation between function systems, as it creates different levels of abstraction, namely the societal, the systemic and the organisational levels (Pelikan, 2007, p. 75).
- for the discussion of the topic from different points of view because Luhmann's systems theory is versatile and adaptable to many contexts (Müller & Larson, 1994, p. 40).

Instead, the fact that systems theory is not fully accepted by some of the international scientific community is considered here to be irrelevant for the choice of the theoretical framework. However, the fact that 'the reception of Luhmann in Anglo-American countries is still made difficult by the relative scarcity of translations of Luhmann's work into English' (Albert, 2004, p. 22) has surely been a challenge for this dissertation. This rejection is probably caused by Luhmann's original affiliation with Talcott Parsons and structural functionalism.

However, Luhmann progressively distanced himself from his mentor, especially in the late period of Luhmann's work (S. Fuchs, 1999, p. 119), after the so-called *autopoietic turn*. In fact, during the 1970s and the 1980s, his theories were significantly rewritten and gained additional shape and clarifying power 'by adopting the concept of autopoiesis from cognitive biology and elements of observation theory from the domain of second order cybernetics' (Müller & Larson, 1994, p. 39). In particular, the attribution of 'autopoiesis' (Maturana & Varela, 1987) as fundamental characteristic of social systems constitutes indubitably a relevant step away from Talcott Parsons's systems theory.

Even if the Stanford University Press has undertaken the project (Albert, 2004, p. 22), the translation of Luhmann's works into English remains incomplete (S. Fuchs, 1999, p. 119) and among the missing works are some cornerstones like '*Die Wissenschaft der Gesellschaft*' (Luhmann, 1990a). This presented a challenge for the present research because the translation of Luhmann from German into English often represents a difficult task even for professional translators (Luhmann, 1995b, p. XXVII). Hence, this doctoral thesis is based on the words, definitions and concepts of the translated works of Luhmann (principally Luhmann, 1977; 1982a, 1982b, 1992, 1993, 1995a, 1997b, 2003, 2008a) and always specifies whether the translation is from these works or from the author of this dissertation. When required, the German word is left in parentheses and italics after its translation in English to allow for a better comprehension of the terms. Leading an international-comparative enquiry in the perspective of Luhmann's systems theory in the English language is also expected to contributing in the never completely accomplished mission of exporting systems theory across the German borders.

Although the research's 'puzzle' (Eckstein, 1975, p. 91) will be answered with Luhmann's systems theory, it is impossible to offer a compendium of this theory here as this would be a costly, long and over-ambitious endeavour. However, some central arguments of the systems theory are prerequisite and necessary in order to understand the arguments contained in this dissertation. Hence, the choice of the systems theory approach will have many implications upon the analysis and the interpretation of the empirical data of this doctoral thesis and it is essential to provide the keys to understand them. In the following paragraphs, some basic topics of systems theory, which are strictly connected with this dissertation's argumentation, will be summarised. Instead, for a complete description of the systems theory, the reader can refer directly to the works of Luhmann (specially 1993, 1995b, 1997a, 1997b) or to the voluminous introductive literature (for example Baraldi et al., 1997a; Berghaus, 2004; Kneer & Nassehi, 1994; Krause, 2005; Luhmann, 2008b; Reese-Schäfer, 1992; Willke, 2001b, 2005, 2006b).

By claiming generality, systems theory tends to occupy all possible theoretical space and indeed often presents itself as being appropriate for an enormous number of subjects. On the one hand, its characteristics allow for the description of complexity in a simplified and workable format (Bette, 1999, p. 76). On the other hand, this theoretical closeness raises accusations of being autoreferential and incapable of self-criticism (Luhmann, 1990c, p. 37). This doctoral thesis considers systems theory to be a powerful theoretical framework but not a dogma, and sees it instead as being open to criticism and demands it to acknowledge its limits.

3.2.3 The Relationship between Theory and Empiricism

Generally systems theory rarely has been posed in relationship to empirical questions of social enquiry (Mayer, 2009, p. 43; Vogd, 2007, p. 295). In fact, even if the constructivist epistemology of systems theory is a good candidate for being a meta-theory of qualitative research, Luhmann never explicitly clarifies how to connect theory with empiricism (Vogd, 2005b, p. 25; 2007, p. 297). For this reason, systems theory has often been accused of being empirically blind (*empirieblind*) or of being inadvisable for empirical analysis. Even if some empirically-based analyses have already been carried out in sport sociology with an empirical-qualitative approach, it is useful in this place to clarify the relationship between theory and empiricism.

From a systems theory perspective, theory and empiricism represent two different levels of communication, both circularly organised. Their relationship is hence not a case of direct interdependency. Instead, it is a form of structural coupling, in which theory can be irritated through empiricism and vice versa (Bette, 1999, p. 103; Vogd, 2007, p. 312). In the best case, a situation like this allows both the empirical and theoretical levels to observe each other as an environment and, in turn, include each other in their self-referentiality (Bette, 1999, p. 103). This requires as a premise that the language of empirical research can be translated into the language of theory and that scientists can develop awareness for the results of these perturbations (Bette, 1999, p. 103; Vogd, 2007, p. 301). If these premises are fulfilled, empiricism can profit highly from being contextualised within the theoretical framework of a developed theory like systems theory (Bette, 1999, p. 103). Qualitative or quantitative empiricism of every field needs to be tied to a theoretical concept for fostering scientific progress and in order to avoid conducting research while missing its sought purpose (Bette, 1999, p. 103; Vogd, 2007, p. 297). Instead, it is exactly this combination of both theoretical and empirical levels, which can foster scientific progress (*problemangemessene Kombinatorik*) (Bette, 1999, p. 104). In light of these arguments, the analysis of strategies for enhancing PA will be a theory-guided empirical analysis, whose results will be interpreted in the perspective of the systems theory.

3.3 Health and Sport Systems

Within the preliminary theoretical choices outlined in the previous chapter, Luhmann's system has been selected for developing the theoretical framework of this dissertation. This chapter outlines the basis of systems theory. It deepens in particular the topic of the differentiation of function systems within modern society and their fundamental characteristics. After that, the discussion focuses on the description of health and sport as function systems. The description of both systems is necessary because the research involves the perspective of the health system on the sport system. Hence, one in the active and the other in the passive roles they are the protagonists of the discourse.

3.3.1 Function Systems in Systems Theory

Because 'system' is the constitutive term of systems theory (Thiel, 1997, p. 24), the explanation of the theoretical framework starts with the concept of 'system' in systems theory.[54] Systems' principal features are that they 'are constituted by a difference between system and environment and are communicative systems' (Luhmann, 1997a, p. 35; translated in Albert (2004, p. 7)). They therefore have two principal characteristics.

Firstly, systems define themselves through their boundaries to their environment (Baraldi, Corsi, & Esposito, 1997b, p. 211). The environment is not a typology of system but it is instead defined by systems as a strategy for reducing complexity: it constitutes everything that doesn't belong to the system (Willke, 2006b, p. 251). The environment has a central role for the differentiation and interaction of systems (Luhmann, 1994b, p. 288ff): on the one hand, it sets systems boundaries by establishing what does not concern the communicative topic of a system; on the other hand, through its boundaries the environment does not isolate a system but instead it allows the creation of interdependences between a system and the environment. Also, systems are environment for each other. In the case examined in this doctoral work, that means the health and the sport systems perceive each other as environment.

Secondly, systems are 'made of operations, which produce the system itself. For social systems, the basic operation is communication' (Berghaus, 2004, p. 39). In the systems theory, communication is the unity of three selections: of announcement, of information and of understanding (Hagen, 2000, p. 36; Moeller, 2006, p. 22). This implies that communication is not limited to the emission of a message and involves instead always the presence of Ego (sender of the communication) and Alter (receiver of the communication). Moreover, the communication includes the understanding of the message which is also the premise of new communications. Understanding is not to be confused with right comprehension: messages are instead often misunderstood without hindering the chance of further communications. For example, the sport and the health systems definitely have a strict communicative relationship, but their messages are often not commensurable with the logic of the other system.

As they differ from the environment and are made of communications, systems are 'islands of lesser complexity in the world' (Bednarz, 1985, p. 58). In particular, social systems constitute recursive networks of specific communication and observation. Even if 'system' as a term is often used in relation with other concepts, it always indicates a multitude of specific components which are in relation to each other and show specific differences when compared with their environment (Thiel, 1997, p. 24). These two characteristics are fundamental to understanding the health system's perspective on the role of sport in strategies for the promotion of PA.

[54] Because the systems theory is a circular theory without a top and bottom or a beginning and end, it is particularly hard to decide how to begin to explain this theoretical framework.

There are different typologies of social systems branded by the characteristics of their own communications (Krause, 2005, p. 35): *function systems*; *interaction systems*; and *organisation systems*. As previously stated, both the sport and health systems are function systems. In the following, the process which determined the emergence of function systems in modern societies will be briefly explained.

Complexity is the basic state of the world and is the condition required for the rise of modern societies (Willke, 2006b, p. 18).[55] In order to understand this sentence, it is useful to explain the terms 'society' and 'complexity':

- For Luhmann, society is a particular social system consisting of and including every existing communication (Baraldi et al., 1997b, p. 218). In the systems theory society is not constituted by individuals, but instead by communications. Its boundaries are not set geographically but they demarcate the social boundaries of possible communication. Society does not have a centre or an apex nor it is hierarchically organised (Hagen, 2000, p. 31). However, it is internally differentiated because it contains many autonomous communication-based systems, like the ones for sport and health.
- Complexity is a phenomenon caused by the immense growth of communications and of their interconnections. Not every communication in modern society can be related to each other at the same time and it is impossible to coordinate all of them. Furthermore, communications can be perceived, ignored or misunderstood at every state of a communicative network. This contingency tends to make relationships between social communications complicated and inextricable (Willke, 2006b, p. 18).

In modern societies, complexity is tremendous and implies a reduction of possible options through selection. As a naturally reaction to manage this, society develops different forms of differentiation (Willke, 2005, p. 73). Differentiation[56] comprises the creation of partial systems within society and of a structure for a relationship between this systems and the environment. Different typologies of differentiation are suitable for diverse degrees of complexity. Luhmann identifies three forms of differentiation: *segmentation*, which differentiates society into equal subsystems; *stratification*, which differentiates society into unequal subsystems; and *functional differentiation*, the more complex form, which organises

[55] Around 380 BC, Socrates in a dialogue with Adeimantus also affirms that the enhancement of complexity relies at the basis of the emergence of society (Plato, 1892b, pp. 49-50).

[56] For Luhmann, differentiation is the 'replication within a system of the difference between a system and its environment' (Luhmann, 1982a, p. 230) or, more detailed, the process that 'multiplies specialized versions of the original system's identity by splitting it into a number of internal systems and affiliated environments which is a process of internal disjunction' (Luhmann, 1982a, p. 231).

communication processes around special functions to be fulfilled at the level of society (Luhmann, 1982a, p. 232).

Modern societies are characterised by different types of social differentiation, but, in contrast with segmentary or stratified societies, modern societies tend to extend the differences of activities and occupations to specialised organisations, role sets and logics (Willke, 2005, p. 57). Hence they are primarily differentiated functionally 'and only secondarily by stratification and segmentation' (Pelikan, 2007, p. 86).[57] In Europe and, subsequently, the world during the 18th century, functional differentiation became the primary type of social differentiation (Moeller, 2006, p. 41). Through functional differentiation, modern society is 'relatively stable even though it has no single centre and no subsector that can claim unchallenged supremacy' (Luhmann, 1982a, p. XV).[58]

From the perspective of systems theory, modern societies host several autonomous function systems specialised in particular societal fields like economy, health, law, politics and sport. Each function system fulfils a precise task for society by means of the execution of specific communications (Baraldi et al., 1997a, pp. 89-92). Function systems are highly autonomous (Bauch, 2004, p. 24; Willke, 2006b, p. 192) and 'fulfil important functions for the whole of society, as well as, solve problems and/or offer solutions, achievements, performances necessary for the functioning of other function systems, as well as for organizations and individuals' (Pelikan, 2007, p. 86).

The constitutional criterion of a function system is a specific meaning (*Sinn*) which permits the creation of a specific logic and, in turn, permits the identification of specific operations (Mayntz, 1988, p. 16). Each function system differentiates itself from the environment and fulfils a fundamental function that contributes to the reproduction of society (Bauch, 2004, p. 43; Schimank, 1988, p. 183). This happens automatically and without a global or strategic vision of whole society because systems work strictly in autopoiesis, according to their own logic and without any understanding for the way other systems perceive their environment (Bauch, 2004, p. 43). In other words: 'social systems are entities that observe problems and select solutions. There may be many, but not an unlimited number, of functional alternative solutions to the same problem, and several, but not an unlimited number, of problems with the same solution' (Hagen, 2000, p. 30).

---

[57] In this sense, 'Luhmann's theory of a functionally differentiated society is simultaneously a theory of modernity' (Müller & Larson, 1994, p. 39).

[58] Furthermore the phenomenon of functional differentiation 'is seen as the basis of individualization and globalization, world-wide urbanization, and of what some would call a society of organizations' (Pelikan, 2007, p. 86).

3.3.2 *Health and Sport as Function Systems*

The preliminary question to answer when undertaking the description of health and sport as function systems is to clarify whether the sport and health systems can be considered function systems.

Regarding the health system, there is concordance among the system theorists that within modern societies an *ad hoc* function system for health matters has differentiated. First, Luhmann (1983a, 1983b, 1990d) assumed the emergence of this specific health-related function system. Also Mayntz & Rosewitz (1988),[59] Bauch (1996, 1997, 2000, 2004) and Pelikan (2007; 1999; 2001) agree with this assumption. Nevertheless, the fact that the 'sociological system theory has been applied to analyses of health only marginally' (Pelikan, 2007, p. 75) has, for a long time, limited the possibility of offering a deep description of the health system in this sociological perspective. This lack has been justified in the subject-related literature for two reasons: Luhmann didn't write a complete description of the health system;[60] and the health system suffers from a lack of self-reflection (Bauch, 2004, p. 56; Vogd, 2005a, p. 258).[61] The degree of this deficit in self-reflection is still discussed within the scientific community. In particular, Luhmann (1983a, p. 173) assumes that the health system has a deficit of self-reflection caused by its orientation to its environment. Bauch (2004, p. 56) shares Luhmann's opinion about the absence of a reflection theory in the health system and its orientation to the environment. However, he states that the health system possesses a rudimental self-description (such as the Hippocrates ethic or the World Health Organisation's definition of health). In contrast to Luhmann and Bauch, Pelikan (2007, p. 89) assumes that the health system does have a specific medium of communication and a specific symbiotic mechanism. Regardless of this issue, in recent times some system theorists have fulfilled the health system's deficiency of system theoretical analysis. Taking advantage of this situation, the following discussions are based principally on the works of Niklas Luhmann (1983a, 1983b, 1990d) but also on the latest extensions of mainly two authors: Jürgen M. Pelikan (1993, 2007; 1999; 2001) and Jost Bauch (1996, 2000, 2004).[62]

---

[59] The two authors are representatives of the action theory.

[60] However, Luhmann dedicated three papers to the topic of the health system (Luhmann, 1983a, 1983b, 1990d).

[61] Self-reflection is the faculty of systems to observe and describe themselves and to understand themselves as environment for other systems (Luhmann, 1997a, p. 757; Willke, 2006b, p. 248).

[62] However, these authors have in turn been largely influenced by the work of Talcott Parsons (1939, 1963) as one of the founding fathers of medical sociology. In particular, the tradition of systems theory regarding the description of health system refers often to Parsons's application of social role theory to interactional relations between sick people and others.

Coming to the sport system, Cachay (1988, p. 33; 2000, p. 40; translation EM) stresses that: 'the sport system cannot only be seen as the simple ensemble of sports clubs, academics and schools. It has to be functionally explained as a complex process, born to solve a specific problem in society.' While arguing about the topic of interpenetration, Luhmann (1984, p. 336) also mentions sport as one of the fields of modern body culture. In these observations, he recognises that sport has emerged as an institutionalised form of reducing meanings about the body's performances within society (Luhmann, 1984, pp. 336-337). However, Luhmann does not furnish a full description of sport as a function system either within these first thoughts or in any other of his works.[63] Fortunately, other authors filled this gap. For example, almost at the same time as Luhmann, Bette (1984, pp. 9-17) affirmed that at least professional sport can be fully considered as a function system. Subsequently, the lack of descriptions of the sport system by means of systems theory has been fulfilled by the work of various sport sociologists (for example: Bette, 1989; Cachay, 1988; Cachay & Thiel, 2000; Schimank, 1988), who all agree about the existence of the sport system as a function system. In this dissertation it will be also assumed that the sport system is a function system. This is a fundamental assumption (*Grundannahme*), based upon the fact that it can be clearly identified and differentiated (Spencer-Brown, 1979, p. 3) from other function systems.

Once took for granted that the health and the sport systems are function systems it is possible to wider describe and compare their features. This will represent the theoretical basis for enquiring into and discussions about how the health system conceives sport as a medium of health in programmes for the promotion of PA.

3.3.3 Characteristics of Function Systems

From the viewpoint of systems theory, both the health and sport systems are function systems within society. In order to apply systems theory to the description of sport and health systems and to allow for their comparison, it is now important to classify and explain the basic characteristics of function systems. Not only do all social systems operate by means of communication, but they also share similar structures and can be described in a comparable way. The binary code is the fundamental feature of function systems (Luhmann, 1986, p. 94; Schimank, 1988, p. 184). However, the characteristics of function system are not limited to different codes. Albert (2004, p. 8), for example, affirms that each function system in a society 'is characterized by a specific function, a specific

[63] Nevertheless, he has never denied that sport could be described as such.

code, and a specific medium'. Mayntz (1988, p. 41) affirms that all function systems have three basic characteristics: (1) a specific identity in difference with the society and which is understood as such from other systems, (2) an own, independent and distinctive logic, and (3) specific roles and formal organisations. Schimank (1988, p. 185) and Thiel (1997, p. 25) identify two fundamental features of function systems: (1) an operational logic at the orientation level and (2) specific roles and formal organisations at the socio-structural level.

In the following sections, this dissertation describes sequentially five features of the health and sport systems: the function, the binary code, the programme, the organisations and the roles. These features have been identified as being suitable for a deep description of the systems and for assessing the useful aspects for the theoretical and empirical discussion of this doctoral thesis. Even if function systems' characteristics are strictly related, the previously mentioned features will now be artificially separated and explained in order to allow a more comparable description.[64]

3.3.4 Functions of Health and Sport Systems

The function is the contribution of system to the reproduction of society. Basically, there has to be a social problem or problems that a function system is able to solve. A founding problem is a basic condition of birth, persistence and stability for a function system and allows the creation of its own identity and differentiation (Cachay, 1988, pp. 31-34).

For Luhmann, the health system's function is 'to fix the body' (*die Körper wieder in Ordnung zu bringen*) (Luhmann, 1983b, pp. 169-170; translation EM). More specifically, Luhmann theorises a structural indifference between body and psyche which is altered by illness and pain and which medicine has the function to re-establish (Luhmann, 1983b, p. 174). Vogd (2005a, p. 238) also affirms that the special function of health system is to heal ill people, who embody the patient's role when they are included in the health system. This function is representative of only a part of health system's operation and particularly that of curative medicine. This dissertation instead analyses operations orientated towards health promotion. For this reason it is useful to complete the panel of the health system's functions with the one proposed by Bauch, who theorises that the aim of the health system is to fight illness and to promote/create health (Bauch, 2004, p. 43).

[64] This explanation is fundamental to understanding the discussion on the health and the sport systems in the following sections.

The function of the sport system is debated[65] in the sociological community and is relevant for the argumentation of this doctoral thesis. For these reasons the current state of this topic needs to be briefly summarised.

For Cachay (1988, p. 157), this function is the 'production of social adequate personal environment' (*Produktion gesellschaftsadäquater personaler Umwelt*). From this view point, the sport system works together with the health and the education systems for the perfection (*Vervollkommnung*) of people through the empowerment of their bodies (Cachay, 1988, p. 177). This constitutes, in turn, an important performance[66] for society and for other function systems (Cachay, 1988, pp. 179-275). Starting with the assumption that the sport system does not have a specific function, Bette (1984, p. 10) concludes that the function of sport is represented by its multiple performances, which are needed by society and other function systems. In this way, it gains stability and continuity within society by means of cooperation with other systems. Some years later, Bette (1987, pp. 609-610) affirms instead that the function of the sport system is to make people fit and this, again, represents the important performance for other function systems. Also Schimank (2001, pp. 13-15) affirms that the function of the sport system consists of the performances it carries out for other function systems. In particular, professional sport implements relevant performances for the systems of economy, politics and media (Bette & Schimank, 2006, pp. 90-116; Schimank, 2001, pp. 13-15; 2008, p. 72),[67] and amateur sport carries out important tasks for the systems of health, education, politic, family and economy (Schimank, 2008, p. 72). For Stichweh (1990, pp. 378-380), the sport system is the function system whose operation is the communication of body performances (*Sport ist jenes Funktionssystem, das aus allen Handlungen besteht, deren Sinn die Kommunikation körperlicher Leistungsfähigkeit ist*). Its function is therefore the process of all communication of and about body performances (Stichweh, 1990, p. 380). From this viewpoint, sport's communications are particular reductions and interpretations of body movements through sports' institutionalised vocabulary and meaning (Stichweh, 1990, p. 379), which summarise them much better than long descriptions. In fact, sport descriptions permit the abstractions of many qualities and motivations of sport movements by reducing them in measur-

[65] Differently from the functions of other social systems, the one of the sport system is sometimes not considered fundamental for the reproduction of society (Bette, 1989, p. 170; Schimank, 1988, p. 183; Willke, 2001b, p. 101). However, this does not represent a contradiction, because Luhmann himself abandoned the opinion that social systems emerge and gain autonomy only if they have fundamental functions for the reproduction of society long before his death (Bette, 2007, p. 204).

[66] In the lexicon of systems theory, 'performance' is the result of the function of a system in the society.

[67] Professional sport profits from the performances of the systems of economy, politic, law, military, science, media, health, education and intimate relationship (Schimank, 2001, p. 17).

able and relevant actions (Stichweh, 1990, p. 379).[68] This reduction into a performance-orientated perspective ensures not only the chance to understand, but also to compare sport facts. Indeed, sport's communication compares performances expected and carried out, the difference between these two performances causes the spread of communication (Stichweh, 1990, p. 379). Several authors (Guttmann, 1979; Heinemann, 1998; Steinkamp, 1983) share this opinion about the fundamental role of competition and/or performance within sport.

In summary, from the review of the existing opinions on the functions of the sport system, it can be stated that two polarised positions emerge: on the one side, the communications of body performance (Stichweh, 1990); on the other side, the empowerment of bodies (Bette, 1987; Cachay, 1988). Within this dissertation, these are both considered to be the functions of the sport system.

3.3.5 Binary Codes of Health and Sport Systems

A function system must have a binary code, which makes its logic explicit to ensure its own reproduction and to develop mechanisms in a specific and recognisable way (Bette 2010: 90). It serves for the system's closure, a demarcation of boundaries and also as a primitive distinction upon which all the other characteristics of a function system solidify. The code is characterised by a binary structure that reduces the description of meaning with a rigid semantic form, which respects an 'either ... or' (*entweder ... oder*) formula.

The binary code of the health system has been intensively discussed in the scientific community. In particular, Luhmann's first proposal has been widely criticised by Bauch and Pelikan, who have changed and extended Luhmann's theory and reached different outcomes.[69]

In summary, Luhmann's binary code 'health/illness' (Luhmann, 1983a, p. 31; 1990d, p. 186) is not appropriate alone for the description of the operation of health promotion. In fact, this code orientates the system's processes principally at the negative value 'ill', and not at the positive value 'healthy' (Luhmann, 1990d, pp. 187-188) which is one of the central topics of this research. Hence, the choice has been limited between Bauch's and Pelikan's codes. Both codes could suit the aims of the following discussions. Pelikan's double health code 'presence/absence of illness for ill physical health' and 'suboptimal/optimal

[68] For example, sentences like 'they lost with a last minute penalty' (for football) or 'he awarded an ippon after 20 seconds' (for judo) are clear examples of sport specific reduction of complexity particular to sport system, which summarise information to an extreme and, at the same time, give adequate information on the unfolding of a sporting event.

[69] This discussion has been thoroughly described in the literature review.

health for positive physical health' (Pelikan, 2007, p. 89) offers indubitably useful extensions for the analysis of salutogenetic operations (Antonovsky, 1979) of the health system.[70] However, Bauch's opinion regarding the co-existence of the binary code 'health/illness' and 'promoting/hindering health' (Bauch, 1996, p. 130; 2004, p. 66) has been chosen for this doctoral thesis because it permits the isolation and therefore the ability to better examine the aspects of health promotion and health education. Furthermore these codes are more accepted in the systems theory tradition. Hence, in this dissertation it is assumed that the code health / illness remains the code for the core operations of acute medicine and the new code has been adopted for new functions of the health system like prevention, health promotion and rehabilitation (Bauch, 2004, p. 75) as illustrated in the graph below:

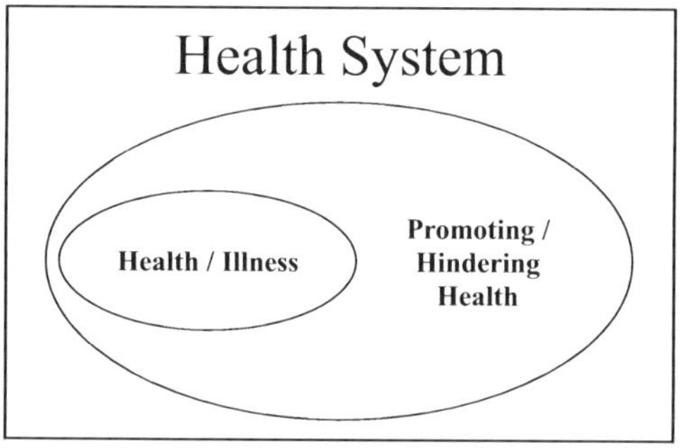

Figure 2 Codes of the Health System

For the sport system, there is a concurrence among many sport sociologists that the sport system's binary code is 'victory/defeat' (*Sieg / Niederlage*) (P. Becker, 1987, p. 24; Bette & Schimank, 2006, p. 37). For example, Schimank (1988, p. 185; translation EM) affirms that victory and defeat 'are the two poles that include the possible horizon in which all sport facts can be interpreted. At any time and in any sport discipline, players have this aim: they want to win against their opponents and avoid defeat'.[71] In comparison with other codes, 'victory/defeat' is not rigorously polarised. In fact, it can be interpreted and concedes degree (Cachay & Thiel, 2000, p. 138), for example in the cases of rankings and draws.[72] Even if the sport code is sometimes flexible, it is at the same

[70] For more details see Bauch (2004, p. 69).

[71] Some authors propose slightly different versions of this code. For example, Bette (1989, p. 171) affirms that the code 'victory/defeat' can be translated into the semantics of the sport system as 'superior/inferior performance'.

[72] Another peculiar characteristic of modern sport is the universalization of the comparison of performances through the institutionalisation of world records.

time highly self-referential: in the evaluation of a sport performance as victory or defeat, any non-sport criteria are not permissible.

Instead, Stichweh (1990, pp. 384-387) proposes a wider code which can also include healthy and recreational aspects of modern sports: 'performing/not performing' (*leisten / nicht leisten*). Stichweh acknowledges many examples of sport in modern times, which are not competition-orientated and which are only hardly explainable with the logic of 'victory/defeat.' In Stichweh's opinion (1990, p. 387), 'victory/defeat' instead represents the motivation of participants in official competitions as well as a reason for leaving them. Nevertheless, the code 'performing/not performing' is also still referred to the interpretation of autotelic bodily accomplishments.

This dissertation acknowledges two codes of the sport system: 'victory/defeat' (Schimank, 1988) as the core code for professional and competitive sport; and 'performing/not performing' (Stichweh, 1990) as the wider code for the amateur and recreational sport, as illustrated in the schema below:

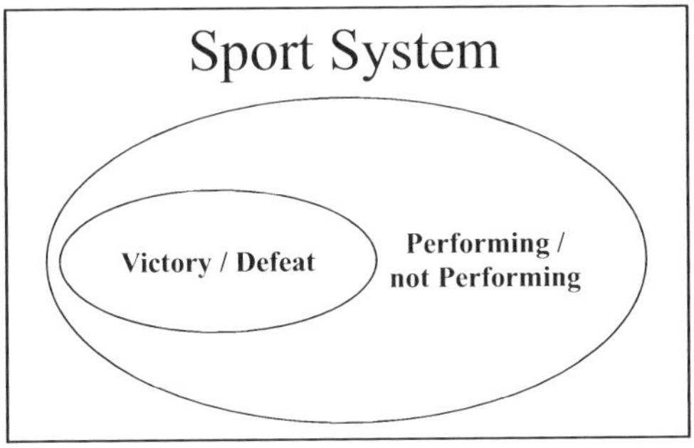

Figure 3 Codes of the Sport System

With slight differences, this model has been acknowledged by some system theorists (Schimank, 1988, p. 210; Stichweh, 1990, p. 383) and it is useful to furnish a more precise focus, an enhanced capacity of reasoning within the theoretical framework and a deeper differentiation of sport phenomena.

3.3.6 Programmes of Health and Sport Systems

Programmes specify the logic of the code and allow the systems to make logical distinctions (Schimank, 1988, p. 188). They can be (Luhmann, 2006, p. 261): output-orientated and consist of a planned intention in relation to a project (purpose programme); or input-orientated and determine specific reactions of the function system to possible situations and scenarios (conditional programme).

There is a lack of scientific literature regarding the health system's programmes (Pelikan, 2009, p. 38). For Luhmann (1990d, p. 190), Vogd (2005a, p. 239) and Pelikan (2009, p. 38), the core operations of curative medicine bases its reproduction mode on decision-making programmes, which rely on the schema of diagnosis-therapy. Indeed, the task of physicians and doctors is to offer a therapy for any illness (Vogd, 2005a, p. 239). These programmes need to be flexible because they change in relation to the progresses of science, knowledge and practice (Pelikan, 2009, p. 38).[73] For the programmes directed towards the prevention of illnesses or health promotion, two health-theories have been more influential than technological advances (Michelini, 2011, pp. 308-310; Vogd, 2005a, p. 252): the salutogenetic theory (Antonovsky, 1997); and the risk factor model (Dawber, Meadors, & Moore Jr, 1951).[74] The rise and consolidation of these theories turned health's focus from curative medicine towards preventive programmes (Hurrelmann, 2006, pp. 124-126). The production and implementation of preventive health programmes are today a relevant task of many health system organisations. In this context, physical inactivity also began to be considered as a relevant risk factor. Therefore, programmes to promote PA have gained continuous significance in the global health arena.[75] Probably, the world's best known programme for the promotion of physical activity is the WHO's 'Global Strategy on Diet, Physical Activity and Health' (WHO, 2004) and the European Commission's 'White Paper on Sport' (2007).[76]

The programmes of the sport system operationalise the difference between victory and defeat or between good and bad performances. To interpret a sport performance, they distinguish, for example, between men and women, young and adult, fairness and unfairness (Bette, 1999, p. 39). Typical sport programmes normally consist of specific rules for sport disciplines. Schimank (1988, pp. 185-190) categorised sport programmes into three orientations: *evaluative, normative* and *cognitive*. The *evaluative orientation* is based on the performance principle, which is both medium and purpose in sport. The *normative orientation* specifies the performance's conditions (what is allowed and what not, or simply what the rules of the game are) for the specific sport disciplines.[77] *Cognitive orientation* is the specific interpretational pattern of sport disciplines like tactic, strategy and definition of situations. However, also programmes without precise sport discipline-orientation exist. For example, the international

[73] The empirical analysis of this dissertation regards health-strategies for the promotion of PA, which are considered as being programmes of the health system.
[74] The two theories will be discussed in detail afterwards.
[75] A selection of these programmes will be analysed in the empirical chapter.
[76] The World Heart Federation and the International Diabetes Federation along with other health organisations are also extremely relevant and active in the promotion of PA.
[77] For example, sport's overreaching normative orientation is the concept of 'fairness'.

campaign 'Sport for All' implies a self-observation of the system as a whole and the establishment of an overwhelming programme of inclusion into the sport system in general (Schimank, 2008, p. 70). Furthermore, through systemic structural couplings sport organisations' programmes also orientate towards aims external to the logic 'victory/defeat' like social inclusion, education and, frequently, health.

3.3.7 *Organisations of Health and Sport Systems*

Function systems need formal organisations as specific mechanisms of the stabilisation of expectations, which will be fulfilled following the specific operations of the systems (Schimank, 1988, p. 85). For Luhmann (1999, pp. 39-53), organisations are special forms of social systems, which differentiate themselves from interaction and society through a set of rules of recognition (*Anerkennungsregel*). These rules consist normally of memberships, which are determined by personal recruitment, and role specifications. Organisations possess a limited number of members. Furthermore, organisations permit the structural coupling between systems (Luhmann, 2002a, pp. 396-401).

Modern medicine and the development of its knowledge are embodied particularly in hospitals (Vogd, 2005a, p. 240). Further specific health system organisations are medical practices, surgeries and other forms of supply devices (Pelikan, 2007, p. 88; 2009, p. 40). As well as function systems in general, the health system tends to optimise its capacity to fulfil its functions without any stop-rule. This phenomenon is particularly tough for the health system and determines its constant tendency to improve its performance and enhance its tasks' spectrum (Bauch, 2004, p. 43) by creating new specialisations and subdisciplines. Generally, this process creates organisations which work at non-competitive levels but also generates a lack of governance and problems of internal coordination (Vogd, 2005a, p. 245).[78] For example, after a knee injury one can refer today to different professional figures within the health system's organisations: physiologist, osteopathic, sport doctor or hospitals' personnel. Each one of these roles will probably apply different programmes of diagnosis and treatment. Furthermore, the hypostatisation of the health system has other relevant consequences such as the explosion of the costs of health care (Düllings, 1993) and the integration and extension of health system's functions over areas normally occupied by other systems. An example of that is the health system's interest in the promotion of PA, which has been historically a core function of the sport system.

[78] This topic is assessed extensively in Badura & Feuerstein (1994).

The health organisations which steer the governance, coordination and agenda setting of health matters at both international and national levels play the main role in this dissertation. With reference to the Lateral World System (LWS) theory (Willke, 2007a, pp. 138-140),[79] the health system is considered here to be a global system because it manages a communicative context that ensures its self-steering. Furthermore it has a unitary structural form which is hierarchically organised. This doctoral thesis assumes that under the pressure of globalisation, health has become a global topic and has started to have a global political agent, embodied in the WHO, which has the role of integrating, coordinating and convening the global health agenda as well as the role of a coordinator between systems. Furthermore, national health ministers, representing their respective national health organisations, are the principal connections of the WHO for the implementation of programmes. In fact, the WHO assumes that health programmes can be carried out 'by working primarily, if not exclusively, through governmental institutions, notably the ministries of health' (Dodgson, Lee, & Drager, 2002, p. 11). Although these organisations are examples of structural couplings between economic, political and health systems, they are highly influenced by the logic orientated toward the codes 'health/illness' and 'promoting/hindering health,' because the members composing them are sourced from within the health system (Dodgson et al., 2002, p. 11; K. Lee, 2003, p. 26; Michelini, 2011, pp. 305-306).

Also the sport system operationalises its peculiar logic through organisations (Krause, 2005, p. 60). In this dissertation, the organisations of the sport system have been sorted into four categories created *ad hoc* for the interpretation of the empirical analysis and organised starting from a macro-level to micro-level:

– sport system organisations in general: to be understood at the highest level of abstraction as the ensemble of organisations, whose communications and decisions regard the performance of bodies (Thiel & Meier, 2004).
– sport governing bodies: every organisation with regulatory or sanctioning functions in the field of sport has been collected under this category. Examples of governing bodies in sport are the sport federations (Schimank, 1988, p. 191), the National Olympic Committee (NOC), the National Paralympics Committee (NPC) and professional sport leagues.

[79] This theorises that in modern societies, function systems have grown beyond national boundaries and have formed global function systems (Willke, 2007a, pp. 138-140).

- national sport ministries (NSM): these organisations are an example of structural coupling between the political and the sport systems.[80] Their function is to represent sport within the political system and to implement policies regarding sport.[81] Sport ministries, sport ministers and regional or local sections are parts of this organisation.
- sport clubs: the typical organisation of the sport system is the sport club (Schimank, 1988, p. 191), considered at large as including all organisations whose principal purpose is the direct organisation of one or more sports. Examples of this typology of organisation are: sport associations, gyms, athletic clubs, private organisations for economic profit and public sport facilities.

Professional and amateur sport normally share their organisations. To be more precise, professional sport normally uses amateur sport's infrastructures and their members as a recruiting container. However, some organisations are strictly related only to professional sport, like athletes' training centres (Schimank, 1988, p. 216).[82]

Finally, sport organisations are also places, which permit the structural couplings with other function systems. For example, within sport organisations it has become normal to offer facilities and programmes for health-related physical activities such as rehabilitation sport and adapted sport variations alongside traditional sport disciplines such as football, basketball, and volleyball. The same can be said about the integration of sport-borrowed programmes in health organisations. Another example is the education system. In schools, there are several projects and concepts, such as the Health Promoting Schools (WHO, 2011e) and the *Comprehensive School Health Program* (Allensworth & Kolbe, 1987), which aim to incorporate health education into the classical school curriculum. Within this tendency, health education and physical education are often assumed to be instructed together. Hence, physical education teachers are encouraged to integrate health education modules into their lesson plans (Dauer & Pangrazi, 1975).

---

[80] In fact, '[o]rganizations are not necessarily confined to the communicative borders of just one function system' (Moeller, 2006, p. 31) and are indeed the concrete place for structural couplings between systems.

[81] Here it must be anticipated that the sport system has different power and functions depending on the country. The topic will be assessed in the chapter: 'Methodology.'

[82] This is only one example which testifies the parasitic relationship of professional sport towards amateur sport. Other examples of this relationship are: that from an economic perspective, at least in sport disciplines without mass audience, professional sport is sponsored by amateur sport incomes; that at the legitimating level, professional sport participates at the high social estimation (Wertschätzung) of amateur sport (Schimank, 1988, pp. 224-225).

3.3.8 Roles in Health and Sport Systems

Through the assignment of persons to specific roles on the basis of distinguishing marks (*Merkmal*) such as career typology, the system's operations can be implemented more selectively (Luhmann, 1975, pp. 41-45; Schulze, 2005, p. 72). For the operationalisation of organisations' programmes, each workplace has a task, is allocated to a department, and is occupied by a person. Furthermore, roles allow for the inclusion or exclusion within a system through the concept of membership. Someone who is included in the operation of a function system sees themselves as a member of such (Schimank, 1988, p. 85). In relation to the membership in a specific system, specific roles can be divided into performance (*Leistungsrolle*) and complementary roles (*Komplemänterrollen*).

The health system possesses specific institutionalised roles like doctors, physicians, and surgeons. These roles permit the inclusion of people, in a complementary role, into the health system by establishing the relationship doctor/patient (Pelikan, 2009, p. 41). Through this relationship, an ill person becomes a patient in the health system and will be treated with a diagnosis and with therapies (Vogd, 2005a, p. 238).[83] In addition to these classic organisations, the previously mentioned guiding organisations (the WHO and the National Health Ministries) also have their own personnel and representations, which are in and of themselves also specific role positions within the health system. Finally, forms of structural couplings between different systems generate hybrid roles, which have emerged and consolidated as a distinct entity in health care. Examples of these roles are sport and exercise doctors, who are influenced not only by the health system's codes, but also toward the logic of bodily performance.

As a differentiated function system, sport is also defined through its specific roles, which are permanently established within a society: trainers, practitioners and spectators (Cachay, 1988, p. 172).[84] Within this dissertation, Schimank's (1988, pp. 190-191) classification will be used as a theoretical framework. He proposes on a socio-structural level the roles of:

– Athletes who perform sport in the form of participation in formal or informal competitions. This role has different characteristics in relation of its

[83] The value for inclusion in these health system organisations is debated. For Luhmann, illness is the value for connectivity and health the value for reflection (Pelikan, 2007, p. 88). Instead, Pelikan (2007, p. 88) argues that the deficit in positive health is the value of connectivity and the optimal positive health is the value of disconnection (Pelikan, 2007, p. 89).

[84] Spectators can be considered as having a complementary or passive role in the sport system. For this reason, although spectators gained progressive notable importance with the differentiation of professional sport (Schimank, 2001, p. 20), they are irrelevant in the following discussion.

membership to professional or amateur sport; in a broader sense, this category can include all those who are involved in the practice of sport activity;[85]
- Trainers, together with instructors and coaches, who enhance the performances of players through training's routinisation. Trainers steer the sport-specific 'reflexive mechanism' and, in this sense, they are a reflective instance in sport.
- Functionaries, who perform different tasks in the field of sport, such as management of sport organisations, representational tasks, or coordination and arbitrage of competitions. They are a consequence of the formal organisations of modern sport, which create the chance to have stable employment within the sport system without being involved in its implementation.

Notably in the sport system, the phenomenon of inclusion is more intensive than in other subsystems because it implies stronger and more formalised participation, although it normally remains on a voluntary basis (Schimank, 1988, p. 194).

3.4 Relationships between Sport and Health Systems

At this point an important question for this dissertation is raised: 'How is communication between systems possible?' In fact, in systems theory, society is made up of reciprocal interactions of systems (Seven, 2008, p. 15). At the same time, systems have been described above as operationally closed and blind to each other. Furthermore, the communicative coupling faces a situation of contingency because systems have no need to communicate with each other.

To assess this topic, this section explains how relationships between function systems are possible and then uses this theoretical framework to perform a review of the structural couplings between the health and the sport systems. In particular, after briefly analysing the structural couplings of the two systems in general within the society, the section focuses on the relationships between the two systems in order to create an historical context and explain the context in which the empirical analysis has been carried out.

3.4.1 Relationships between Systems in the Systems Theory

In systems theory, function systems are generally characterised as being operationally closed. This means that 'different elements of the system interact in such

[85] For an operational definition of what is considered as being sport in contrast with PA, see the chapter 'Defining Health, Physical Activity, Sport and Their Relationship.'

a way as to produce and re-produce the elements of the system' (Seidl & Schoeneborn, 2010, p. 6). For example, the health system communicates everything which concerns with health. By doing this it sets the boundaries with the environment and contemporary produces the health system itself. Because 'there are no operations entering the system from outside nor vice versa' (Seidl & Schoeneborn, 2010, p. 6), all those that exist outside the system are perceived as being its environment (Baraldi et al., 1997a, pp. 89-90; Luhmann, 2008a, p. 86). Nevertheless, the environment plays an essential role in the auto-determination of function systems and is the precondition of systems' relationship.[86] In fact, from the perspective of a function system, other function systems constitute the environment, which is, in turn, able to create reactions in the internal processes of function systems by stimulating impulses.[87] It is through this phenomenon that relationships between function systems are explicable. Systems are connected with each other because each one fulfils a function for society and is simultaneously part of the society (Kuchler, 2006, p. 19; Luhmann, 1997a, p. 746).[88] Two function systems being capable of stimulating each other create, in systems theory, a structural coupling:[89] 'a state in which two systems shape the environment of each other in such a way that both depend on the other for continuing their autopoiesis and increasing their structural complexity' (Moeller, 2006, p. 19).

For example, sport performances are important for many function systems. Because relationships between systems are never univocal, they in turn suggest the existence of many structural couplings, which are fundamental to the sport system's development and existence. These couplings are particularly important with the education, religion, politics, military, health and economic systems (Schimank, 1988, p. 198).

The structural couplings of the sport system can be distinguished in relation of its two logics:

– Professional sport has strong relationships primarily with the mass media system, as a telegenic and newsworthy product; politics, as a medium for enhancing the population's national identification; and economic, as a medium of product advertising (Schimank, 1988, pp. 217-223);

[86] Luhmann differentiates two typologies of relationship: one between function systems and society, through function and performance, and one of systems with themselves, through self-reflection (Krause, 2005, p. 66). This section refers to the first typology of relationship.
[87] Coupling does not explain how or why a system interacts with the environment produced by other systems; it is simply the result of the relationship.
[88] The debates that have emerged out of the structuralist-functionalist approach in the sociology of sport around this theoretical model must be acknowledged here (for example in: Ingham & Donnelly, 1997; Pronger, 2002).
[89] In fact, even if 'structural coupling' is often preferred by Luhmann, the term can be considered a synonym of 'relationship' (Krause, 2005, p. 66).

– Amateur sport shows strong couplings with the systems of: education, as a pedagogic and socialisation medium, normally institutionalised in schools' curricula; politics, as a medium to solve urbanisation and integration problems; military, as a medium of recruiting, maintaining and enhancing the population's bodily performances; economy, in form of a market segment; religion, as a medium of recruiting and inclusion; and particularly with the health system[90] (Schimank, 1988, pp. 198-210).

Also the reproduction and development of the health system have been characterised by many structural couplings (Pelikan, 2009, p. 41). Luhmann, Bauch and Pelikan assume that the health system is coupled with the economy, science, politics, law, the media, family and the education system (Pelikan, 2007, p. 91). In particular from the perspective of the health system, the following couplings are highly relevant (Pelikan, 2009, p. 41):

– with science and education systems for recruiting and training of health personal;
– with economy and science systems for the development of new knowledge, treatments and medicines;
– with politics and law and also with economy and media for the determination of the health system's operational environment;
– and with family as a means of taking care of family members.

Pelikan (2007, p. 90) argues that the strongest coupling of the health system is with the scientific and education systems, followed by the coupling with the economic system and the political system, whose strength varies in dependence with the state's welfare policies. Bauch (2004, p. 44) assumes that a relevant role is played by the coupling between the economic and health systems because money is seen as the only limitation to the hypostatisation of the health system.

Irritation is the capacity of responding to a stimulus (Østerberg, 2000, p. 24). This enables the adaptation of an autopoietic system to the environment's perturbations through structural coupling: 'Systems can "irritate" each other, possibly leading to the creation of operational and structural couplings between systems. One system may irritate another by observing a part of its activities and strategically interfering with its operations. Structural couplings emerge as a system struggles to find a way to cope with a recurring source of environmental irritation. An effective coupling communicates information about the environment in a self-referential manner' (D. Lee, 2000, p. 328). An important characteristic of this phenomenon is that it is not univocal, instead '[t]here are always two

[90] The structural coupling between the sport and the health systems, particularly relevant for the development of sports system, will be discussed separately in the following as a fundamental topic of this dissertation.

sides to structural coupling. A system that irritates another cannot, in turn, avoid being irritated' (Moeller, 2006, p. 39).[91]

This can only involve the cognitive processes of a system but doesn't determine them (Wiesenthal, 2006, p. 63). In fact, autopoietic functional systems have no operational coupling but only structural coupling (Luhmann, 1990d, p. 102f). In practice, the logics of two function systems can be combined only at the organisational level (Kuchler, 2006, p. 18; Luhmann, 1990a, p. 396ff).[92] For example, the sport system offers health-orientated programmes to their customers in its organisations. However, this does not modify its evaluative orientation towards sport performances. In fact, structural coupling does not imply a fusion of the systems' logics, which instead remain highly independent (Luhmann, 2002a, pp. 396-401). In this cognitive relationship, systems are stimulated by the environment and not by external intervention in their internal processes. That is why autopoiesis and structural coupling are completely compatible (Wiesenthal, 2006, p. 62).

If the two systems have a privileged structural coupling in which there is reciprocal stimulus in a particularly efficient way, one can speak of the systems' interpenetration (Baraldi et al., 1997b, p. 139). This can be defined as a reciprocal reduction of the degrees of the freedom of systems, which still allows the pursuance or improvement of their self-reproduction (Lange, 2004, p. 12; Luhmann, 1995a, p. 48). Integration always has a negative connotation: over or underintegration. Underintegration means that a system does not perform adequately for the other systems or that its performance limits the operations of other systems. Overintegration is the excessive coupling of systems and represents a risk for them (Lange, 2004, p. 16). Indeed, if the structural coupling between two function systems is too high, it can cause negative effects to one or both systems, worsening their efficiency, innovative power and performance (Lange, 2004, p. 12). In this sense, systemic integration, which is, in its common sense, often considered as something desirable (Lange, 2004, p. 11), is a dangerous situation from the perspective of systems theory (Luhmann, 1997a, pp. 617-618) because through the integration, systems are no longer as free as they were in a disintegrated situation. For the purpose of this dissertation, the integration of systems is particularly significant. In fact, the communication of the health system on the role of sport in the promotion of PA is a clear manifestation of an important aspect of the stable and historical relationship between the two systems.

[91] In this quotation and in the following the term 'irritation' is used in its systems theory's specific meaning and can be transcribed as 'stimulus'.

[92] Instead, the structural coupling between the society and the personal consciousness systems (*Bewusstseinssysteme*) or, roughly, persons is realised through language (Wiesenthal, 2006, p. 63).

3.4.2 Different Relationships between the Sport and the Health Systems

The relationship between sport and health systems[93] represents one of the most fascinating topics in both the sociologies of health and illness and of sport. In fact, both the health and the sport systems have continuously influenced each other, evolved in their functions, and gained great social significance.

Functional differentiation became the primary type of social differentiation in Europe and in the world during the 18th century (Moeller, 2006, p. 41). The process of functional differentiation leading up to the birth of modern societies has been characterised by the differentiation of function systems from the environment (Cachay, 1988, p. 61; Cachay & Thiel, 2000, p. 60). In particular, the sport system first emerged as one of the last function systems in the 19th century (Stichweh, 1990, p. 374). Consequently, the following enquiry starts to review the relationship between the two systems from the end of the 19th century. A modified version of the following two sections has been published in an article of the European Journal for Sport and Society (Michelini & Thiel, 2013). Because this topic constitutes a crucial point of the theoretical framework of this dissertation, this has been argued in a modified and briefer version. The discussion identifies two different attitudes of the health system regarding the function of 'sport' as a medium of health. In these two phases,[94] the essence of the relationship between the two systems assumes brand new characteristics by paradigmatically changing after periods of stability.

3.4.2.1 Qualification of Sport in the Health System's Communications

The qualification of PA and sport to the health system's communication has allowed the coupling between the health and the sport systems. In particular, the acknowledgment of these as health-medium by the health system represents the basis of a phase, in which the sport system is fundamentally dependent on the health system. In fact, there is consensus in the literature on the claim that the birth of the sport system was enabled by the development of the health system and the expansion of its themes. Indeed, a decisive factor in the emergence of the sport system has been the creation by the health system of the societal need for more PA for health reasons (Cachay & Thiel, 2000, p. 79; Schimank, 2005, p.

[93] A modified version of the following sociological analysis has been published in Michelini and Thiel (2013). As this topic constitutes a fundamental part of the theoretical framework of the present dissertation, it needs to be discussed in the following.

[94] Within this section, these phases are roughly connected with time spans. However, temporal specifications do not represent precise indications of the beginning and end of phases due to overlapping.

21). This plays a key role in the present discussions and obliges to briefly sketch the history of the emergence of the health system.

The low rate of population growth due to high death rates led to the differentiation of the health system (Cachay, 1988, p. 62; Cachay & Thiel, 2000, pp. 61-62). In this context, PA started to be considered by the health system as being relevant for health (Cachay, 1988, p. 72) and subsequently was recommended as both a preventive and curative medium (Cachay, 1988, p. 92). In this way, the health system offered the basis for the emergence of a system for the implantation of PA both at the level of justification (PA is good for health) and at the level of structures (places and structures for doing PA) (Cachay & Thiel, 2000, p. 79). This led to a quantitative[95] and qualitative[96] explosion of health-related scientific and pedagogic programmes for PA in the 18th century. In turn, the differentiation of programmes permitted a successful differentiation of an independent system of PA (Cachay & Thiel, 2000, p. 82).[97]

Almost simultaneously (between the 17th-18th centuries), modern sport disciplines like cricket, fox hunting, horse racing and boxing emerged in England as principal pastimes (Maguire, 1994, p. 405). Different from physical activities born in the same period in German speaking regions, the English sporting disciplines were not health-related in the beginning. In fact, they started to be coupled with health firstly in Victorian England (19th century), where sports became to be used as medium against social and health dangers induced by the mass migration from rural areas into the cities (Schimank, 1988, p. 204). However, also in this case the integration of sport and PA in the health system's communication led to the symbiotic relationship, which was fundamental for the consolidation of the sport system (Schimank, 1988, p. 204). Through the development of the health system, a social problem (the protection of public health) was identified, the solution to the problem (sport as compensation for the lack of physical exercise) was proposed and institutionalised solutions to the problem (establishment and administration of public facilities) began to be offered.

Even if based on the stabilisation of the idea that 'sport is good for one's health,' the further development of the relationship between the health and the sport systems is characterised by the increasing degree of independence of the sport system. In particular, the health system entrusts the sport with the autonomous functions of creating proper environments and offers for population's PA.

---

[95] For example the number of professional figures of medical specialisation as well as the number of hospitals and healthcare practices (Cachay, 1988, p. 63; Cachay & Thiel, 2000, p. 63).

[96] For example, this is the case of the development of medical technology and knowledge (Cachay, 1988, p. 63; Cachay & Thiel, 2000, p. 63).

[97] A different perspective on the emergence of the health system has been offered by Foucault's concepts of biopower and biopolitics (Foucault, 1998). This perspective is highly interesting yet not compatible with the present discussion.

This turn has been allowed by a process of the systems' self-reflection (Cachay & Thiel, 2000, p. 105) and accompanied by a considerable consolidation and growth of the two systems. These phenomena are characteristic for the 20th century.

During this period, alongside other couplings, the sport system still had its strongest binds to the health system (Schimank, 1988, p. 204). Indeed, despite radical changes lived by the two systems, the coupling between the health and sport systems remained stable: the health system 'acknowledged' the sport system as responsible for bodily activity within society and assigned it some typologies of prevention and therapy functions. At the same time, the sport system legitimised its societal role by successfully supplementing the performances of the health system (Stichweh, 1990, p. 204). In fact, the main line of reasoning for justifying the societal relevance of sport in the 20th century referred to the consequences of the substantial change in lifestyle habits (city life, public transport, office jobs). Since the late 1970s, the major health problems of modern society were increasingly identified as being caused by modifiable risk factors (stress, tobacco consumption, unbalanced dietary intake and sedentariness). The increased health system focus on NCDs was fundamental in reinforcing the nexus between the concepts of health and sport: sport was considered an outstanding activity in relation to its (theoretical) benefits for fighting many prominent diseases (Heinemann, 2007, p. 59). For this reason in this period '[t]here are probably few ideas which are as widely and uncritically accepted as that linking sport and exercise with good health' (Waddington et al., 1997, p. 165). Indeed, the positive impact of sport as a form of PA was normally taken for granted and this is still the reason for including it in school curricula and strategies for health promotion (Lüschen et al., 1996, p. 197).

Besides this characteristic relationship, the two systems enhanced their social relevance. This process of growth can be explained as an adaptation of the systems to the environment of a dynamic and developing society. To respond to the stimuli of this social environment, both the health and sport systems adapted their functions and continuously enhanced their complexity. To be more precise:

- Through several paradigmatic changes caused by both theoretical[98] and technological[99] developments, the health system sensibly expanded its functions and its relevance in society. This has been widely described in the scientific community with various terms such as 'healthism' (Crawford, 1980; Rose, 1999; Skrabanek, 1994) and 'medicalization' (Conrad, 1992; Conrad

[98] For example, Antonovsky's salutogenesis (Antonovsky, 1979), and the risk factors model, used first by Dr. Thomas Royle Dawber in the Framingham Heart Study (Dawber et al., 1951).

[99] For example, the advances in the diagnosis and treatment of different life sciences' specialisms like pharmacology, toxicology, virology and hematology.

& Schneider, 1980; Zola, 1991). The inclusion of (theoretically) all members of the society and the expansion of its functions brought even to speak about the birth of a super system (Bauch, 1996, 2004).[100]

– Sport became 'an ever present element of modern society' (McPherson et al., 1989, p. 2) and 'institutionalized in practically all societies, thus denoting its universal character' (Grupe & Baitsch, 1972, p. 119). The sport system plays a significant role in modern societies acknowledged by the massive participation (amateurs and professionals) and audience, but also by the social relevance of many events and by its influence on social behaviour. Referring to this phenomenon, some sociologists and sport scientists speak about a 'sportification of society' (Cachay, 1990; Digel, 1990; Grupe, 1988).

The drawing in of more and more segments of the population characterises in this period the process of hypostatisation. For the health system, inclusion became widespread in the 19th century by including the disadvantaged classes and by providing services free of charge (Cachay & Thiel, 2000, p. 81). Instead, the sport system successfully 'sportified' pastimes (Dunning, 1995, p. 8). This process had three main spurts: in the 18th century the 'sportified' version of some traditional forms English diversions (cricket, golf, foxhunting, horseracing and boxing) emerged as principal pastimes; in the 19th century new sport disciplines (athletics, soccer, rugby and tennis) grew and sport clubs became less exclusive; and, at the end of the 19th century, many of the 'English sport forms began to spread around the world' (Dunning, 1995, p. 10).[101]

The growth of the sport system and its acknowledged responsibility for the population's PA origin the main change in the relationship between the two systems: the release of the sport system from the health system. This is certainly connected with the successful 'sportification' of pastimes (Dunning, 1995, p. 8) and the institutionalisation and relevance of sporting events such as the Olympic Games and the FIFA World Cup. However, these successes are the consequences rather than reasons of the release of sport system from the health system. In fact, the sport system's path to independence matches the development of an efficient sport canon, which distinguished sport from other forms of PAs through specific rules, organisations and roles (Cachay & Thiel, 2000, p. 105). This process includes the differentiation of programmes that permitted the creation of a wide range of activities on offer. Heinemann (2007, pp. 57-60) acknowledges this phenomenon by dividing sport along five different models: traditional-competitive sport, professional sport, expressive sport, functional sport and tradi-

[100] This thesis has been criticised (for example Pelikan, 2009, p. 42) and never fully accepted in the scientific community.

[101] The word 'sport' itself with minor linguistic variations established in many European countries (Dunning, 1995, p. 11).

tional-game sport. All of these models are characterised by the presence – with different relevance – of four constitutive elements of sport: bodily performance, competition, rules and non-productivity (Heinemann, 2007, p. 56).[102] The growth of the two systems also permitted the birth of new 'minor' structural couplings within both systems. For example, Schimank (1988, p. 204) argues that the sport system's coupling with the health system determined the birth of a health-sport subsystem within the sport system, which includes activities such as jogging, aerobics, trimming and rehabilitation sports.

Within this period, the responsibility of health and sport systems for the population's health is not easy to discern (Stichweh, 1990, p. 382). In fact, sports have something in common with well-being and the health system is the function system responsible for it. This confusion can be overcome by: dedicating the health system to deal with the issue of illness more than with that of health; and by identifying the sport system as the 'health system' of modern society (Stichweh, 1990, p. 382). Indeed, bodily health is a fundamental prerequisite, only for the sport system, while for all other systems the body plays an insignificant role if the physiological bases are intact. At the same time, for Stichweh (1990, p. 383) the development of the sport and health systems is a complementary process that positively enhances their autopoiesis. In this situation, 'the longer the health care system becomes accustomed to the fact that regular sport activities prevent certain serious illnesses, the less it could do without this support of its own operations' (Schimank, 2005, p. 23).

3.4.2.2 Disqualification of Sport in the Health System's Communication

The latest trends in the health system's logic demonstrate that Stichweh's aforementioned theory on 'the sport system as health system of modern society' is charming yet questionable.[103] Recent developments in the relationship between health and sport systems show the weakening of the general belief that 'sport is good for the health'. This new perspective of the health system about sport as a health-medium generated a more fragmented and ambiguous scenario.

Indeed, between the late 20th century and the early 21st century, the relationship between sport and health has been characterised by an apparent contradiction: on the one hand the belief that 'sport is good for the health' is consolidating in the mass media, in part of the scientific community, in politics and

[102] In this section, the provision of constitutive elements of sport instead of its definition has been favoured because the latter appears to be particularly debated within the scientific community (Bette, 1995, p. 33; Heinemann, 2007, pp. 53-54).

[103] At the same time, other concepts which were seen for decades as unquestionable milestones of sport began to be put in question (König, 1995).

generally in society (Klaus Bös & Walter Brehm, 1998, p. 7; Rütten et al., 2010, p. 18); on the other hand, the connections between sport and health are becoming openly disputed by some scientists and these critiques are being increasingly accepted by the health system (S. Becker, 2011, p. 15). Indeed, '[a]fter more than a century of involvement of medical science in the analysis of sport there are still many open questions, and the final verdict on the impact of sport on health is still pending' (Lüschen et al., 1996, p. 200). In this regard, the main argumentation of the health system is that even if several studies have established objective connections between PA and health, one should not automatically extend these conclusions to sport activities. In fact, such studies normally 'do not suggest that all exercise is beneficial; rather, they indicate that exercise of a particular kind, amount, and intensity has a beneficial impact on health' (Waddington et al., 1997, p. 168).

The analysis of this paradox implies an operative distinction between sport and PA. PA is 'any bodily movement produced by skeletal muscles that results in energy expenditure' (Caspersen et al., 1985, p. 126). A further characteristic of PA can be made by specifying its mode, frequency, intensity, duration and continuity (Ainsworth et al., 2000; Caspersen et al., 1986; Dishman et al., 1985; Evenson et al., 2002; Hagströmer, 2007; King, 2001). Sport is a subset of PA, characterised by being recreational and governed by rules and orientated to performance (modified version of Heinemann, 2007, p. 56). This somewhat general characterisation allows for evidence of some features of sporting activities. Firstly, they are not easily adaptable to everyday life because they normally require planned time, special fields, equipment and/or partners. Secondly, their intensity is not predictable, because 'the fact that sport involves not only cooperation but also competition, means that sport, and particularly team sport, is usually a considerably more complex social activity than is non-competitive exercise' (Waddington et al., 1997, p. 170). This implies that 'the frequency and intensity of these bursts of activity are, at least in complex games, largely beyond the ability of any single player to control; […], that players are almost inevitably constrained by the moves of their opponents to engage in activities which are anything but rhythmic; and […], that many of these movements, such as those involved in rapid acceleration and deceleration, or the twisting or turning movements involved in rapid changes of direction, impose considerably greater stresses on the body than do the much more rhythmic movements involved in non-competitive walking, jogging or swimming' (Waddington et al., 1997, p. 171).

Since the beginning of the 1980s, many studies (British Medical Association, 1992, p. 14; J.N. Morris et al., 1980; Paffenbarger Jr et al., 1986; Smith & Jacobson, 1988, p. 126) have started to emphasise the beneficial effects of moderate and regular forms of PA (Waddington et al., 1997, pp. 168-169).

The idea that 'daily PA of moderate intensity, e.g. brisk walking, is sufficient for health benefits in many sections of populations' (Oja, 2004, p. 169), also called the 'moderate-intensity' concept, has consolidated during recent years in the scientific health-community. Indeed, the formula of 'at least 30 minutes of regular, moderate-intensity PA on most days' (WHO, 2004, p. 4) has become the standard of health-orientated recommendation on the dosage of PA. Because the health benefits of intense PA are more disputed, they have been marginalised in these recommendations. Indeed, as Waddington et al. (1997, p. 169) point out: 'one cannot assume that the health benefits associated with moderate exercise will simply be duplicated - still less can one assume that they will be increased – by exercise which is more frequent, of longer duration and of greater intensity, for exercise of this kind, as we shall see later, may generate substantial health 'costs' in terms of additional stresses or injuries.'

In defence of classical sport as a medium for improving health, there are no reliable studies establishing that competitive and professional sports are, in general, unhealthy.[104] In fact, statistical inquiries regarding sport injuries in top-athletes do not demonstrate a general bad influence on health understood broadly as 'a state of complete physical, mental and social well-being and not merely the absence of disease or infirmity' (WHO, 1946, p. 1). Moreover, it should be kept in mind that '[r]egardless of the causal relationship between sport and the objective state of health, there is of course the matter of cultural interplay and lifestyle' (Lüschen et al., 1996, p. 199). Sport, not as a subset of PA but as a complex social phenomenon, tends to have a healthy influence on the lifestyle of the practitioners and of the athletes. In addition, by considering only the implications of sport on physiological health, the health system forgets the socio-psychological implications of sport which can have important beneficial influence on general well-being (R. Fuchs, 2003, p. 1).

This demonstrates that the reason for the deligitimisation of the sport system in the area of health promotion does not rely on scientific reason, but rather on the paradigmatic developments of the health system already started in the second half of the 20th century. These developments brought about a new logic in addition to the one of 'healthy/ill', namely the code of 'hindering/promoting health' (Bauch, 1996). This new code emerged in the background of a decline in the population's health caused by NCDs and shifted the focus of the health system from the classical curative praxis to the prevention of illness and the promotion of health. In this contest, the promotion of PA once again became one of the

[104] Critical positions and disputes about what is good for one's health without (or with poor) evidence-based data are not new to the scientific community. Furthermore, it has to be remembered here that some scholars also claim that healthcare is having negative influences on population's health (Illich, 2003).

functions of the health system (Lupton, 1995, 1999). However, the acceptance and co-habitation of the two codes within the health system is often problematic, in particular in the case of PA promotion. In fact, even if the health system focused on PA promotion in the perspective of the code 'hindering/promoting health,' it kept evaluating the benefits and disadvantages of PA by referring to the old code 'health/illness'.

Conversely, the causes for this re-appropriation of the promotion of PA are not only related to the health system's developments. Indeed, the sport system has been incapable of singularly carrying out the function of making people sufficiently active. Despite the processes of growth and augmented inclusion as well as the birth of ad-hoc solutions such as the sport-for-all movement, the sport system proved unable to include some parts of the population, especially risk groups particularly affected by NCDs. Moreover, the intrinsic need of enhancing sport performance, particularly present in professional sport but also to a lesser degree in amateur sport, is characterised by risking the health of athletes (Nixon, 1994). Nevertheless, the sport system today offers a broad spectrum of activities that are explicitly health-orientated (Haag & Haag, 2003, p. 238). This wider differentiation of the sport system permitted its expansion but it has also raised questions about the loss of its real constitutive elements: a social phenomenon called 'de-sportification of sport' (Cachay, 1990; Digel, 1990). This implies the diversification and consolidation within the sport system of new sporting disciplines that are not characterised by the classical code of 'win/lose'. The de-sportification of sport demonstrates that 'sport has lost its hitherto established form and has been complemented by elements which contradict its classical definition' (Bette, 1995, p. 34). Moreover, successful trends such as jogging, body-building and mountain biking embody a category of activities which 'require no membership, are easier to synchronize with the segmented timing of complex societies and do not carry the burden of honorary participation commitments' (Bette, 1995, p. 43).

Even by taking into account all these tendencies, the sport system has not been able to fulfil its function to ensure PA in the population. Indeed, many people's health is in decline because of illness caused by physical inactivity (Cachay, 1988, p. 9). In other words, even in its 'expanded' form, the sport system is incapable of handling the problems that justified its birth. This justifies health system's reappropriation of PA promotion after a period in which it no longer cared about it (Cachay, 1988, p. 10), as this function had been delegated to the sport system. In summary, the historical function of sport as a medium of health in the health system's communication is undergoing a phase of deligitimisation.

However, the whole relationship between health and sport is not experiencing a period of crisis. Many new and old forms of 'secondary' couplings still bind the two systems together, for example in the cases of: rehabilitation, health preservation through PA, medical assistance of top athletes, adapted sports for illness sufferers and many others.

In order to exemplify how these new connections evolve and become an important adhesive for the binding between the two systems, the example of medical assistance for top athletes will be commented upon in the following. Today in top-level sports, '[t]he modern successful athlete is likely to be surrounded by - or at least to have access to - and to be increasingly dependent upon, a whole group of specialist advisers, including specialists in sports medicine' (Waddington, 1996, p. 180). In this case a new function of the health system has been created for the sport system (and not vice-versa) and this coupling has bilateral characteristics. In fact, not only are 'top-class athletes more and more dependent on increasingly sophisticated systems of medical support in their efforts to run faster, jump further, or compete more effectively in their chosen sport' (Waddington, 1996, p. 180), but the health system also needs sporting injuries as a justification for the consolidation and institutionalisation of new operational procedures created ad-hoc to combat illnesses which would barely exist (or would not be relevant) without the sport system.[105]

This leads to the discussion on a final phenomenon regarding modern developments of the health system's process of medicalisation. This '[...] describes a process by which nonmedical problems become defined and treated as medical problems, usually in terms of illnesses or disorders' (Conrad, 1992, p. 209). The process of medicalisation expands the responsibilities of the health system to functions that were once performed by other systems and specifically by the sport system. This is 'worrying' some sociologists (Cachay & Thiel, 1999b) who observe that the health system includes several sport operations in its organisations, and yet exclude sporting staff (for example trainers) from the administration and execution of these operational procedures. At the same time, personnel from the health system are progressively finding professional opportunities in sport organisations. Furthermore athletes, by sole virtue of being athletes and disconnected from any form of pathology, receive special consideration by the health system (Waddington, 1996, p. 179).[106] In this sense '[a]thletes have thus become yet one more group to add to Illich's list of those - the unborn, new-

105 Examples of illnesses caused by sport are lateral epicondylitis, also known as tennis elbow, and patellar tendinopathy, also known as jumper's knee.

106 For example, 'athletes require routine medical supervision, not because they necessarily have any clearly defined pathology but, in this case, simply because they are athletes' (Waddington, 1996, p. 179).

born, infants, and so on - who are held by definition to require routine medical supervision, irrespective of the presence or absence of any specific pathology' (Waddington, 1996, pp. 179-180).

3.5 Governance in the Promotion of Physical Activity

The previous section assessed the topic of the relationship between function systems. In particular, the mechanism of mutual influence through irritations called 'structural coupling' has been pointed out as the means for establishing relationships between independent and autopoietic function systems. However, this still does not explain how the function systems can be steered for example in the case of the cooperative implementation of a strategy. In fact, the sport and the health systems are surely linked by a strict relationship, but this situation creates also conflict potential because parts of the operations of the two systems overlap. This is also the case for the promotion of PA in which the two systems not only irritate each other, but also aim for a common goal using two different logics. Furthermore, in the promotion of PA the health system is assuming an acknowledged leading role, which raises questions about its ability of coordination and about the sport system's capacity to react to these stimuli. In order to cover this final missing piece in the theoretical framework, the following section introduces the concept of 'governance' from the perspective of the systems theory, which will be the theoretical basis for the analysis of the role of sport in health-related communications on the promotion of PA.

3.5.1 Governance in Systems Theory

'Governance' is a word with multiple meanings and it has been discussed in different academic disciplines. For this reason it is necessary to give a brief overview of them to explain the implication of the use of a systems theory perspective for the concept of governance and to clarify how it is different from other perspectives.

Although the term 'governance' has a long history,[107] it was still unknown to the majority of the subject's experts until the 1990s (Benz et al., 2007, p. 10). In fact, the word was long associated with the term 'government' and was rarely used in the period following the Second World War until it first re-

[107] Etymologically the term derives from the ancient Greek *kubernan*, which meant to pilot or steer. In the Middle Ages the word *gubernare* indicated piloting, rule-making or steering (Kjær, 2004, p. 3).

emerged in the 1980s with a broader meaning (Kjær, 2004, p. 1). However, it is first at the end of the 1990s that 'governance' became a central scientific concept for many of the humanities (Kjær, 2004, p. 1). Today its usage has become prominent in many scientific and organisational discussions, particularly the ones on changes in the nature and role of the state and of social coordination (Bevir, 2009, p. VII). However, similarly to many other authors (Benz et al., 2007, p. 9; Bevir, 2009, p. 3; Kjær, 2004, p. 1; Lange, 2004, p. 18; Willke, 2007b, p. 10) Jordan, Wurzel and Zito (2005, p. 478) observe that 'there is no universally accepted definition of governance'.

For Bevir (2009, p. 29), this is due to the fact that 'the term "governance" can be used at various levels of generality and within various theoretical contexts'.[108] Bevir (2009, pp. 3-4) acknowledges three different levels of generality connected to the concept of governance which can be referred to: changes in the nature and role of states after the reforms of the 1980s and 1990s; the pattern of rules that arises if the state plays little or no steering role; and in general the entire pattern of coordinating rules. Also within its theoretical contexts, the word 'governance' is extremely multidisciplinary (Benz et al., 2007, p. 10) because its key concepts are derived from diverse disciplines (rational choice, new institutionalism, regulation theory, social constructivism and systems theory),[109] which often rely on different assumptions (Bevir, 2009, p. VII). Hence, the meanings of 'governance' depends greatly upon the theoretical context (Bevir, 2009, pp. 16-21).[110] For Benz (2007, p. 13), the governance concept's multidisciplinary nature can on the one hand be confusing, but on the other hand it can constitute a bridge-concept between disciplines.

In sociology, governance broadly refers to the mechanism 'for steering social systems toward their goals' (Rosenau, 1998, p. 296).[111] This topic is directly related to a fundamental question of the sociology: 'How is social order possible?' (Luhmann, 2008b, p. 13). However, the word 'governance' has been borrowed by sociology from neighbouring disciplines like economics and politics. Within sociology, the usage of the term today has become prominent, particularly in systems theory, regulation theory, social constructivism and actor

[108] Moreover, Benz et al. (2007, pp. 14-15) also recognise different usages of governance: analytical, descriptive, normative and practical.

[109] In the 'Handbuch Governance', Benz et al. (2007, pp. 10-12) acknowledge two prominent perspectives: the one of institutional economy and the one of political science. In the first case, governance is understood as a mode of non-market organisation. In the second case, governance is understood as counterpoint to government defined as hierarchical social steering.

[110] Or, from another point of view, 'governance' can be even seen as an 'empty signifier' (Offe, 2009).

[111] Rosenau is not a system theorist and he borrowed the term 'social system' from complexity science.

centred institutionalism[112] (Bevir, 2009, pp. 16-21). Among these approaches, systems theory offers particular advantages because 'the new governance has arisen because we live in a centerless society, or at least a society with multiple centers' (Bevir, 2009, p. 19).

As anticipated in the introduction, the concept of structural coupling is not sufficient to explain the social phenomenon at hand because if 'there is an explicit goal to be implemented, resulting from a project, a plan or a strategy' (Willke, 2007b, p. 10), the relationship between systems becomes a question of governance. In fact, the health system not only cooperates with the sport system for the promotion of PA, but it also produces new approaches to the problem of PI and it tries to involve the sport system in its strategies.

In this dissertation, governance is defined as: 'the activity of coordinating communications in order to achieve collective goals through collaboration' (Willke, 2007b, p. 10).[113] In systems theory, communication is the unity of three selections: of announcement, of information and of understanding (Hagen, 2000, p. 36; Moeller, 2006, p. 22). The empirical analysis of this doctoral thesis will involve the announcements of the health system regarding the topic of sport's participation in strategies for the health-orientated promotion of PA. By being a self-referential and autopoietic operation defining the unity of systems (Albert, 2004, p. 7), communication plays a principal role because governance 'produces patterns of communication and the need to organize communication creates the demand for governance' (Willke, 2007b, p. 25). In order to better understand the definition of governance and how it is possible in the perspective of systems theory, the following sections focus on the problems and chances related to governance, the cases of relationship in governance and the role of super-experts in it.

---

[112] The actor-centred institutionalism, whose biggest representatives are Renate Mayntz and Fritz W. Scharpf, is a highly relevant and well accepted scientific stream. This theory is a reaction to Luhmann's scepticism about the chance of steering systems and putting the relevance of social actors in the centre of analysis (Pöllmann, 2005, p. 172). This theory has been considered a candidate for this dissertation's theoretical framework, but it has been dismissed for being less functional for the discussion at hand.

[113] The word 'governance' has not been used in Luhmann's works, even if the topics of integration and structural coupling are central to systems theory. Furthermore, the problematic integration of function systems within society has long remained at the periphery of the discussions of systems theory (Schimank, 2000, p. 449).

3.5.2 *Problems and Chances of Governance*

The chances of cooperation between systems are dependent upon the specific form of differentiation within a specific society. In modern societies,[114] functional differentiation implies independence of function systems, but also creates interdependences between them through society itself (Hagen, 2000, p. 31; Luhmann, 1997a, p. 746). However, systems normally perform their functions independently and do not need to communicate outside their boundaries: they observe society from their peculiar perspective without the chance of understanding the logic of other systems (Willke, 2001b, p. 100). This autonomy and autopoiesis[115] cause communication, steering and control problems (Willke, 2001b, p. 106; 2007b, p. 25).

Luhmann gives no solid theoretical basis for the analysis of governance mechanisms (Wiesenthal, 2006, p. 68) and for the problem of relationships between social systems (Krause, 2005, p. 65).[116] Furthermore, Luhmann has been highly sceptical about the chances of steering systems (Krause, 2005, p. 65). Despite this, a summary of Luhmann's thinking about these topics is necessary because they serve as theoretical basis for the introduction of the Willke's theories. For Luhmann, 'when specific forms of speech are differentiated from noise and given meaning in a social context, a language emerges that can function as a structural coupling between communicants' (D. Lee, 2000, p. 326). This is also the case for governance, in which function systems can develop a common understanding, which allows for inter-systemic cooperation. However, this still doesn't create a sufficient environment for positive governance. Indeed, systems interpret the attempt to steer them using their own logic and the operative closeness of self-referential systems hinder the chance of prescriptive steering for society and for systems (Wiesenthal, 2006, p. 66). This can determine differences between the original steering impulse and its implementation by the system (Wiesenthal, 2006, p. 67).

---

[114] In this dissertation, the adjective 'modern' has been preferred to 'postmodern' when describing society. However, the term 'postmodern' has been widely discussed in sociology, principally by Habermas (1986, 1990, 1993), but also by Luhmann (1995d) in an article titled 'Why Does Society Describe Itself as Postmodern?'.

[115] Autopoiesis means that social systems are operationally closed (Luhmann, 1984). It refers to the mode of internal operations of the system; autonomy is the relationship of systems to their environment. In functionally differentiated societies, the relationship of social systems to society is determined by a specific function, while the relationship with other systems is determined by their performances (Luhmann, 1990b, p. 73).

[116] Krause (2005, pp. 68-70) even stresses a certain imprecision in Luhmann's arguments and lexicons regarding these topics, which normally represent the very strengths of the systems theory.

Instead, Willke[117] is more optimistic than Luhmann about the chances of systems' steering, governance and cooperation (Wiesenthal, 2006, p. 68). In this perspective, function systems are able to cut across functional domains, take into account societal needs and 'are credited with a capacity for integration' (Hagen, 2000, p. 34). In particular, they can react to external stimuli and modify themselves in order to allow positive cooperation if it constitutes a win-win situation for all subjects involved. Premise for this is the establishment of particular patterns of communication that crystallise through repetition and confirmation (Willke, 2007b, p. 27) and allow for the inclusion of foreign meanings in the systems' self-referential processes (Wiesenthal, 2006, p. 72). In fact, 'from a systemic view, there is no operational coupling of two distinct complex, self-referential systems' (Willke, 2007b, p. 15), but 'coordination of different systems poses no problem of identity, since it simply requires an agreement on common rules or perspectives' (Willke, 2007b, p. 15). This can happen because systems operate through organisations, which can act in multiple contexts with diverse environments and can communicate in a multilingual way (Wiesenthal, 2006, p. 70). From this point of view, a governance situation between the health system and the sport system is theoretically possible. In this case, the health system would produce communication that is able to irritate the sport system with the aim of achieving a form of cooperation between their organisations for reaching the common goal of PA promotion.

The aforementioned situation in which a system stimulates another system in order to obtain cooperation to achieve a common goal does not give any insight about the success of the effort. In fact, the attempt to steer of one system by another can produce three different scenarios (Willke, 2005, pp. 106-107): indifference, conflict or coordination. The typical relationship between systems is one of indifference and it continues until the operations of one system cease to interfere with the competences of others.[118] Also, the relationships between experts of different systems are often conflict-free because they have nothing to say, they live in different worlds and they speak different languages (Willke, 2001b, p. 106). Systemic communications directed to another system is generally unable to irritate it or to be translated in the logic of the system. This does not change the *status quo* of indifference between systems and does not create the premise for governance.

[117] Helmut Willke (born 1945) is a German sociologist, whose scientific work on systems theory led to further developments of Luhmann's work, particularly regarding social control and Lateral World Systems theories. These two extensions are highly relevant for this dissertation.

[118] To ensure this, the systems' operations have to be characterised by operative fairness, humanity and efficiency and do not have to create negative effects that damage other systems (Willke, 2001b, p. 101).

The case of negative governance or of a conflicting relationship is instead a more complex scenario (Willke, 2001b, p. 106). Conflicts are social systems originated by a negative or unexpected reaction to a previous communication, which does not set the end of the network of communications (Luhmann, 1984, p. 530). In this sense, they are connections of communicated contradictions (Thiel, 2003, p. 42) which tend to absorb the resources of other systems like parasites (Baraldi et al., 1997b, p. 74). Conflicts generally stimulate an immune reaction of systems which protect their autopoiesis from dangerous external irritations (Baraldi et al., 1997b, p. 76). The purpose of this reaction is to defend the system from outside disturbances (*Störungen*) without concrete changes to the area of competence or to operations and especially without changes in the systems' logic (Willke, 2001b, p. 106). Because systems tend to ignore each other, conflicts are rare and normally limited to peripheral questions. They are normally characterised by delimitation of words, protection of meanings and the fighting for competence on certain boarder fields (Willke, 2001b, p. 106). This provokes a situation of negative governance in which a system perceives the attempt to steer the environment, but it simply reacts by protecting its autopoiesis and without changing its operations.

Positive governance is the most complex situation. In this case, the coordination of autopoietic systems is needed to obtain cooperation toward operations directed to a common goal (Willke, 2007b, p. 14). The goal of coordination is 'to provide frames and templates for common understanding of communications' (Willke, 2007b, p. 15). Common understandings do not refer to a consensus or to solidarity. On the contrary, 'most understandings pertain to agreed zones of disagreement' (Willke, 2007b, p. 15). The need for coordination increases because modern societies are highly complex. This 'requires strong self-steering of the subsystems, maintaining their autonomy and specialized problem solving capabilities, and [...] a substantial strategic purpose of the entire system that does not submit to the fallacy of central coordination but combines the distributed capacities of the parts to build emergent properties of the whole' (Willke, 2007b, p. 15). The aim of cooperation is to coordinate[119] operations directed towards a common goal, which is expected to be better achievable through the combined effort of various players (Willke, 2007b, p. 17). In fact, 'under circumstances of distributed expertise, knowledge, competencies etc., under conditions of specialization and functional differentiation of systems, cooperation makes sense because it produces results that cannot be obtained by single actors' (Willke, 2007b, p. 17). Cooperation is not the property of the parts involved, but instead of the mode of communication which instigates and allows positive gov-

[119] Coordination is the condition for cooperation (Willke, 2007b, p. 17), which 'creates results from combining operations in a complex and purposive action' (Willke, 2007b, p. 14).

ernance (Willke, 2007b, p. 17). If the systems involved in pursuing a common goal can achieve coordination and cooperation, they will be able to pursue a common goal together without endangering their autopoiesis.

3.5.3 Super-Experts as a Premise of Governance

Because of the autopoiesis of systems, positive governance is hard to achieve and must be justified because 'if I don't see the need of cooperation, I don't want to pay for it' (Willke, 2001b, p. 109, translation EM). This is a challenging task to solve, because function systems see society in different ways and have different logics. Furthermore, cooperation is always a limitation of freedom for function systems and implies a change of the operational *status quo*. This is dangerous because it influences the autonomy and operations of systems, which are the basis of their existence. The biggest risk is the de-differentiation (*Entdifferenzierung*) (Willke, 2001b, p. 112): an extreme case of operational coupling between function systems which destroys autopoiesis and causes the disappearance of one or both systems.

For this reason, even the acknowledgment of the need of cooperation represents a delicate phase and normally requires the creation of super-experts (*Über-Experten*) for creating an environment which allows positive governance (Willke, 2001b, p. 108).[120] Expert knowledge has a great importance as steering method because systems suffer of a 'flood' of information, which needs to be processed through systemic internal logics of selection and interpretation. Over-experts are able to observe a complex situation, create an understandable stimulus and provoke a systemic operative change (Wiesenthal, 2006, p. 72). Showing different scenarios and the clear chance of a win-win situation are usually the techniques required to justify the need of cooperation (Willke, 2001b, p. 109).

Nevertheless, the consequences of intervention do not depend only upon the over-expert's communication, but also upon its variation caused by the integration in the circle of operation. The intervention has to achieve an internal differentiation and change the rules of the operation without destroying the autopoiesis of the system (Willke, 2001b, p. 106). Furthermore, over-experts are unable to observe the complexity of society from all its perspectives and are, for this

[120] For example, for Willke, the modern state is a mediator and a communication intermediary between subsystems, which provide for the creation of collective gains not obtainable from the operation of a single system (Wiesenthal, 2006, p. 70). For Willke, 'because of the exceeding complexity, specialization, and efficiency of societal subsystems, the state becomes dependent on at least three capacities of these corporated subsystems: their capacity for detailed and specialized information and know-how; their capacity for decentralized implementation; and their capacity to withhold compliance and social consensus' (Willke, 1990, p. 236).

reason, always biased. Often super-experts cannot act in diverse contexts because they use the logic of a system and are perceived as impartial and as defending the interests of one specific system. In this case, the system will ignore its information or will filter the message and operationalise it through its logic. This can generate different outcomes from the one desired by the super-expert and hinder cooperation. A solution for this problem is the creation of an independent over-expert. Examples of this *ad hoc* creation are ministers for political and coordinating agencies in organisations. However, professional over-experts are also perceived as being neutral at the beginning and tend to be rapidly perceived by the systems as defending the interests of one system or their own interests. This makes the work of over-experts in most situations difficult in absence of steering media materials (money, power or expertise). In this dissertation the over-expert, which communicates the need for cooperation, are health systems' organisations, namely the WHO and the health ministries. For this reason they are biased from the beginning by using the particular logic of the health system. However, this still need not hinder their chance of creating understandable communications for the sport system *per se* and achieving its cooperation.

3.5.3.1 The WHO as a Super-Expert in the Promotion of Physical Activity

To assess the central question 'What role does sport play in the health-orientated promotion of PA?' it is possible to make enquire at different levels. The international discussion on PA as a medium of health is particularly relevant because it represents the context of the present enquiry.

In particular, the WHO plays an important role in this area: it is the most relevant organisation for steering the international health agenda and has had, from its founding onwards, a particularly influential role in the switch to preventive strategies against NCDs (Dodgson et al., 2002, p. 7; C. H. Schneider, 2009, p. 7). Furthermore, it is one of the most relevant international health organisations, which advises an extensive cooperation founded upon forms of cooperative governance for the efficient promotion of PA (Brettschneider & Naul, 2004; Kickbusch, 1992; WHO, 2004). The *Global Strategy on Diet, Physical Activity and Health* (SDPA)[121] (2004) represents the most significant effort on the part of the WHO to promote PA and openly recommends the cooperation of the sport and health systems. In this sense it can be considered as being the most relevant super-expert in the health related promotion of PA.

[121] The *Global Strategy on Diet, Physical Activity and Health* will henceforth be called 'SDPA' or simply 'the Strategy.'

The role of the WHO in the promotion of PA has already been analysed in a section (Michelini, 2011) of the book '*Welten der Bildung? Vergleichende Analysen von Bildungspolitik und Bildungssystemen*' (Schmid, Amos, Schrader, & Thiel, 2011), but at the same time constitutes a part of the theoretical framework of this dissertation. For this reason, the content of this section has been restated below in a modified and briefer version. In particular, the summary will focus upon the WHO's organisational function and the causes for its transformation into the coordinative body of global health. These processes are particularly important because they also put the WHO into the role of the super-expert for a broad systems cooperation in the fight against PI.

For understanding the relevance of the WHO in the governance of international public health (Karns & Mingst, 2004, p. 55), it is necessary to briefly describe its main structures and the characteristics.[122] The WHO is a specialized agency of the United Nations (UN) that is concerned with international public health. It was established on 7 April 1948 and has headquarters in Geneva, Switzerland. The WHO's constitution (1946) 'provides the organization with a variety of instruments for directing and coordinating international cooperation' (K. Lee, 2003, p. 26). Even if formally coordinated by the Economic and Social Council (ECOSOC) and under the authority of the UN General Assembly (K. Lee, 2003, p. 26), the WHO is highly autonomous in its decisions, has its own interests and operates mostly independently. Indeed, it has been able to gain legitimacy in health governance by steering the medium of knowledge (Willke, 2007b) even in absence of executive powers. The WHO's constitutive and general programme is 'the attainment by all people of the highest possible level of health' (Grad, 2002, p. 981; WHO, 1946, p. 2). This programme governs the general goal, implements the organisation's logic and evaluates the correctness of its decisions. For the WHO, health is 'a state of complete physical, mental and social well-being and not merely the absence of disease or infirmity' (Grad, 2002, p. 981).[123] The WHO's normative, directive and coordinative functions permit the organisation to play roles in advocacy, surveillance and standard-setting at the global level. Moreover, the WHO is actively involved in health-research. Finally, its hierarchical structure based on regional offices provides it with operational functions of technical support in almost every region and country (Ruger & Yach, 2008, p. 3; Yach, Wipfli, Hammond, & Glantz, 2007).

[122] An exhaustive description of the WHO is not the aim of this section. For such an exposition, see for example: Schneider (2009), Karns and Mingst (2004), Porter (1999), Rosen (1993) or Siddiqi (1995).

[123] See the chapter 'Defining Health, Physical Activity, Sport and Their Relationship' for deeper reflections on the definition of health.

The WHO exercises its functions through three organs: The *World Health Assembly* (WHA), the *Executive Board* (EB) and the *Secretariat* (WHO, 2011b). The composition of these three organs is largely technical and composed of experts from various medical disciplines. Further to this, the national health ministers are the WHO's principal connections for the implementation of its programmes. In fact, the WHO assumes that health can be achieved 'by working primarily, if not exclusively, through governmental institutions, notably the ministries of health' (Dodgson et al., 2002, p. 11). This is particularly relevant for understanding the WHO's operational mode because the background, education and career of an organisation's members are highly influential for the logic of the organisation (Baraldi et al., 1997a, p. 168). By having its members sourced from within the health system, the WHO is highly influenced by this systemic logic, even if the WHO requires a multiple contexts and languages for its role in the coordination of international cooperation in order to be understood by other systems. This characteristic has been frequently discussed (Peabody, 1996; Ruger & Yach, 2005; Siddiqi, 1995) because global health has 'undergone a radical transformation over the past 10-15 years' (Fidler, 2008, p. 2) with regards to its political nature. Within this turn the collaboration with non-medical organisations and implementation of horizontal strategies have become fundamental in modern health-strategies (Fidler, 2008, p. 5).

After the Cold War, the relevance of health matters has constantly increased and today health matters occupy an important position in world politics (Fidler, 2007, p. 1; Sridhar & Gostin, 2009). In this context, the WHO has played a key role in enhancing the global interest in health matters and in revolutionising the scenario of global health governance. In order to achieve these accomplishments, the WHO has undergone profound transformations, which explain its contemporary role as the political body of the global health system as well as its interest for PA promotion. The reasons for these radical changes are external and internal stimuli, which have penetrated the internal processes of the organisation, have been processed by them and have changed the internal rules of the organisation. In the following, globalisation[124] and the progress of science in relation to public health will be discussed as external influences.

Indubitably, globalisation represents an important driving force for the extension of health matters beyond national boundaries because it has caused (Ricci, 2009, p. 2): the intensification of trans-border health risks, the increase of non-state health actors, the worsening of some socio-economic, political and environmental problems and the acceleration of the political and practical decline

[124] Broadly defined as 'the growing of economical, political and cultural interaction across state borders' (Bevir, 2009, p. 89). For Robertson (1992, pp. 7-8) globalisation is 'the compression of the world and the identification of consciousness of the world as a whole'.

of various governments. Under the pressure of globalisation, health has started to engage a global political agent, the WHO, with the role of integrating, coordinating and convening the global health agenda.

Within a Global Health Governance (GHG)[125] arena characterised by the cooperation of many transnational and international organisations, the WHO's coordinative function and dissemination of ideas cover the key role (Dodgson et al., 2002, p. 7; C. H. Schneider, 2009, p. 7). The WHO emerged within the process of globalisation of health as the point of reference for global health cooperation and as the key standard-setting organisation (Ruger, 2005; Ruger & Yach, 2008). The globalisation has offered favourable circumstances for wider decision-making and new challenges for health and its distribution, which has been rapidly understood and assessed by the WHO. Additionally, the much more complex and pluralistic scenario, the increased fragmentation of the global health agenda and the need for new leadership created favourable circumstances for increasing the relevance of the WHO's position (Ruger & Yach, 2008, p. 3). Nevertheless, this cooperative shift emerged not only under the WHO's influential ideas dissemination, but also in an independent way under the influence of globalisation so that 'the WHO itself has had to adjust to the evolution in global health's source code' (Fidler, 2007, p. 12). This context produced the basis for a more complex and ambitious range of health objectives and a 'governance effect far more vigorous than WHO ever managed to create as an intergovernmental organization' (Fidler, 2007, p. 10). This also raised problems of governance, concerning the implementation of some typologies of health-strategies (Fidler, 2007). For example, this adaptation has been successful especially in the cases of new governance approaches to some infectious and tobacco-related diseases (Fidler, 2007, p. 12). At other times, though, this model of governance has faced hard challenges in its implementation (Irwin & Scali, 2007). In particular the concurrent participation of several systems, the role of the market and the decreased role of states negatively affected some health-strategies, mostly those concerning NCDs (Thomas & Weber, 2004, p. 193).

The second relevant stimulus for the changes of the WHO has to do with scientific progress in the fields of medicine and public health. In particular, two health-theories, rather than technological advances, have been particularly influential: first, the salutogenetic theory (Antonovsky, 1997) moved the operational focus of the health system from the genesis of diseases to the genesis of

[125] Health Governance (HG) is defined here as 'the actions and means adopted by a society to organize itself in the promotion and protection of the health of its population' (Dodgson et al., 2002, p. 6). GHG concerns instead the health of society in general, not linked to any specific territorial control (Hein, Bartsch, & Kohlmorgen, 2006, p. 2; Ricci, 2009, p. 3), and the 'collective efforts of a variety of actors within institutionalised settings' (C. H. Schneider, 2009, p. 30).

health; second, the risk factor model justified the assessment of variables related to an increased risk of diseases, even if they are correlational to, but not causal of, illnesses. The rise and consolidation of these new health theories not only turned the health focus to preventive strategies (Hurrelmann, 2006, pp. 124-126) but also generated the birth of a new logic for the health system: that of 'hindering/promoting health' (Bauch, 1996, 1997, 2004).[126]

This change in the logic of the health system provoked increased interest in NCDs and primary healthcare by the WHO.[127] Therefore, the way to define and address health determinants changed by directing attention towards the determinants of health and by including areas external to classic health issues (Dodgson et al., 2002, p. 13). In this context physical inactivity started to be considered one of the most relevant risk factors of many chronic diseases by the WHO. Therefore, over the last decades, discussions about strategies and governance models to promote PA have continuously gained significance in the global health agenda. The contemporary high degree of worldwide interest on this topic is partially related to the WHO's 'Global Strategy on Diet, Physical Activity and Health'.[128] This Strategy is the tip of the iceberg of a precedential debate documented in the resolution on prevention and control of NCDs (WHO, 2000), the WHO's *Global Initiative for Active Living* (WHO, 1997, 2011c) and the *World Health Day 2002* 'Move for Health' (WHO, 2002, 2011a).

In summary, the WHO is an organisation that occupies a central role in the *Global Health Governance*. It has moved through several phases and approaches, which were discussed here in relation to the globalisation and the change in the logic of the health system. These cause the re-focus of the WHO on the prevention of NCDs through broad cooperative strategies. At the same time, this ambitious governance model multiplies the problems of coordination (Ruger & Yach, 2008).

3.6 Summary of the Theoretical Framework, First Results, Next Steps

This chapter has made explicit the theoretical fundamentals, which lie at the basis of this enquiry. This dissertation is grounded on a constructivist epistemological position and has a theoretical framework based on Luhmann systems theory. Its aim is to describe a social phenomenon through the particular perspective of the systems theory, which will help to shed some light upon the blind spots typi-

[126] A deeper argumentation of these topics is contained in the chapter 'Health and Sport Systems.'
[127] Representative for that change of focus are the Health for All (HFA) strategy and the Alma Ata conference (WHO, 1978).
[128] The efforts of other health organizations such as the World Heart Federation and the International Diabetes Federation in the promotion of PA also have to be mentioned here.

cal of societal viewpoint. In order to achieve this, empirical data will be posed in relationship with the theory in a circular process, which is expected to furnish progress in the empirical and theoretical knowledge of the phenomenon. This implies by no means a claim to universality or an attempt to furnish normative indication. Instead, this is supposed to create new questions and theoretical models concerning the phenomenon observed.

From the perspective of systems theory, function systems have emerged through a process of differentiation in modern societies. Function systems are autopoietic, which means that they are operationally closed and tend to ignore other function systems. They are specialised in a particular function and perform a special task, which contributes to the reproduction of society. The essential characteristics of function systems are: functions, binary codes, programmes, organisations and roles. These notions have been applied to the description of both the sport and the health systems in the tab below:

Systems / Features	Health	Sport
Function	Fighting illness and promoting/creating health (Bauch, 2004)	Communications of body performance (Stichweh, 1990) and empowerment of bodies (Bette, 1987; Cachay, 1988)
Binary Codes	Ill/healthy (Luhmann, 1990d) and promoting/hindering health (Bauch, 2004)	Victory/defeat (Schimank, 1988) and performing/not performing (Stichweh, 1990)
Programmes	Pathogenesis-orientated (Luhmann, 1990d) and salutogenesis-orientated (Antonovsky, 1996)	Sport disciplines' evaluative, normative or cognitive orientations (Schimank, 1988)
Organisations	Hospitals, medical practices and governing bodies (Vogd, 2005a)	Sport clubs, sport federations and governing bodies (Schimank, 1988)
Roles	Doctors, physicians, surgeons and representative roles (Pelikan, 2009)	Athletes, trainers and functionaries and representative roles (Cachay, 1988)

Figure 4 Features of Sport and Health Systems

After having described the two systems, their emergence, development and relationship have been inquired. In particular, the review of different acceptances of the health system regarding the function of 'sport' as a health-medium suggests two main forms of relationships:

– The qualification of 'sport' as a medium of health in the health system's communication allows for the coupling between the sport and health systems. Also, it constitutes the basis for the differentiation of the sport system.

Through this, the sport system legitimises its existence through its function for the health system. In a further development, the consolidation of this fundamental structural coupling and the hypostatisation of the two systems permit the release of the sport system from the health system and the birth of new minor structural couplings.

– The disqualification of 'sport' as a medium of health in the health system's communication is the basis for the health system's reappropriation of the responsibility of PA promotion. This turn is caused by changes within the logic of the health system and by the failure of the sport system in including the risk group most affected by NCDs. At the same time, the hypostatisation of the systems causes issues (de-sportification and medicalisation) and the health system tends to medicalise some of the sport system's functions. Nevertheless, the increasing number and relevance of 'minor' structural couplings still binds tightly the two systems.

This description establishes an account of the context of the social phenomenon analysed in this dissertation. However, for completing the theoretical framework, a final step has been carried out: it has been described how, in a situation of strict relationship between function systems, a plan or a project can be implemented in a cooperative way. In order to assess this issue, the topic of 'governance' has been inquired from the perspective of the systems theory. Starting with the general meaning of this term, the doctoral thesis focused on its meaning in systems theory, particularly in the works of Luhmann and Willke.[129] In fact, the communications of the health system analysed in this dissertation are directed in order to gain the cooperation of the sport system and achieving the common goal of the promotion of PA.[130]

As an example, the WHO has been described as a health organisation responsible internationally for the coordination of systems in the implementation of health-orientated strategies. The WHO implements the logic of the health system by making decisions regarding the management of international public health. This role has been legitimised and consolidated by the globalisation of health matters and by the change of the WHO's orientation towards salutogenesis and risk factor models. However, its reference to the health system's logic

[129] The theories of Willke regarding governance in systems theory are fundamental for this dissertation's theoretical arguments and interpretation of the empirical data

[130] Precisely, the empirical analysis involves announcements produced by health system's over-experts. These should stimulate the cooperation of the sport system in the promotion of PA. Not at least, this dissertation inquires whether they constitute an understandable impulse for creating positive governance.

can constitute an obstacle to the comprehensibility of its message directed to obtain the cooperation of systems with different logics.[131]

Especially two of the phenomena assessed in the last sections play relevant roles in this dissertation: the paradigmatic change of health system's code and its tendency to expand its societal functions; and the changes regarding the acceptance of sport as health-medium by the health system. Sport in the following sections will be spoken about as a system, as a social phenomenon and as a sub category of PA. As stated in the definition of the basic terms of this doctoral thesis, sport is a bodily activity, which involves performance, rules and unproductivity, but it has different meaning depending upon the context. In order not to transfer this ambiguity to the basis of the present sociological analysis, the discussions will individually specify whether it refers to the broad or to the specific traditional-competitive meaning of 'sport' whenever necessary.

At this point, it is possible to furnish the first conclusions regarding the sub-question 'Which central documents have been developed for the health-related promotion of physical activity?' Nowadays, health organisations have been identified as producing the most relevant communications on health-related promotion of PA as a consequence of a change in the logic of the health system which permitted its development and the broadening of its function. The logic of the health system orientated towards health promotion made the health system seeking for cooperation for the promotion of PA. Nevertheless, in the scientific literature the troubles of the health system in its function of super-expert and the conflict with the logic orientated towards illness are widely discussed.

For making enquiries into the perspective of the health system regarding the role of sport as a health-medium, the programmes of health organisation with governmental tasks have been identified has being the most representative. Programmes of health organisations are often communicated through health-strategies. In the next chapter, the development of an empirical approach of the dissertation will furnish the logic for the selection of the health-strategies to be analysed and for setting the instruments for a scientific enquiry of their contents through the research method of content analysis.

[131] This context constitutes also the basis for the conception WHO's of the 'Global Strategy on Diet, Physical Activity and Health' (WHO, 2004). This strategy has been analysed in the methodological chapter as a test for the empirical instruments and as an exemplary analysis of international communications on health-related promotion of PA.

4. Methodology

'Methodology, as I see it, is a product of common sense applied to circumstances'
(Morison, 1951, p. 263)

The present chapter contains the methodological approach used for selecting and analysing the health orientated strategies for the promotion of PA issued by national health ministries. At first, considerations regarding the aim and mode of comparison and the sampling of documents have been made. The second step explains in depth and tests the mixed design used for the document analysis. With the exception of some peculiar characteristics of the codes used for the document analysis, this chapter contains all the necessary information to justify, understand and reproduce the empirical analysis performed in this dissertation. As 'real research is often confusing, messy, intensely frustrating, and fundamentally nonlinear' (C. Marshall & Rossman, 2010, p. 21), the following discussions aim to explain the procedures carried out for the empirical analysis without hiding their openness, circularity and reflexivity through 'highly standardized reporting practices' (Bargar & Duncan, 1982, p. 2). Instead, the aim of this chapter is to 'create an account of method and data which can stand independently so that another trained researcher could analyse the same data in the same way and come to essentially the same conclusions' (Mays & Pope, 1995).

4.1 Comparison and Sampling

This doctoral thesis analyses national communications regarding the health-related promotion of PA with particular focus on the role of sport in these documents. The comparison of countries as a method for gaining knowledge and the strategy for the sampling of the case studies has been gathered from political classics such as: Almond (1966); Almond and Powell (1966); Hague and Harrop (2007); Laitin (2002); Landman (2002, 2003); Lijphart (1971); Mair (1998); Øyen (1990); Przeworski and Teune (1970); Sartori (1970). In fact, this research is in its core a classic sociological analysis but it has been deeply influenced by the multidisciplinary environment[132] in which it was conceived and particularly by comparative politics (CP).[133] Namely, if the theoretical framework based upon the systems theory would not play such a relevant role and if some methodological choices would have been different (for example if a hypothesis would have been made instead of posing a research question), this dissertation could be considered to fully belong to CP. This does not pose problems of commensurability because some streams[134] of this discipline (in particular post-behaviouralism) are strongly linked to sociology. Furthermore, comparative politics aims to explain how political problems are treated by comparing different political contexts. This aim is commensurable and can be fulfilled with sociological descriptions. In particular, this doctoral thesis borrows from CP:

- The objective of the comparison,
- Countries as comparison units,
- The logic for the choice of the number of countries to be compared,
- The Przeworski and Teune (1970)'s 'most similar systems design' as framework for choosing the countries to be compared,
- and Esping Andersen's theory on welfare states as theory for selecting the countries.

[132] The doctoral programme: 'International and Comparative Research on Education and Education Policy in the Welfare State.' This programme took place between 2009 and 2012 at Eberhard Karls University in Tübingen. It has been advised by Prof. Amos, Prof. Dr. Schmid, Prof. Dr. Schrader and Prof. Dr. Thiel and financed by the Hans-Böckler foundation. The research programme focused on an international comparison of the relations between various types of welfare states, steering, governance-practices, structures and processes of selected educational areas. The theoretical basis of the international comparative programme drawn on two concepts: first, the older and meanwhile revised model of welfare states (Esping-Andersen, 1990; Lessenich, 1995), and second, the newer concepts of steering and governance in the education system (Altrichter, 2007; Kussau & Brüsemeister, 2007).

[133] Comparative politics is a sub-discipline or a movement within political science (Almond, 1966; Laitin, 2002; Lijphart, 1971). Even though political comparison was born in the 4th century BC with Aristotle (Mair, 1998, p. 309), it started to concretise as modern science during the first half of the 20th century (Hague & Harrop, 2007, p. 6). Its goal is 'to encompass the major political similarities and differences between countries' (Hague & Harrop, 2007, p. 83).

[134] The old tradition of comparison in political science was the *comparative government* and was focused on the comparison of institutions. With the birth of comparative politics, the focus of comparison switched to comparing political systems by taking into account polity, politics and policy and by having a functionalist approach. For this change, historical events (in particular the Second World War) as well as further theoretical and methodological development played a great role. In particular, CP started to become more interdisciplinary and be linked to foreign policy and modernisation theory or combined with assumption of systems theory (Easton, 1965) and functionalism (Almond & Powell, 1966). Furthermore, the rise of behaviouralism brought CP new approaches and methods orientated towards statistics and surveys.

These topics will be discussed in the following sections.[135] At the same time, as a whole this discussion also clarifies the reasons for the comparison of the case studies France, Germany, and Italy.

4.1.1 Objective and Logic of Comparison

Through the use of empirical data, the comparison is one of the fundamental scientific methods[136] which can be used to test the validity or to develop new theoretical propositions (Lijphart, 1971, pp. 683-685). The general aim of comparison is to understand and explain the similarities and differences between the units of comparison (Landman, 2003, p. 4). For Landman (2003, p. 4), there are four main objectives in CP: *contextual description, classification, hypothesis testing* and *prediction*. The objective of this dissertation is the description of political systems aimed at finding their similarities and differences. Contextual description is considered to be the fundamental and first objective of CP because 'systematic research begins always with good descriptions' (Landman, 2003, p. 5). Furthermore, out of the four objectives it is the most commensurable with the characteristics of sociological statement which are impartial, empirically based and descriptive (Willis, 1996, pp. 37-40). By offering the advantages discussed above and by being commensurable with sociology, the comparison has been chosen to generate theories and knowledge on the topic analysed.

In CP, there are different logics for comparative research (Lijphart, 1971, pp. 685-691): inter-state comparison of political systems existing at the same time; intra-state comparison of one state at different points in time; supra-state comparison of supra-national processes; and ideal/real types comparison of models and their implementations. For assessing coherently the research question of this dissertation, a comparison of political systems from the same period has been chosen. In particular, it has been decided to analyse documents produced by a political organisation, specifically the health ministry, in different countries. The health minister is the member of a country's government responsible for the protection and promotion of public health and for the provision of welfare and other social security services. The ministry of health has been chosen as the issuing body of the documents because, in almost every country in the world, it is the highest governmental department responsible for health. Its relevance is not only motivated by its hierarchical position in national health sys-

[135] These steps have not been considered separately and successively during the natural research process, which was circular and explorative instead.

[136] The other fundamental scientific methods are the case study approach, the experimental and the statistical methods (Lijphart, 1971, pp. 683-685).

tems, but also by the funds available to it.[137] Hence, from a systems theory perspective, this organisation possesses both the steering powers given by its peak position on the organisation chart and by its financial powers. Furthermore the ministries of health are organisations strictly connected to each other. Namely, through the WHO they constitute a (virtually) unique organisation or, in the language of systems theory, a *lateral world system* (Willke, 2006a, pp. 38-39) for health matters worldwide. In this scenario the WHO embodies the global political body of the health system and the health ministries its national manifestation. For these reasons, making enquiries into the programmes of these organisations has been considered particularly representative and relevant for an analytical description of the health system's attitude towards the role of sport in the promotion of PA. Furthermore, the comparison of these programmes in different countries offer the chance to discuss the development of the global discussion, the influence of international guidelines and the relevance of countries' alternative paths for assessing the topic.

4.1.2 Number of Case Studies

After deciding to compare national political organisations, the question of 'How many countries should be compared?' is still open. The choice of the number of countries is deeply connected with the level of abstraction of the comparison: the more countries are analysed, the more abstract the comparison (Mair, 1998, p. 316). This concept has been represented in the graph below:

[137] In fact, the health ministry is one of the ministries with the greatest expenditure capacity in many countries of the world. In particular, the total expenditure on health as % of GDP in 2010 was: 9.5 in Italy; 11.6 in Germany; 11.9 in France (WHO, 2012).

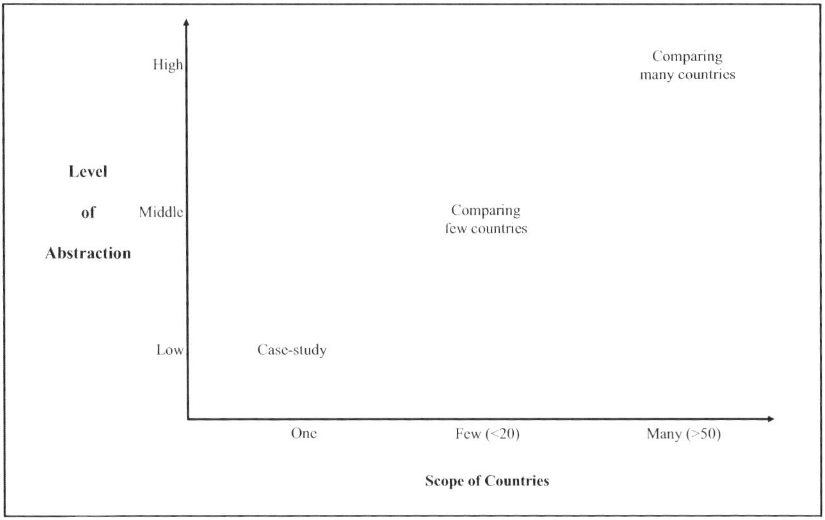

Figure 5 Number of Countries and Abstraction of the Comparison (Landman, 2002, p. 4)[138]

Usually it is impossible to examine all the relevant cases (complete sampling) and it is necessary to identify a limited sample. Consequently, there are three choices concerning the number of countries to be compared (Landman, 2002, p. 4): one, few and many. Each one of these options has advantages and disadvantages.[139] For the social phenomenon at hand, a comparison of a few countries has been selected. This can involve between 2 and 20 or more countries (Landman, 2003, p. 27). The empirical analysis compares three countries, a number of units which permit a very low level of abstraction within the group of 'small-n' comparisons. Such a 'focused comparison' permits the careful selection of cases (Landman, 2002, p. 13) and thereby a very detailed enquiry (Kohn, Naoi, Schoenbach, Schooler, & Slomczynski, 1990, p. 95; Øyen, 1990, p. 11), which represents an advantage for the purpose of the present dissertation. However, in the absence of a clear logic for the selection, a small-n sampling can provoke selection bias[140] and produce incorrect inferences (Landman, 2003, p. 28). For this reason, the type of research design used for the sampling will be explained in the next section.

[138] Based on Mair (1998) and Sartori (1970).
[139] For further insight into this topic, see Mair (1998) and Landman (2002).
[140] In brief, this is the phenomenon which makes the sampling influential for the result of an analysis (Berk, 1983).

4.1.3 *Framework and Sampling of the Case Studies*

The welfare policies[141] play a great role in many socio-political areas and particularly in healthcare (Lampman, 1984).[142] This justifies a choice of countries based on the typology of welfare. Although many theories on welfare policies exist, in recent times the discussion has been dominated by Gøsta Esping-Andersen (Hicks & Kenworthy, 2003, p. 1). Indeed, his works (Esping-Andersen, 1990, 1999) have stimulated a great body of research and are highly accredited in politics (Hicks & Kenworthy, 2003, p. 1). In particular, the book 'Three worlds of welfare capitalism' (Esping-Andersen, 1990) theorises a different degree of countries' 'decommodification', which points out how much a citizen is protected by the state from the insecurity of market. Among other argumentations, Esping-Andersen differentiates three typologies of welfare states in capitalist economies (Esping-Andersen, 1990, p. 74):[143]

Typology of Welfare	Description	Countries
Liberal	Market logic and private insurance dominate this typology. Even if a wage minimum is normally secured, welfare state benefits are mild and coupled to population's needs	USA, Canada, Switzerlan, Australia, Japan
Conservative (Corporatist-statist)	This type increases the welfare basic benefits with pensions, unemployment assistance and social insurance. It tends to preserve people's living standards. Social security is paid according to the equivalence principle and depends on the amount and duration of previously contributions	Italy, Austria, Belgium, France, and Germany
Scandinavian (Social-democratic)	This type reduces the tradability of work as a commodity and offers government-guaranteed salary replacement benefits. Monetary hedging is completed by networks of social services, active labour market policies and quality childcare	Norway, Sweden, Denmark, and Finland

Figure 6 Typologies of Welfare States in Capitalist Economies (Esping-Andersen, 1990)

[141] For Luhmann, welfare policies are an intervention of politics outside its areas of competences (Kuchler, 2006, p. 7): they endanger the autonomy of function systems because they directly intervene into the internal operations of function systems through the medium of power (Luhmann, 1981a, p. 140). His assumption is presumably connected with the political situation at the beginning of the 80s in which states were substantially reducing their investments in welfare policies (Kuchler, 2006, p. 7) and has been considered right-wing from some authors (Kuchler, 2006; Østerberg, 2000).

[142] For some authors welfare policies play a major role also in sport matters (Heinemann, 2003). However this connection has never been clearly demonstrated or taken for granted in the scientific community and has instead been often proved inconsistent.

[143] Although many authors still debate the categories of welfare capitalism and the country memberships of those categories (Arts & Gelissen, 2002; Castles, 1993; Castles & Mitchell, 1993; Huber & Stephens, 2001; Ragin, 1994; Scharpf, 2000), a new classification accepted by the scientific community has never come forth from these discussions.

After deciding to compare a few countries and to choose them based upon their welfare typologies, a final step has must take place in order to complete the sampling. Generally there are fundamentally two main types of research designs used for the sampling of a comparison of few and very few objects (Landman, 2003, p. 28): some studies compare different outcomes across similar countries, which is known as the Most Similar Systems Design (MSSD); others compare similar outcomes across different countries, which is known as the Most Different Systems Design (MDSD).[144] In particular, Przeworski and Teune (1970) have described these two approaches for selecting case studies: the MSSD is based upon the assumption that a sample of similar cases which present different outcomes permits the explanation of these outcomes. This research logic intends to find and explain meaningful differences in a sampling that is otherwise as homogeneous as possible. The MDSD also aims at explaining the outcomes, in this case similar, of a sample of intentionally selected heterogeneous, cases. In this case, the heterogeneity of the cases allows for focusing on the variables, which determine similar outcomes.

In a comparison of a few countries based on Esping-Andersen's categorisation of welfare typologies, a researcher has two choices: comparing different countries (MDSD) or comparing similar countries (MSSD). The comparison of different typologies of welfare has been discarded because it has been considered too ambitious and difficult to defend by having a country for representing each group. For this reason, this dissertation compares three similar countries in a slightly modified version of the MSSD. In fact, enquiries based on this design are normally strongly premise-bounded because they test the most similar cases based upon a priori assumptions about mechanisms of action. Instead, in this case, a research question and not a hypothesis guides the research. This overcomes the problem bound to the case of a similar sample with similar outcomes, which is normally considered as a failure of the experiment (Przeworski & Teune, 107: 38). Furthermore, this dissertation does not focus on the relationship between dependent and independent variables and concentrates on qualitative and descriptive tasks. This is expected to add value because many social processes in the area of policy research are highly complex: the various influential factors for the characteristics of the cases are not easily able to be reduced and they can not be controlled in a quasi-experimental design like the classic MSSD (Scharpf, 2000, pp. 54-60).

Within the three typologies of welfare capitalism, the conservative group has been chosen. In fact, among the three welfare typologies, these coun-

[144] Hybrid typologies of these two designs have reached a good level of acceptance within the scientific community, but they did not offer particular advantages for the present enquiry and have been discarded.

tries are expected to offer a more balanced scenario than the liberal or social-democratic typologies. More specifically, the analysis of France, Germany and Italy is considered a generalisation for the entire group of the five welfare conservative countries, which also includes Belgium and Austria. Indeed, the analysis of the whole group of conservative countries has been excluded for the purposes of reduction discussed previously in this section. Nevertheless, this sampling entails the majority and most populous conservative countries.[145] Finally, this sampling offers a further advantage: the comparison of these three countries with similar welfare systems can prove whether a different sport system has influence on the social phenomenon being enquired into. In fact, the sport system of the three countries differs in many aspects:

- The French sport system is characterised by being highly politicised and extremely centralised (Defrance & Renard, 2003, p. 221; Digel & Fahrner, 2003, p. 259; Hartmann-Tews, 1996, p. 191; Tokarski & Steinbach, 2001, p. 184);
- Germany has a federal system in which the sport system is formally highly independent, but in practice influenced by regional policies (Engelhardt & Heinemann, 2003, p. 139; Hartmann-Tews, 1996, p. 129; Tokarski & Steinbach, 2001, p. 178).
- the Italian sport system is characterised by the relevance of the Comitato Olimpico Nazionale (CONI), an independent public body which relies on public funds and which entails both the functions of NOC and of an umbrella organisation for sport federations (Digel & Barra, 2004, p. 287; Ferrari, Porro, & Russo, 2003, p. 275; Porro, Bizzaglia, & Conti, 2003, p. 33; Tokarski & Steinbach, 2001, p. 193).

The comparison of France, Germany and Italy is expected to find conclusions able to be generalised for the group of conservative countries and to understand if a different sport system influences its ascribed role in strategies for the promotion of PA, issued by the health system. Given the theoretical and methodological premises of this dissertation, this sampling has been acknowledged as being the best country-clustering for the research at hand.

[145] The three countries entail more than the 75% of the conservative countries' population.

4.2 Choice of the Documents

The analysis of all documents published in Italy, Germany, and France about PA as a medium of health promotion constitutes a workload too great to be covered by a single researcher and far too unfocused a sample to answer the research question. For these reasons a limited sampling has been necessary for this dissertation. This section explains the procedure implemented for the selection of the relevant documents to be analysed. After this, the documents chosen for each case study have been listed and described in order to furnish their basic contextual information and make the reasons for their selection explicit.

4.2.1 Logic Behind the Choice of the Documents

The rough principle which orientated the collection of available written communications in the first explorative phase for the construction of a relevant catalogue of documents was to look for all health-strategies dealing with the promotion of PA and available for the case studies France, Germany, and Italy.

The WHO's 'International inventory of documents on physical activity promotion' (WHO, 2013) and the WHO's 'European database on nutrition, obesity and physical activity' (WHO, 2011f) have been used to develop an initial, general idea of the existing documents regarding the promotion of PA. However, even though these inventories might have been helpful, they could not constitute the basis for sampling the documents because they are neither scientifically based nor up-to-date enough to fulfil this aim.

In order to limit the number of documents and better the focus of the sampling, only documents on the promotion of PA produced by the ministries of health of the selected countries have been considered.[146] These documents encompass a variety of different typologies such as: policies, legislations, programmes, reports, conference proceedings, and information. This does not represent a problem *per se,* because the typology of the documents plays a secondary role for the relevance of the enquiry. Indeed, the analysis generally focuses on the role of sport in the health systems' communication, which regards PA as a medium of health independently from the typology of the communication.

Even if all the documents were available on the website of the health ministries of the selected nations, the official websites of the ministries themselves do not furnish adequate tools for the selection of appropriate documents. In fact, these websites' maps and contents differ greatly from one another. For

[146] The reason for this choice is argued to a more thorough extent in the section containing the logic of the sampling.

this reason, they cannot represent a basis for the development of a standardised path to access the documents appropriate for all the websites. For example, thematic sections dealing specifically with the topic of PA are present on the German and French websites but not on the Italian one. Furthermore, not even the health ministries' website search engines represent a tool reliable enough for the identification of the documents because of technical reasons: they do not appear to function correctly and some documents are not listed in the search results.

For these reasons, the web search engine 'Google Web Search' by Google Incorporated has been preferred for identifying the documents rather than direct research on the health ministries' websites. In particular, the following structured web search query has been developed and used for finding the documents: *site:*health ministry's website domain* "*physical activity*" sport filetype:pdf*[147]

This query aims to find all documents which contain the key word "sport" and 'physical activity' on the health ministries' websites and which are, for this reason, expected to treat relevant topics for the assessment of the research question. In practice, this search query has been translated for each case study and produced the following results:[148]

Country	Search Query	N. of Results	Date
Italy	site:www.salute.gov.it/ "attività fisica" sport filetype:pdf	127	2011-07-20
Germany	site:www.bmg.bund.de/ "Bewegung" sport filetype:pdf	22	2011-07-20
France	site:www.sante.gouv.fr/ "activitè physique" sport filetype:pdf	307	2011-07-20

Figure 7 Results of the Web Search

The substantial disparity in the number of documents found on the Health Ministries' websites is due to their different publication strategy. In particular:

- The German Health Ministry's website contains only a few focused documents. In fact, for the case study Germany just 22 documents were found through web research.
- The Italian Health Ministry's website contains more documents (127) which are incomplete or not issued by the health ministry, which have the form of ministerial covenants of understanding, laws, or which assess a specific illness.

[147] The asterisk indicates that the words have been translated differently for each case study.
[148] The date for carrying out the research is casual and the results have not been updated afterwards.

- The French Health Ministry's website has the same characteristics as the Italian one and, in addition, contains a multitude of regional and local documents. Here, a total of 307 documents were found.

For obtaining a more focussed and representative selection, the documents found via online research were sorted in a further step. In particular, the documents with the following characteristics were discarded at this stage:

- documents issued before the year 2000, because the social phenomenon analysed is relatively new and an older sample would falsify the results,
- documents with regional or local scope,
- documents not issued by the national health ministries,
- documents orientated towards the prevention or rehabilitation of particular diseases (for example arteriosclerosis),
- documents related to the promotion of a particular mode of PA (for example cycling or walking),
- documents containing the words 'sport' and 'PA' and 'movement' only occasionally.

After this second step, the number of documents considered suitable for the analysis became manageable for each of the case studies: six for France, seven for Germany and nine for Italy. This means that the filter process conducted for the selection of a limited number of documents was independent from the starting number of documents found via online research.

In a final step of selection, the documents, which satisfied all the rules established, but which did not appear to be relevant for the assessment of the research question, have been excluded. In contrast to the previous steps, this last action has prevalent qualitative characteristics and has been conducted by reading the documents and by collecting information on their context. The logic and results of this last selection have been summarised below.

In conclusion, the method for the selection of the documents presents a mix of quantitative and qualitative characteristics, which ensure both a highly standardised, scientific and repeatable procedure and the security of having chosen documents, which have relevant contents for answering the research question.

4.2.2 List and Description of the Documents per Case Study

In the following, the list of documents taken into account until the last step for the analysis will be listed for each case study, briefly described, and accompanied by basic contextual information. This also includes the explanation and the logic for the final documents' selection.

4.2.3 French Documents

The French Health Ministry's website also contains downloadable materials. However, only few of these documents are suitable for answering the research question. The documents selected are three subsequent versions of the '*Programme national nutrition santé*' (PNNS) for the years 2001-2005 (French Ministry of Health, 2001), 2006-2010 (French Ministry of Health and Solidarity, 2006) and 2011-2015 (French Ministry for Employment and Welfare & French Ministry of Health, 2011). The PNNS has been launched in January 2001 and aims at improving the general health conditions of the French population by principally changing nutritional behaviours. The first programme was issued in 2001, the second extended, clarified, and strengthened the original PNNS and, in early 2011, a third version of the PNNS was released. The goals and strategies of this third document are developed in close collaboration with the 'Obesity Plan', launched in 2010. Even if these documents focus mainly on nutrition, the promotion of PA also plays a key role.

Within the context of the PNNS, the documents *'Activité physique et santé. Arguments scientifiques, pistes pratiques'* (Physical Activity and Health) (French Ministry of Health and Solidarity, 2005) and *'La santé vien en bougeant. Le guide nutricion pour tous'* (Health Comes by Moving) (French Ministry of Health, 2004) have also been analysed; the former aiming to confront the topic of PA promotion more exhaustively than in the PNNS and the latter being an informative document for the population.

Instead, even if relevant at first sight, the document '*Plan National de Prévention par l'Activité Physique ou Sportive*' (PNPAPS) (French Ministry of Health, Youth, Sports and Community, 2008) has been discarded after a thorough analysis. In fact, the PNPAPS is a national prevention plan through physical activity or sports. However, it has a different format,[149] it is deeply influenced by the perspective of the Sport Ministry,[150] and resulted as less representative for the analysis at hand.

[149] The document consists of six different and independent strategies.

[150] The document is based on the report of the Commission on Prevention, Sport and Health, written in 2008.

Title of the document	Author	Date	Type	Pages
PNNS 2001-2005	French Ministry of Health	2001	Policy	40
PNNS 2006-2010	French Ministry of Health and Solidarity	2006	Policy	51
PNNS 2011-2015	French Ministry for Employment and Welfare and Ministry of Health	2011	Policy	66
Physical Activity and Health	French Ministry of Health and Solidarity	2005	Information	58
Health Comes by Moving	French Ministry of Health, Youth, Sports and Community	2004	Information	36

Figure 8 French Documents

4.2.4 German Documents

The website of the German Ministry of Health provided fewer resulting publications when compared to the Italian and French results. The publications, however, constitute a solid basis for a document analysis as well as for the other case studies. In fact, of the 22 results, more than ten documents were found to be suitable for the analysis and five of them have been chosen as most representative for the German case.

Among the documents analysed is the national plan '*IN FORM Deutschlands Initiative für gesunde Ernährung und mehr Bewegung*' (IN FORM) (German Ministry of Health & German Ministry of Nutrition, 2008). This national action plan regards the prevention of malnutrition, physical inactivity, obesity and related diseases and has been presented jointly by the Federal Ministry of Food, Agriculture and Consumer Protection and the Federal Ministry of Health. The aim of the plan is to permanently improve the diet and PA behaviour of German population by 2020. The action plan sets out concrete goals and fields of action and establishes measures to improve the knowledge about the relationship between health, a balanced diet and adequate exercise. Within the context of this campaign, not only the main document has been analysed, but also two further documents related to this campaign: '*Aktiv für mich*' (Active for Myself) (German Ministry of Health, 2010b), dedicated to women, and '*Geistig fit im Alter*' (Mentally Fit in Old Age) (German Ministry of Health, 2010c) dedicated to the elderly. Together, the three documents related to the campaign 'IN-FORM' give a comprehensive overview of the strategy in all its facets.

However, the topic of PA promotion in the German case study is not just assessed through the national plan 'IN FORM' but also in generic strategies for health promotion. In order to also include this second viewpoint on PA promotion, the following documents have been selected: '*Ratgeber zur gesundheitlichen Prävention*' (Advisory Guide to Health Care) (German Ministry of

Health, 2010a), an informative document containing advice on health promotion; and '*Nationales Gesundheitsziel gesund Aufwachsen: Lebenskompetenz, Bewegung, Ernährung*' (National Health Objective) (German Ministry of Health, 2010d), dedicated to the health of teenagers and written in cooperation with the project 'gesundheitsziele.de' of the Gesellschaft für Versicherungswissenschaft und -gestaltung e.V. (Society of Insurance Studies and Development). Instead, the '*Strategie der Bundesregierung zur Förderung der Kindergesundheit*' (Strategy for Children's Health) (German Ministry of Health, 2008), which focuses on the health of children, has been discarded for only very superficially assessing topics related to sport and PA.

Title of the document	Author	Date	Type	Pages
Advisor on Health Care	German Ministry of Health	2010	Information	120
IN FORM	German Ministry of Health, German Ministry of Nutrition, Agriculture and Consumer Protection	2008	Information	52
National Health Objective	German Ministry of Health	2010	Information	72
Mentally Fit in Old Age	German Ministry of Health	2010	Information	40

Figure 9 German Documents

4.2.5 Italian Documents

The Italian Health Ministry's website contains several publications containing the key words 'sport' and 'PA.' However, many of them are not useful for the present research. The documents selected have fundamentally been chosen from two distinct thematic series, which embody the Italian Health Ministry's attitude towards PA promotion, namely ones relating to the national health plan '*Piano Sanitario Nazionale*' (PSN) and the campaign '*Guadagnare Salute*' (Make Gains in Health).

The PSN is the main tool for defining the objectives, programmes and organisational actions for protecting the public health of the Italian population. It is foreseen by the article n. 1 of the Legislative-Decree no. 502 from 1992 (President of the Italian Republic, 1992) and its further changes and/or amendments. Each PSN comprises a National Health Plan as well as Regional Health Plans and is valid for three years.[151] It is adopted by the government upon the recommendation of the Ministry of Health after having consulted the committees responsible for health matters, the most representative labour union confederations, the regions and a Joint Conference (President of the Italian Republic,

[151] More precisely it is adopted by the government by the 31st of July of the last year of validity of the previous plan. The national health plan may be modified during the three years.

1992). On the Health Ministry's website (2012), 6 PSNs are available. Of these, the one for the triennium 1998-2000 is outdated, the one for 2001-2003 is damaged[152] and the versions for 2010-1012 and for 2006-2008 do not assess the topic of PA. For these reasons they have been discarded from the sample. The PSN taken into account are those for the years 2003-2005 (Italian Ministry of Health, 2003) and 2011-2013 (Italian Ministry of Health, 2011). The analysis of these two versions of the PSN constitutes a thorough overview of the perspective on PA within these plans.

The campaign 'Make Gains in Health' is the Italian programme for the promotion of health as a collective good. It is characterised by a change in the logic of preventative strategies which provides a broader approach of intervention, the coordination between actions and the shared responsibility for health between citizens and the community (Italian Ministry of Health, 2007, p. 5). The main document of this programme is the strategy 'Make Gains in Health' (Italian Ministry of Health, 2007), published as a Decree of the President of the Council of Ministers in 2007. Within the context of this campaign, several informative fliers and documents have been issued. Many of them are highly interesting for this research, but are almost identical in their contents. In particular the documents '*Guadagnare salute in 4 mosse*' (Gaining Health in 4 Moves), '*La tre giorni della salute*' (Three Days for Health) and '*Un'Italia in salute è una questione di stile... di vita*' (A Healthy Italy is a Question of Style... of Life) are so similar that a separate analysis of each document proved to be unnecessary. Consequently only the most exhaustive documents have been chosen for this analysis, namely 'Gaining Health in 4 Moves' (Italian Ministry of Health, 2009) and the informative pamphlet 'Pages of Health' (Italian Ministry of Employment, 2009). The analysis of these three documents is highly representative for the campaign 'Gaining Health'.

Title of the document	Author	Date	Type	Pages
PSN 2006-2008	Italian Ministry of Health	2003	Policy	100
PSN 2011-2013	Italian Ministry of Health	2011	Policy	123
Make Gains in Health	Italian Ministry of Health	2008	Policy	44
Gaining Health in 4 Moves	Italian Ministry of Health	2009	Information	24
Pages of Health	Italian Ministry of Health	2009	Information	16

Figure 10 Italian Documents

[152] The problem has been reported to the Health Ministry's mail service, which could not provide a fixed version of the document.

4.3 Document Analysis

By adopting both quantitative and qualitative steps, this dissertation uses a mixed approach to content analysis for assessing the research question: 'What role does sport play in the health-related promotion of PA?' However, it has to be specified from the beginning of this chapter that quantitative procedures are used as a tool to facilitate the documents' exploration and to support the research argumentations. Instead, the qualitative analysis constitutes the very core of the analysis. This leaning towards qualitative logic determines the fact that the central methodological principles (Lamnek, 1989, pp. 21-30)[153] and the criteria of rigour (Lamnek, 1989, pp. 152-192; Mayring, 2002, pp. 144-148) followed in this dissertation are principally the ones of qualitative analysis. Furthermore, the work on the documents has an explorative and descriptive aim and doesn't intend to verify or falsify a hypothesis, which has not been previously formulated. The following sections explain extensively the main characteristics of mixed methods and how to apply them to content analysis. Furthermore, particular attention will be paid to the integration of the two methods and to the strategies to ensure rigorousness.

4.3.1 Mixed Methods

The disputes between advocates of quantitative and qualitative research paradigms has continued for over than a century (Johnson & Onwuegbuzie, 2004, p. 14). The emergence of purists on both sides even determined the formulation of an incompatibility thesis (K. R. Howe, 1988). Instead, it is here believed that qualitative and quantitative methods are not incommensurable (Westle, 2009, p. 335)[154] and that they can be strategically mixed. Furthermore, the multiplication of research designs created a methodological constellation more similar to a continuum than to a polar distribution. Because of this, it is sometimes difficult to say whether a design is to be categorised as quantitative or qualitative (Westle,

[153] For Lamnek (1989, pp. 21-30) these are: the openness (Offenheit) of the researcher to the object investigated; the communicativity (Kommunikativität) of the research which aims to enquire into social reality by involving symbolic-communicative acts and by respecting their rules; the procedural character of the enquiry means (Prozeßcharacter), which can be modified during the whole research process; the reflexivity (Reflexivität) of the enquiry to the stand of analysis and to its interpretation; the explicitness (Explikation) of the enquiry's steps which are ruled and structured and at the same time open; the flexibility (Flexibilität) of the research process to the context of the research.

[154] Generally it can be stated that 'objectives, scope and nature of enquiry are consistent across methods and across paradigms' (Dzurec & Abraham, 1993, p. 75). For example, both have the use of empirical observation for addressing the research question and the procedures for avoiding the selection bias in common.

2009, p. 336). With the establishment of mixed methods in the scientific community, the two approaches started to be combined at the beginning of the 20th century in a quite unstructured way and have progressively been better systematised. In the last three decades, concepts, methods and standards of quality for studies that combine qualitative and quantitative approaches have been widely discussed (Tashakkori & Creswell, 2007, p. 3). Without trying to replace either the quantitative or the qualitative paradigms, mixed methods offer a third paradigm which tries to minimise the weakness of both and in this sense constitutes a bridge between the two poles (Johnson & Onwuegbuzie, 2004, pp. 14-15). On the one hand, many research designs today based upon mixed methods are fully developed, tested and accepted in methodological literature (Westle, 2009, pp. 352-353). On the other hand, mixed methods research, even in the light of their development and consolidation, are still evolving and the discussion of some important and unresolved core issues is far from being concluded (Tashakkori & Creswell, 2007, pp. 3-4).

A mix of methods roughly indicates the use of both qualitative and quantitative approaches in the same research project. Starting from this definition, a radical distinction can be made on the way the two methods are integrated. Indeed, some studies 'simply' use the two approaches[155] whereas others put efforts into combining them (Tashakkori & Creswell, 2007, pp. 3-4). This second case is also utilised in this dissertation, which not only mixes quantitative and qualitative methods but also puts efforts in integrating them in a structured and rational way (Westle, 2009, p. 353).

After this theoretical introduction, it is important to explain why and how mixed methods will be applied to this doctoral thesis. A mixed method is believed to be suitable here because it offers better chances for analysing the data and obtaining useful answers to the research question. In fact, the investigation of the analysis unit, composed by the health-strategies for the promotion of PA in Germany, Italy, and France, presents difficulties related to its size and the heterogeneity of forms and languages. A mixed method is expected to add precision and to provide more evident results than qualitative analysis alone would by adding standardised steps. More specifically, a quantitative content analysis is useful because it permits a less time consuming exploration and analysis of the data, research results which are relatively independent from the researcher and research that is both able to be generalised and replicated (Johnson &

[155] Sometimes the literature is not even clear whether this approach also belongs to the mixed methods.

Onwuegbuzie, 2004, p. 19).[156] Instead, the qualitative content analysis permits an increased depth of analysis, the chance to describe in detail the complex phenomenon being enquired into and, finally, the chance to assess the research question (Johnson & Onwuegbuzie, 2004, p. 20).

4.3.2 Integration of the Methods

When a mixed method is used, one must answer the question 'How one can best integrate the qualitative and quantitative approaches?' This is essential for maximising their contribution to the research project. In order to answer this query, two primary decisions have to be made (Morgan, 1998, p. 366): (1) which paradigm should be dominant, in other words, which method should be the principal tool for the analysis[157] and (2) whether the two methods are used concurrently[158] or sequentially. In turn, the combination of the decisions on the time order (concurrent or sequential) and on the paradigm emphasis (equal or dominant status) establishes nine options. Each option represented in the table below involves particular benefits and disadvantages:

[156] Johnson and Onwuegbuzie (2004, p. 19) list two further advantages, which do not apply to the present dissertation: a higher credibility with institutions and the production of objective and quantitative data.

[157] The alternative of giving the two methods equal priority is often considered to be impractical (Morgan, 1998, p. 366) and has been here excluded.

[158] The simultaneous use of the methods is considered generally hard to manage (Morgan, 1998, p. 367) and has therefore not been utilised here.

Paradigm Emphasis Decision	Time Order Decision: Concurrent	Time Order Decision: Sequential
Equal Status	QUALITATIVE + QUANTITATIVE	QUALITATIVE → QUANTITATIVE QUANTITATIVE → QUALITATIVE
Dominant Status	QUALITATIVE + quantitative QUANTITATIVE + qualitative	QUALITATIVE → quantitative qualitative → QUANTITATIVE QUANTITATIVE → qualitative quantitative → QUALITATIVE

Note. '+' stands for concurrent, '→' stands for sequential, capital letters denote high priority or weight, and lower case letters denote lower priority or weight

Figure 11 'Priority-Sequence Model' from Morgan (1998, p. 368)[159]

For this dissertation the following option has been chosen: (1) the qualitative method is dominant and (2) the methods will be used sequentially, first the quantitative and then the qualitative procedures. This solution is represented in the right lower quadrant of the table above. The reason for these choices is that the quantitative method is useful for exploring and collecting data on such a large and heterogeneous unit of analysis. This step will constitute the basis for the qualitative method and has a dominant position because it offers a set of strengths, which can ensure the achievement of the project's aim.

For Westle (2009, pp. 356-357)[160], after the fundamental questions on sequence and preponderance, a researcher is called to also answer questions regarding: (3) the point in which the methods have to be integrated and (4) what the role of the theoretic perspective will play. In the research in this doctoral thesis, (3) the integration point of the two methods is the start of the qualitative analysis. In fact, this dissertation uses the quantitative data as the basis for extending and deepening the analysis. Also within the interpretation, quantitative and qualitative results will be discussed together. The use of the systems theory

[159] Retrieved in a modified version in Johnson and Onwuegbuzie (2004, p. 22)

[160] Westle theorises that the combination of four criteria (sequence, priority, point of integration and role of theory) gives researchers the chance to choose from among 72 different mixed-methods designs (Westle, 2009, pp. 356-357).

(4) aims to reduce the complexity of the phenomenon, to guide the construction of the categories and to serve as a framework for the description and the interpretation of the results.

In summary, this doctoral thesis will use a mixed method consisting of a sequential design starting with the use of quantitative analysis with explorative and data collection functions and continues with qualitative methods for a deeper understanding of the data (Westle, 2009, pp. 356-357). The results of the quantitative and qualitative analysis will be discussed and interpreted together in the light of the systems theory perspective at the end of this dissertation.

4.3.3 Mixed Methods in Content Analysis

In the case of content analysis, the mix of quantitative and qualitative paradigms is facilitated by the fact that both work with similar terms and common empirical steps. Both methods foresee the classification of the material in a communication model, working with categories, the dissection and definition of the unit of analysis in succession, a systematic, standardised and theory-guided procedure and the use of similar criteria of rigour (Mayring & Brunner, 2009, pp. 672-673). In other words, the two paradigms, although diverse, offer the basis for a commensurable synthesis. It is therefore possible to mix them in order to produce a 'superior' product. The following section offers a detailed description of the quantitative and qualitative procedures carried out in the research for the content analysis.

Content analysis has been variously defined. Krippendorff (1969, p. 103) defines it as 'the use of replicable and valid method for making specific inferences from text to other states or proprieties of its source.' For Früh (2007, p. 25), content analysis can be described as the systematic, rule-guided and intersubjective description of the contents of a communication. In this dissertation, content analysis is considered as the method to 'identify and describe the properties of the information of a text in an objective and systematic way in order to make inferences on non-language properties of individuals and social aggregates' (Mayntz, Holm, & Hübner, 1974, p. 151. Translation EM). The aim of content analysis is the systematic treatment of communication-related material (Mayring, 1995, p. 209) for making inferences from this symbolic medium (R. P. Weber, 1983, p. 127).

Because of its historical development,[161] content analysis designs can be still distinguished on the base of the classical categorisation of 'qualitative' and

[161] The origin of content analysis dates back to the beginning of the 20th century. This procedure was established in the United States in the academic field of communication sciences and has been prin-

'quantitative.' The use of these categories is often controversial in the scientific community. By over-simplifying this distinction it can be stated that the quantitative paradigm is closer to the model of natural science: the aim is to test a hypothesis by analysing principally quantifiable data through statistical procedures and that the qualitative paradigm is closer to the social science model: it aims at understanding and interpreting symbolic-communicative mediated interactions with a focus on subjective meaning (Lamnek, 1995, p. 173; Westle, 2009, p. 335).

A document is all informative material related to a social phenomenon which exists independently of the researcher's actions (Corbetta, 1999, p. 437).[162] Working with existing documents involves three advantages: firstly, non-reactive information is free from the alterations due to the enquiry's procedures; secondly, the documents are independent of time and always up-to-date, even if referred to the past; thirdly, document analysis can be conducted with low research costs (Corbetta, 1999, pp. 437-438). Corbetta also speaks about the disadvantages of document analysis generally connected to the fact that documents can not be interrogated (Corbetta, 1999, p. 468):[163] information can be incomplete and there is an official dimension to the information.

The documents can be roughly categorised in addition to their form on the basis of their contents. Modern societies produce an infinite amount of doc-

---

cipally developed to permit the analysis of large amounts of material originating from mass media like radio and periodicals (Mayring, 2002, p. 114). Content analysis has been characterised from its beginnings by principally systematic and quantitative methods in order to achieve this aim (Mayring & Brunner, 2009, p. 672). This quantitative orientation raised general critique of superficiality and of poor reliability. In fact, quantitative methods applied to content analysis: (1) do not take into account latent meanings and the context of the texts; (2) do not have profound linguistic foundations; and (3) are insufficiently systematic and verifiable (Mayring, 1995, p. 209). Other critiques reflect the limits of such an approach for not taking interesting unique cases and all that is absent in the texts into account (Ritsert, 1972). These critiques opened the way to qualitative designs, whose aim is to preserve the benefit and to avoid the problems of quantitative procedures (Mayring, 1995, p. 209). The advantage of content analysis is its qualitative characteristics added to a systematic and method-controlled proceeding, which differentiate this method to both hermeneutic and grounded theories (Mayring, 2002, p. 114).

[162] The wide definition of 'document' includes all sorts of recorded communication such as films, photos or, more commonly, written documents which represent protocols of communication (Lamnek, 1995, p. 185).

[163] Socrates in a dialogue with Phaedrus similarly affirms that '[...] writing is unfortunately like painting; for the creations of the painter have the attitude of life, and yet if you ask them a question they preserve a solemn silence. And the same may be said of speeches. You would imagine that they had intelligence, but if you want to know anything and put a question to one of them, the speaker always gives one unvarying answer. And when they have been once written down they are tumbled about anywhere among those who may or may not understand them, and know not to whom they should reply, to whom not: and, if they are maltreated or abused, they have no parent to protect them; and they cannot protect or defend themselves' (Plato, 1892a, p. 485).

uments registering and testifying facts, opinions and proposals. These can be divided into personal and institutional documents. Institutional documents are normally already collected and systematised by administrations and can be analysed by researcher with both quantitative and qualitative methods. The present dissertation only analyses institutional documents. They have been considered as the best form of documents for analysing the perspective of health organisations on 'sport' as a health-medium. The analysis unit[164] in particular is constituted by health-strategies on the promotion of PA produced by the National Health Ministries of Germany, France and Italy.

From its characteristics, content analysis can appear to be a trivial research method (Lamnek, 1995, p. 172) because its aim is to make inferences from linguistic materials (communication) about non-linguistic phenomena (Lamnek, 1995, p. 172). Its principles are therefore founded on the development and standardisation of the proceedings of informal communication (Lamnek, 1995, p. 172). On one hand, it is true that both the aim and the material involved in understanding communicative contents are fundamentally the same in non-empirical social situations and in content analysis (Lamnek, 1995, p. 176). On the other hand, it is exactly this similarity to everyday situations which makes of this method 'the central model for the understanding of social reality' (Lisch & Kriz, 1978, p. 11. Translation EM).

4.3.4 *Quantitative Content Analysis*

For Berelson (1952, p. 18), quantitative content analysis can be defined as 'a research technique for the objective, systematic, and quantitative description of the manifest contents of communication.' The quantitative method used in this dissertation is word frequency analysis (or word frequency count), which is particularly used in linguistic and literary analysis. Word frequency analysis is the most basic art of content analysis and consists in the counting of elements (words, word clusters and/or topics) within the material and its comparison[165] to other elements (Mayring, 2003, p. 11). This quantification is not considered here as a criterion for relevance and/or validity *per se* and it does not attempt to produce inferences. The aim of this procedure instead consists of creating a map of the relevant words, words clusters and concepts contained in the documents, exploring their contextual use and sorting them into fewer content categories (R. P.

[164] The analysis unit is the ensemble of the elements empirically analysed in research (Westle, 2009, p. 337).
[165] Particularly important is the accent placed upon the comparison. In fact, a word frequency count always needs a standard and/or a sample for interpretation (Krippendorff, 2004, p. 109).

Weber, 1983, p. 127). In order to achieve this, the recording units to be counted are selected through the development of a category schema (Lamnek, 1995, p. 192) constructed by categories developed *a priori* in the light of the theoretical framework and *a posteriori* during the document analysis.

The present dissertation uses the software MAXQDA for computer aided content analysis. This programme is here seen to complement to rather than supplement a hand-coded content analysis (R. P. Weber, 1983, p. 128). In fact, its function is to speed up the process of word identification and to limit possible errors during the manual coding. In this doctoral thesis, the frequencies count of a word list has been the basic step for further (qualitative) analysis (R. P. Weber, 1983, p. 127). For the word frequency analysis, single words and word clusters have been identified in the texts. The word count methodology not only includes the precise words in question, but also synonyms, abbreviations, derivate forms and compounds. These are to be understood as groups of words which have similar meanings and/or connotation and that signify the presence of a relevant topic within the passage (R. P. Weber, 1983, p. 140). The method utilised for this aim is the identification of keywords within the documents. The presence of these keywords in the texts implies the addressing of one of the topics related to the research question: 'What role does sport play in the health-related promotion of PA?' The key words identified in the documents are:

Key Word / Language	German	French	Italian
Sport	sport; -sport;* sport-*	sport; -sport;* sport-*	sport; -sport;* sport-*
Physical activity	körperliche Aktivität; aktivität;* Körperliche*	activité physique; activité;* physique*	attività fisica; attività;* fisica*
Movement	bewegen;* Bewegung*	bouger;* mouvement*	muoversi* motorio;* movimento*

*: these words have been always submitted to a disambiguation routine.

Figure 12 List of Key Words

The key words below have been chosen from a broader set of words after conducting a test on the documents and were further adjusted during the analysis of the documents.[166] These words have been selected because they emerged during the tests of the proceedings as the most relevant indicators for the identification of relevant passages within the document. Furthermore, this set of words is present and homogeneous within the documents and can be translated without ambiguity into the three languages involved.

[166] Further words which have been discarded after the test phase are 'inactivity,' 'sedentariness,' 'exercise.'

The wider quantitative works surrounding these key words in the light of this category system and its integration with the qualitative step have been developed. This means that every time that a key word has been found, the whole sentence and paragraph have been read in order to understand whether the piece of text contains elements useful to answering the research question and, if this is the case, then sorted within the category system. This procedure has been useful in speeding up the analysis process, which involves 15 documents on a total of 894 pages written in three different languages and creation of a standardised and repeatable first step of the document analysis.

4.3.5 Strategies to Ensure the Rigour in Quantitative Content Analysis

The criteria of rigour as related to the reliability of the word-count content analysis and to the consistency of measurements will now be discussed. The principal reliability problem is the consistency of the rules applied by the coder for classifying words in a text (R. P. Weber, 1983, p. 132). This stems from two major difficulties caused by: (1) the ambiguity of categories and (2) the ambiguity of words.

The first problem is directly connected with the rules of coding. In the case of disagreements, the solutions are obligatorily produced by changing the rules or by implicit or ad hoc solutions (R. P. Weber, 1983, p. 132). In this case, a manageable quantity of material and of the key words allows the coder to double-check all counting procedures. The second problem derives from the characteristics of language, which allow for structurally ambiguities (R. P. Weber, 1983, p. 132). The disambiguation routine has been performed here through the double-checking of a broad sample of text (sentence, paragraph or section). The same procedure has been applied to error reduction in cases where words can be assigned to more than one category. However, the typology of documents analysed (health-strategies) has limited the difficulty of this task through their implicit nature.[167] Furthermore, the method's procedure foresees the development of qualitative analysis in the quantitative step. This represents a further chance for re-testing the quantitative data.

4.3.6 Qualitative Content Analysis

As already mentioned, the first quantitative step serves the development of the qualitative analysis. In fact, a further revision of the quantitative proceedings has

[167] For example when compared to the format of transcribed interviews.

not been considered useful for the assessment of the research question. In this sense, this dissertation agrees with the general critiques of quantitative document analysis that claim that an analysis of the manifest contents of a text establishes oversimplified results. Instead, qualitative analysis is more interested in the analysis of latent meanings and use of methodologies closer to the hermeneutic tradition for the interpretation of the data (Westle, 2009, p. 335).[168]

Qualitative analysis is an umbrella term, which includes different techniques and procedures to be applied to a unit of analysis. Mayring (2003, p. 46) speaks about an explorative phase in the document analysis, which consists in: (1) the collection of material, (2) the analysis of the context, and (3) the description of material's formal characteristics. After this step, the proper analysis of the contents within the unit of analysis begins. This can be carried out through different interpretative techniques and can have different aims such as reduction, explication or structuring. The present research uses the content structuring technique, which consists of the systematic treatment of selected topics, themes and/or aspects of the documents (Mayring, 2003, p. 89). By using systematic rules, the content structuring technique filters the chosen topics and aspects in the texts and creates a cross-section from the material in order to allow for their evaluation (Mayring, 2002, p. 115).

To achieve this, the core process is the development of a category system and the encoding of the text. The category system is the principal tool for analysis and consists of a regulatory scheme used for the acquisition of information within a text. This serves the systematisation of the analysis, 'associates a set of words with each theoretically relevant concept, and summarizes a document's content in a vector of category occurrence frequencies' (Lowe, 2003, p. 1). The ensemble of categories constitutes the category system (or schema), which describes the relationship between categories and constitutes their distinctive boundaries (Westle, 2009, pp. 336-337). The construction of the coding system in this dissertation has been guided by the research questions and by the theoretical framework. It has been established in order to describe the social phenomenon at hand through two different typologies of categories: the first ones are *a priori*, have been developed by the researcher with the help of secondary literature and are theory guided (systems theory); the second category typology has emerged during the qualitative analyses of the texts, are less structured and more similar to the hermeneutic approach.[169]

[168] For example, given the ambiguity of the word 'sport', its precise meaning needs to be deduced from the context and examples furnished by the documents.

[169] Hermeneutics is the study of the theory of interpretation. It has a long history and it was not established within the scientific arena. In its scientific form, it is related to understanding, which also includes the comprehension of understanding. It explains what understanding theoretically is and how it can methodologically take place (Westle, 2009, p. 300). The development of modern hermeneutics

The category system serves to perform the analysis of the selected documents. The term 'encode' (*kodieren*) means the process of systematic examination of the analysis unit within the category schema (Westle, 2009, p. 337). This presupposes the development of coding rules for describing the exact conditions for including a text (passage) within a category. For applying the categories to the texts, coding instruction have been developed for: (1) defining when a text passage is to be put into a category; (2) finding pieces of a text that will be used as anchor examples to exemplify when a passage applies to a category; and (3) developing particular disambiguation rules for doubtful cases. In this research, the theory-guided categories have first been tested on the WHO's *Global Strategy on Diet, Physical Activity and Health* (2004).[170] After treating the texts with the categories system, the passages are summarised and structured for answering the research sub-questions.

4.3.7 Strategies to Ensure the Rigour in Qualitative Content Analysis

In general, any enquiry has to be tested by criteria of rigour in order to establish its adequacy (Mayring, 2003, p. 109). Within the exponents of the qualitative approach, increased attention for rigour is also created in response to the possible accusation of not being scientific. Among qualitative researchers, two main criteria of rigour can be identified: some scientists think that the classical strategies of scientific (quantitative) methods have to be readapted to the qualitative case (Lamnek, 1989, p. 154); while others think that new criteria must be thought out for qualitative research because the criteria of quantitative methods, even if modified, do not apply to qualitative proceedings (Mayring, 2002, pp. 140-144). In this dissertation, criteria from both these streams have been chosen to ensure the quality of the empirical analysis. These will be briefly explained in the following paragraphs and exemplified in practical examples of their application within the doctoral thesis.

The criteria of rigour explicitly for qualitative analysis and particularly meaningful in this dissertation are (Mayring, 2002, pp. 144-148)[171]:

---

is related to the works of Schleiermacher (1768-1834), Wilhelm Dilthey (1833-1911) and Edmund Husserl (1859-1938), but it was firstly Max Weber who developed hermeneutics into an empirical science (Westle, 2009, p. 298). Weber aims to understand social behaviour (*Handeln*) and, in this way, explain its development and effect. The scope of such proceedings is to find causal mechanisms (Westle, 2009, p. 299).

[170] The results of this analysis are summarised in the following chapter and contained in their original form in Michelini (2011).

[171] The criterion for the closeness to the object (*Nähe zum Gegenstand*) and communicative validation apply mostly for interview proceedings.

- The procedural documentation (*Verfahrensdokumentation*), consisting of the detailed and extended explanation of the procedures for allowing for the examination and repetition of the procedures. Starting from this section, the entire methodology chapter of this dissertation put effort into openly and extensively explaining the procedures followed for the creation of the empirical analysis.
- The rule-guided procedure (*Regelgeleitetheit*), planned for cases in which the necessity of flexibility clashes against the highly structured characteristics of the proceeding. Qualitative analysis is systematic, but it is also ready to re-think analysis steps so they better apply to the documents and to the research question. For the rules' consistency, it is important to also treat these changes systematically and to include them explicitly in the procedures' explanation. For this reason, the results of the encoding of the documents have always been double-checked in order to verify whether the changes applied to the procedure during the encoding process are still coherent with the early encoding. Furthermore, particular attention has been given to the coding phase and to the intra-code reliability. The extensive explanation of the coding rules followed for each category is contained in the five dedicated sections, which answer this doctoral thesis's sub-questions.
- The triangulation, which is a criterion for testing the procedures and/or the research results. It means that a researcher should always try to answer the research question through different solutions and compare these results. In this dissertation, the mix of quantitative and qualitative methods and the analysis of three different case studies are forms of triangulation.
- The argumentative interpretation hedging (*argumentative Interpretationsabsicherung*), which assesses one of the most important, but also less structured, phases of qualitative research: the interpretative phase. Interpretations have to be extensively augmented and not simply explained. The theoretical framework plays a key role in this by explaining the phenomenon.[172] In order to respect this criterion of rigour, the interpretation of empirical data has been kept separate from the empirical analysis and can be seen as a continuum and as an extension of the theoretical framework in the light of the new data created by the analytical process.

[172] Fortunately, systems theory has the virtue of being a general theory and covers the entire argumentative space. For this reason, it has not been necessary to apply other theories or different solutions here.

Coming to the strategies to ensure the rigour mutated by the quantitative proceedings and adapted to qualitative methods, the criteria followed in the present content analysis are *validity* and *reliability* (Lamnek, 1989, pp. 156-157)[173]:

- *Validity* aims to understand if that which one aims to analyse has really been analysed (Mayring, 2002, p. 141) and it is a fundamental criterion in the qualitative research (Lamnek, 1989, p. 162). Lamnek speaks about five methods of validity creation: ecological, argumentative, communicative, cumulative and through practice. In this dissertation, two typologies of validations have been used: argumentative, by using the systems theory for the theory-guided interpretation of the data; and cumulative through the comparison of the data between the case studies.
- *Reliability*, which regards the precision and the accuracy of measurement proceedings (Mayring, 2002, p. 141). As in quantitative proceedings, reliability is also an expected criterion of rigour in qualitative proceedings (Lamnek, 1989, p. 177). The mix of quantitative and qualitative methods, the procedural documentation and the theory guided construction of the categories are particularly thought to enhance the reliability of the enquiry in terms of its repeatability and transparence.

In summary, the dissertation uses the criteria of rigour both developed especially for qualitative methods (procedural documentation, argumentative interpretation hedging, rule-guided procedure and triangulation) and adapted from quantitative methods (validity and reliability) to ensure the quality of empirical proceedings.

4.3.8 Step by Step Explanation of Content Analysis Proceedings

In order to move from theory to practice, this section offers a step-by-step description of the practical actions carried out by the researcher during the execution of the content analysis.[174] During the description of the procedures, particular attention will be devoted to the explanation of how quantitative and qualitative methods have been integrated. For Mayring, the whole procedure of content structuring analysis has to be done in ten steps (Mayring, 2003, pp. 46-99). To precisely describe the processes of content analysis carried out, a slightly modified version of Mayring's model is graphically represented and described afterwards:

[173] The criteria of objectivity and the ability to generalise are partly contained in the strategies of rigour, thought explicitly for the qualitative analysis and partly not applicable to this dissertation.

[174] This is particularly needed to respect the criterion of procedural documentation discussed below.

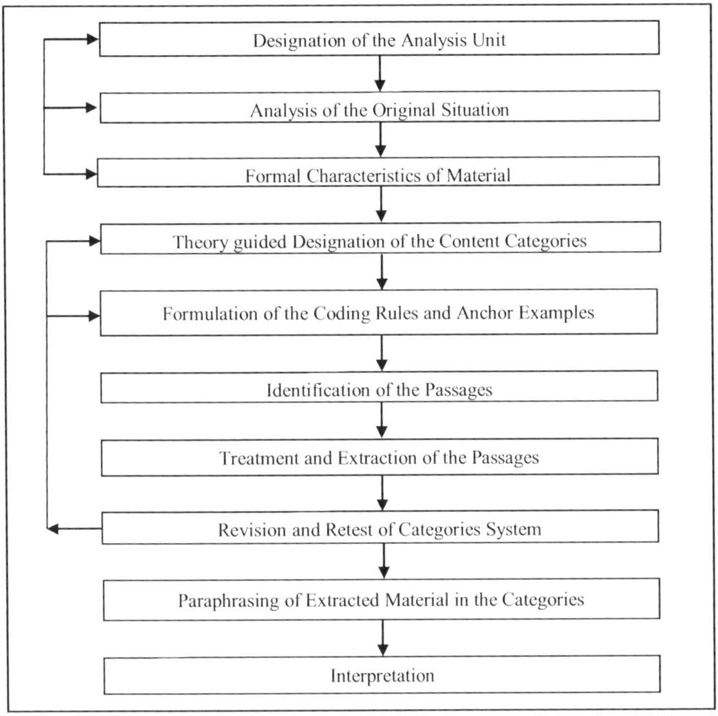

Figure 13 Steps of the Content Analysis (Modified version of Mayring, 2003, p. 89)

1. *Designation of the analysis unit.* The first step of the document analysis regards the choice and collection of material to be analysed (analysis unit or corpus). This dissertation enquires into 15 health-strategies for the promotion of PA, issued by the National Health Ministries of Italy, Germany and France. These have been chosen to look into the research question 'What role does sport play in the health-orientated promotion of PA?' The procedure followed for selecting the case studies and the national documents analysed is explained extensively in separate chapters.
2. *Analysis of the original situation* (*Analyse der Entstehungssituation*). This step consists in the description of the conditions in which the material has been produced. This inquiry offers a brief description for each case study: of the status concerning the promotion of PA; of the sport and the health systems; and of the context behind the documents.

3. *Formal characteristics of material.* This stage regards the description of the material's form. It has been carried out through the use of six criteria of recognition (*Erkenntniswert*) mutated from the methodology of document analysis (Mayring, 2002, p. 48). This aims at answering questions about: the typology of the documents; their external characteristics; the general features of their contents; their level of confidentiality or security; the closeness to the object to be documented with regards to time and space; and brief explanations on the writers of the documents and their relationship to PA promotion.[175]
4. *Theory guided designation of the content categories.* This step foresees the creation of the main content categories. The analysis aims to understand how the role of sport is assessed in health-orientated policies for the promotion of PA. In particular, by basing the research developed categories on the theoretical framework to enquire into how the health system, in the light of its renewed interest for the promotion of PA, deals with the function of the sport system and with the integration of sport activities in its programmes. This step also foresees the wider differentiation of specific sub-questions.[176]
5. *Formulation of the coding rules and anchor examples (Ankerbeispiel).* In this theory-guided step, precise definitions and concrete rules of the application of the category system for the analysis of the phenomena have been formulated. A part of this task consists in establishing one or more anchor examples for each category. The first document, which has been used to test the analysis rules of the further documents (anchor example), has been the WHO's *Global Strategy on Diet Physical activity and Health* (2004).
6. *Identification of the passages.* This step identifies and encodes the text passages which will be analysed through the use of the category system. This step has been made possible by carrying out an analysis of frequency of the keywords: 'PA', 'sport' and 'movement'. The word clusters, sentences and/or paragraphs containing the keywords have been analysed a second time to establish whether they contain important information needed to answer the research question through the category system.[177]
7. *Treatment and extraction of the passages.* The keywords individuated during the last phase constitute the basis for the passages' extraction. The chosen passages have been analysed in light of the categories and the needed in-

---

[175] Normally, this step also involves transcription (Ehlich & Switalla, 1976), which has been an uncomplicated task in this case. In fact, the documents have been imported in their original form (Portable Document Format) to the programme for content analysis *MAXqda*.

[176] By avoiding the formulation of hypothesis the openness in respect to the dissertation's topic has been secured.

[177] Independently from this proceeding, the documents have all been read to permit the eventual accentuation of their special and/or unique characteristics.

formation has been extracted and systemised. The analytical procedure followed in this research is the one of structuring, which aims to filter a particular structure from the material through specific criteria.

8. *Revision and retest of categories system.* The treatment of the passages implies the modification of the coding rules, which have to be open to adaptation for special situations found in the passages. Because the proceeding of content analysis needs to be highly systemised, this step foresees the systemisation of additional rules and the retesting of the material in light of the modified coding rules.
9. *Paraphrasing of extracted material in the categories.* In this stage the information extracted from the passages is paraphrased, reduced and summarised. For this, proceedings similar to reduction techniques are used. The extracted and paraphrased information are structured in the light of the categories for answering the research question.
10. *Interpretation.* In this final step the results of the analysis are interpreted in a separate chapter in relation to the main research question and the theoretical framework with the aim to assess to the research question. In order to achieve this, the phenomena and the language of the documents will be translated into sociological concepts. This is expected to form a step further in the sociological description of the phenomenon.

4.4 Test of the Design

After their theoretical conception, the empirical instruments for the content analysis have been tested on the WHO's 'Global Strategy on Diet, Physical Activity and Health' (WHO, 2004). This step has been carried out for testing and refining the empirical design before applying it to the analyses of the strategies of national health ministries. This health-strategy from the WHO has been chosen because it received resonant attention and it constitutes the most relevant global effort to assess the promotion of PA (Bauman & Craig, 2005, p. 4). Furthermore, it is an example of the WHO's international attempt to coordinate and facilitate the cooperation between the sport and the health systems. Through the cooperation between systems, the WHO expects to create collective gains unachievable by the operation of a single system (Wiesenthal, 2006, p. 70). The results of these analyses have been published in 'Cooperation in the promotion of physical activity. The function of the WHO and the role of sports in the Global Strategy on Diet, Physical Activity and Health' (Michelini, 2011). Because they constitute the test of the empirical design of this dissertation, these have been restated below in a modified and briefer version.

The following sections explain the process that brought about the publication of the SDPA, provides an overview of its main contents and perform the document analysis of this document. In particular, the investigation has been performed using a mix of quantitative and qualitative methods, focussing on the characterisation of PA and the role of sport in the Strategy, which is a prototype of the design used for analysing the health-strategies of the health ministries of France, Germany and Italy.

4.4.1 The 'Global Strategy on Diet, Physical Activity and Health'

Some sections above,[178] it has been argumented that even by recomending cooperation between systems and by trying to mediate between them, the WHO still follows the logic of the health system. This situation gives rise to potential problems of misunderstanding and incommensurability, because the WHO's language and orientation can result in incomprehensibility or cause issues in other function systems.[179] Therefore the messages of the WHO risks being perceived as biased, defending the interests of the health system (Willke, 2001b, p. 108) and unable to create positive governance. This section analyses the context which brought up the conceiving of the SDPA for enabling a deeper understanding of its contents.

The process of the development of the SDPA involved different steps (WHO, 2011d) and generated massive political interest, media attention and debates (Bauman & Craig, 2005, p. 3; Danzon, 2004). However, controversies were particularly related to dietary topics (Cannon, 2004; Danzon, 2004) while the guidelines on PA remained substantially unchanged (Bauman & Craig, 2005, p. 3). This was not caused by a broader concurrence of the recommendation of the promotion of PA. Instead, 'nutrition appeared to be more controversial but was sometimes given more emphasis as the most important risk factor by some writers' (Bauman & Craig, 2005, p. 3). On other occasions, the discussion on health promotion, even by quoting both PA and diet, tends to assess just the

[178] This concept has been deeply assessed in the chapter 'Governance in the Promotion of Physical Activity.'

[179] For example, the manufacturers of foods rich in unsaturated fatty acids do not follow the logic 'healthy/unhealthy' but instead the logic 'selling/not selling.' By promoting a healthy diet the health system surely goes against the economic logic of some food industries. As a result, such organisations will probably ignore or deny a communication of the health system which recommends the use of ingredients poor of unsaturated fatty acids until that is possible. Indeed, only the use of steering media like 'knowledge', 'power' or 'money' (Willke, 2007b) or a situation in which the resistance to the communication of the health system provoke an economical loss will be interpreted as stimuli which justify a change in the operations of the organisation.

problem of promoting a healthy diet. For example, the article '*Diet and physical activity: the public health debate*' (Danzon, 2004) confuses the two risk factors exemplarily. The article is about diet, but PA is sometimes quoted as the two were synonyms. This is confirmed by the fact that, after its last release, the media interest on the SDPA tended to be overly focused on nutrition while the promotion of PA has often been perceived as a secondary objective (Bauman & Craig, 2005, p. 4).

Instead, the Strategy recognises the importance of the promotion of PA as the key determinant of energy expenditure and as risk reduction for chronic diseases. The overall goal of the SDPA is to 'promote and protect health by guiding the development of an enabling environment for sustainable actions at individual, community, national and global levels that, when taken together, will lead to reduced disease and death rates related to unhealthy diet and physical inactivity' (WHO, 2004, p. 3). With the exception of some focused pieces of advice for risk groups, the target group of the SDPA is as broad as possible. The reason for this extensive ambit is that NCDs are now epidemic throughout the world and their related risk factors need to be removed without particular reference to individual or segmented variables (Cannon, 2004, p. 371).

The principles for action are based on the 'life-course' approach, cooperation and reference to scientific evidence. The themes of cooperation and stakeholders' engagement cover key aspects. In particular, one of the four main objectives of the document is strictly related to the topic of governance, and the second half of the Strategy consists of a list of responsibilities of the stakeholders (UN agencies, national governments, international partners, civil society, non-governmental organisations and the private sector). These stakeholders are called to cooperate under the coordination of health ministers. In fact, the SDPA is explicit about the role of the health ministries, which 'have an essential responsibility for coordinating and facilitating the contributions of other ministries and government agencies' (WHO, 2004, p. 6).[180] The SDPA's guidelines also include school policies because these are seen as being influential for the 'lives of most children in all countries' (WHO, 2004, p. 9) and encourage schools to provide children with daily physical education classes and to offer properly substantial opportunities for physical activity. The cooperation between the stakeholders involved is fundamental in order to implement the Strategy and to reach the local

[180] Governments also 'have a central role, in cooperation with other stakeholders, to create an environment that empowers and encourages behaviour changes by individuals, families and communities, to make positive, life-enhancing decisions on healthy diets and patterns of physical activity' (WHO, 2004, p. 3).

levels. The sport system is also mentioned as a potential system partner for the promotion of PA.[181]

In conclusion, the SDPA is an 'advance in the thinking of WHO on global public health' (Cannon, 2004, p. 370) and marks the status of the WHO as the 'intellectual lead in the prevention and control of chronic diseases' (Cannon, 2004, p. 370). The consultation process for the SDPA involved many stakeholders and exemplifies the function of the WHO as a super-expert for ensuring cooperation in the prevention of NCDs.

4.4.2 *Analysis of the 'Global Strategy on Diet, Physical Activity and Health'*

As a programme which implements the WHO's decisions, the SDPA aims to promote diet[182] and PA on a global scale through the cooperation of a wide range of function systems. This section analyses the contents of the final version of the Strategy approved on May 22, 2004 in the 57th WHA. The analyses have been carried out through a mix of word frequency count[183] and content analysis which is the prototype for the analysis of this dissertation. The design has been developed for assessing two topics: the role of the sport system and the characterisation of PA.[184] A frequency analysis first evaluated the occurrence of related terms and identified the most important passages in the document. The content analysis (Mayring 2007: 89) then extracted the information needed from the selected passages in order to describe and make inferences about them (Holsti, 1969). The contents have been than critically discussed by way of personal observations, clarifications found within the texts and secondary literature.

In the following, a mention of the SDPA will only refer to the Strategy without the additional annexes contained in the official document.[185] The SDPA is divided into 14 topics[186] and 67 sections.[187] For reason of synthesis, the parts

---

[181] See section: 'Content Analysis of the *Global Strategy on Diet, Physical Activity and Health*' (pages 15-19).

[182] The analysis of the promotion of a healthy diet is not contained in the analysis below because it is not relevant to the focus of the present research.

[183] The word count methodology includes counting not just the particular word in question, but also derivatives from and compounds of the word in question (example for 'sport': sport; sports; sporting; sport-; sporting-). The document's transcription encompasses the formatting of images, logos, page headers and the page's theme.

[184] The results of this analysis are not to be considered representative for the general logic of the WHO.

[185] The official SDPA document includes: an introduction, the Strategy (pages 1 to 14), the WHA's Resolution 57.17 (pages 15 to 18) and a page containing references and copyright data.

[186] In detail: Global Strategy on Diet; Physical Activity and Health; The Challenge; The Opportunity; Goal and Objectives; Evidence for Action; Principles for Action; Responsibilities for Action; Mem-

of the Strategy will be identified in this section exclusively by the number of the respective section. A copy of the document, available on the WHO website (WHO, 2004), would be helpful to follow the discussion and to reap the full benefits of the analysis.

During the analysis of the Strategy, a general tendency has been identified: 'PA' is a central topic and a recurrent word, but it is often mentioned together with diet.[188] In this regard, section 13 of the SDPA argues that:

> 'Diet and physical activity influence health both together and separately. Although the effects of diet and physical activity on health often interact, particularly in relation to obesity, there are additional health benefits to be gained from physical activity that are independent of nutrition and diet, and there are significant nutritional risks that are unrelated to obesity. Physical activity is a fundamental means of improving the physical and mental health of individuals.'

Even in light of this explanation, this is a questionable characteristic of the Strategy because, from a governance perspective, 'if the effector arms of physical activity programmes are different to nutrition, then strategic implementation and partnerships might be kept separate, although the health-related consequences of poor diet and physical inactivity show large degrees of overlap' (Bauman & Craig, 2005, p. 3).

In the following, the role of sport in the SDPA will be analysed. 'Sport' is mentioned six times, with the six references contained in four sections (38, 41.2, 42.1, and 61), specifically:

- Section 38: 'Health ministries have an essential responsibility for coordinating and facilitating the contributions of other ministries and government agencies.' Among others,[189] bodies 'whose contributions should be coordinated include ministries and government institutions responsible for policies on [...] sports [...]'.

ber States; WHO; International Partners; Civil Society and Nongovernmental Organizations; Private Sector; Follow-up and Future Developments; and Conclusions.

187 Some of them (sections 18, 40, 41, 42, 45, and 46) have additional numerical subsections and others (sections 22, 51, 58, 60, 61, and 63) have additional points listed by means of square-shaped bullet points. The subsections will be referred to in the following way: 'number of the section'.'number of the subsection'.

188 To be more precise, in the 14 pages of the Strategy, PA and diet are mentioned together on 82 occasions, with 37 slightly different formulations. PA is mentioned autonomously from diet 26 times. Furthermore, these are all contained in six sections (out of a total of 67) of the Strategy (sections 13, 23, 24, 29, 39.3 and 42.1-2-3-4), which are in fact the only passages that consider PA as an independent topic.

189 Specifically: food, agriculture, youth, recreation, education, commerce and industry, finance, transportation, media and communication, social affairs, and environmental and urban planning.

- Section 41.2: 'Public policies can influence prices through taxation, subsidies or direct pricing in ways that encourage healthy eating and lifelong physical activity.' The section recommends the usage of 'public funds and subsidies to promote access among poor communities to recreational and sporting facilities' where needed.
- Section 42.1: 'National and local governments should frame policies and provide incentives to ensure that [...] sport and recreation facilities embody the concept of sports for all.'
- Section 61: 'The private sector can be a significant player in promoting healthy diets and physical activity. The [...] sporting-goods manufacturers [...] have important parts to play as responsible employers and as advocates for healthy lifestyles'.[190]

In summary, the sport system, embodied in the ministries and government agencies responsible for sport, sport facilities and sporting-goods, is identified as a partner for the promotion of PA. Moreover, the reference to 'sports for all'[191] can be interpreted as the acceptance by the WHO of the logic of sport in the promotion of PA.

This closely regards the characterisation of PA in the SDPA. PA is a broad concept, defined in this dissertation as 'any bodily movement produced by skeletal muscles that results in energy expenditure above resting level' (Bouchard & Shephard, 1994, p. 77). The activities covered in this broad definition can be further specified on the basis of their mode, intensity, duration, frequency and continuity (Ainsworth et al., 2000; Caspersen et al., 1986; Dishman et al., 1985; Evenson et al., 2002; Hagströmer, 2007; King, 2001). The information contained in the SDPA regarding each one of these attributes of PA is commented in the following:

- Mode: the SDPA furnishes 7 indicators contained in sections 24, 39.3 and 42.1. Three of these -'other forms of physical activity', 'different types [...] of physical activity' and HEPA[192]- are general advice and do not represent examples of PA to be practiced. This reduces the concrete modes of PA to four types: walking, cycling, muscle strengthening, and balance training. The latter two are contained in the sentence: 'Muscle strengthening and balance training can reduce falls and increase functional status among older adults'. They are hence limited to risk groups (older adults) and the sentence

[190] The term 'sporting-goods' is repeated in a very similar context.

[191] Sport for all is 'an internationally accepted term of proclaiming everybody's right and giving everybody access to sport' (Palm, 1991, p. 9).

[192] HEPA is the abbreviation of Health-Enhancing Physical Activity. It is defined as 'any form of physical activity that benefits health and functional capacity without undue harm or risk' (Foster, 2000, p. 9).

is weakened by the use of the verb 'can'.[193] Furthermore, the Strategy does not contain any specific reference to sport disciplines.[194]

- Continuity: the SDPA underlines in its 'Principles for Action' the relevance of a 'life-course' approach. Direct pieces of advice on the continuity of PA are contained in section 24, 'for physical activity, it is recommended that individuals engage in adequate levels throughout their lives' and in section 28 '(The life-course) approach [...] encourages [...] regular physical activity from youth into old age.'
- Intensity, Frequency and Duration: the guidelines of the SDPA are contained in section 24 and can be summarised as being practiced regularly and moderately (intensity), on most days (frequency) and for at least 30 minutes (duration).

The analysis now will focus on section 24 of the SDPA because it is particularly significant for explaining the characterisation of the intensity, frequency and duration of the PA to be promoted in the SDPA (WHO, 2004, p. 4):

> 'Different types and amount of physical activity are required for different health outcomes: at least 30 minutes of regular, moderate-intensity physical activity on most days reduces the risk of cardiovascular disease and diabetes, colon cancer and breast cancer. [...]. More activity may be required for weight control.'

One can notice that the section containing unique precise recommendations on PA is accompanied by introductory and concluding sentences that provide important additional information about the topic. Nevertheless, these are both vaguely formulated and do not refer to any concrete measurement of intensity, frequency and/or duration. For example the sentence 'different [...] amount of physical activity are required for different health outcomes' is vague and the explanation of the different health benefits attainable is completely absent from the SDPA. Furthermore, the sentence 'More activity may be required for weight control' is limited to risk groups (overweight persons) and its content is weakened by the usage of 'may'.[195] On the one hand, the usage within the SDPA of the standard formula '30 minutes of moderate physical activity on most days' is coherent with the Strategy's philosophy on the clarity of the message contained in section 42.4: 'simple, direct messages need to be communicated on the quantity and quality of physical activity sufficient to provide substantial health bene-

[193] The vocabulary generally used in the Strategy is characterised by a frequent usage of weakening verbs such as 'can', 'may' and 'could' instead of clearer imperative formulations (Cannon, 2004, p. 372). This confuses and reduces the strength of the contents by decreasing the sense of scientific urgency and the importance of the guidelines.

[194] As seen above, sport is mentioned 6 times but never as a mode of PA.

[195] See the previous footnote.

fits.' Bauman and Craig (2005, p. 3) also justify this simplification and the absence of recommendations for 'vigorous PA' as follows:

> 'The recommendation of 'half an hour of achievable moderate intensity activity on most days of the week' fits well into social marketing and media campaign efforts. Additional physical activity, or activity at a greater intensity may be required for some health outcomes such as cancer prevention or weight loss, but making the message(s) more complicated may confuse efforts to raise community awareness'

On the other hand, this statement goes against the purpose of the Strategy to stimulate the cooperation of different systems in the promotion of PA. Indeed, the SDPA aims to create a palpable impulse through a message comprehensible for function systems with different logics. Only in this way can it stimulate cooperation for the promotion of PA. The simplification of the characteristics of PA in a unique standard and health-orientated formula does not seek to explain how the sport system could cooperate in the promotion of PA.

In summary, the messages of the SDPA regarding the role of sport and the characterisation of PA do not constitute a clear point of connection for the cooperation of the sport system. Even by recommending cooperation with the sport system, the PA recommended by the Strategy is not compatible with the logic of the sport system. In fact sport organisations promote a PA often orientated towards performance and many classical sport disciplines imply a form of PA that differs from the WHO's standard. Nevertheless, vigorous activity also produces health benefits and sport can have benefits on the dietary habits and lifestyle of the participants that go far beyond benefits related to calorie consumption. Furthermore, sport organisations are appropriate for practicing and promoting PA and allow many forms of structural coupling with the health system, such as in the case of health-orientated sport activities.

4.5 Summary of the Methodology and Next Steps

This chapter has described the empirical design and the methodological instruments for enquiring the research question 'What role does sport play in the health-related promotion of PA?'

As a first step, general reflections on the empirical approach for gaining knowledge on the subject have been made. Developing a reliable research basis is one of the most tenuous phases in planning a research project and has to be carefully carried out in order to prevent the selection bias. In summary, this dissertation:

- uses the comparison of countries over the same time span as a method to gain knowledge about the phenomenon being enquired into;
- takes into account three countries, because a small-n comparison permits a focused and deep analysis;
- analyses France, Germany and Italy, because the comparison of three conservative countries is expected to furnish conclusions that can be generalized for whole group of conservative countries and that can test whether a different sport system influences the social phenomenon inquired.

Alternative samplings exist and have been carefully considered. In particular, the power of comparison could be amplified by expanding the comparison to the groups of liberal and social democratic countries.[196] Even with its imperfection, the comparison of France, Germany and Italy has been identified as being the best choice for it feasibility and relevance. Once clarified these points, the selection of the catalogue of documents to be analysed has been carried out as a further propaedeutic methodological step.

By using a semi-standardised procedure, five documents for each case study have been chosen. These documents have been issued by the national health ministries, are related to the topic of PA promotion and assess the role of sport in this context. In this way, a catalogue of documents (unit of analysis) has been created which is representative for the main topic, offers the chance to compare the results of the case studies and is suitable for answering the research question. The detailed and extensive explanation of the sampling procedure furnishes enough information for allowing another scientist to repeat the selection with very similar outcomes. A first observation of interest can be made regarding the sampling: the selection brought naturally to a profoundly different catalogue in general and within each case study. This reflects the differences regarding the health ministries, their approaches to health promotion and their ways of communicating with their respective populations. Also, it is a demonstration of the fragmentation of the global discourse.

To explore health-strategies issued by the health ministries of France, Germany and Italy, the dissertation uses an approach developed *ad hoc* to content analysis. This procedure[197] has been created by the author himself to better

[196] This topic will be deepened in the conclusions.

[197] By further categorizing this method through the reviewing of methodological literature, the most similarities with an already existing design are with *the summative approach to quantitative analysis*, which is characterised by the mix of the analytical methods of word frequency count and content analysis (Hsieh & Shannon, 2005). Anyway, this further characterization is at least artificial because: the method has been independently developed following the general rules of mixed methods and then acknowledged as being similar to the summative approach; the two methods are only similar and not identical; the constant further differentiation in mixed method of 'new' designs create a kind of 'lost

fit the aim of the analysis and it is based upon a mix of quantitative and qualitative approaches. This design is based on general methodological guidelines for document analysis retrieved in particular from the works of Lamnek (1989, 1995, 2010), Mayring (2000, 2001, 2002, 2003, 2007) and Flick (2011, 2012; Flick, von Kardorff, & Steinke, 2000). A mix of methods indicates the use of both qualitative and quantitative approaches in the same research project, which is believed to enhance the quality of the dissertation by profiting from the strengths of both disciplines. This design: uses sequentially quantitative and qualitative content analysis; gives the dominant role to qualitative methods; and discusses the results in light of the systems theory. More specifically, the passages to be analysed have been identified through the use of word count analysis. In a successive step, these have been analysed in depth with the interpretative technique of content structuring. The treatment of the analysis unit through these categories is expected to furnish a description of the social phenomenon inquired and to furnish the basis for the formulation of hypotheses and generalisations.

The provisory version of the methodology for content analysis has been tested on the WHO's 'Global Strategy on Diet, Physical Activity and Health' (2004). The SDPA is a health-strategy that aims to promote PA on a global scale through the cooperation of a broad range of function systems, mostly external to health. The WHO represents a point of reference for the coordination of systems towards health matters. For this aim, the message of the WHO should be understandable by the various systems, which should mutually cooperate. Only by highlighting the opportunity of a win-win situation and by using a language adaptable to all contexts involved can the message impact other systems. The analysis of the role of sport and of the characterisation of PA in the SDPA demonstrates that the message fails to create a solid basis for the cooperation of the sport system. In fact, the Strategy mentions the sport system as an important partner for the cooperation in the promotion of PA. Nevertheless, it recommends 'at least 30 minutes of regular, moderate-intensity physical activity on most days' and does not specify how the sport system should participate in facilitating the implementation of such a recommendation. In this way, the SDPA limits the potential understanding of how the sport system should contribute to the Strategy's goals and, more generally, what the role of sport in the prevention of NCDs is. This represents an obstacle for the cooperation between organisations within the sport system and other potential partners such as schools, workplaces and transport companies regarding the promotion of PA. Moreover, this can cause a general misunderstanding and limit the potentially substantial contribution of sport in improving the population's health.

in design' effect which the author had to face in first person and which he doesn't want to support further.

However these results cannot be generalised for the discussion on the promotion of PA at national level. In fact, even though the WHO has a large influence on the setting of the health agenda, the health ministries develop and implement health-strategies independently and in different national contexts. For this reason, the national level has been considered particularly interesting for investigating the topic at the hand and will be analysed through the exploration of health-strategies issued by the health ministries of France, Germany, and Italy. In the following chapter, the sub-question 'How are PA and sport spoken about in strategies for the health-orientated promotion of PA?' will be assessed by applying the developed design to the unit of analysis.

5. Empirical Analysis of the Case Studies

'Now obviously the propositions of the system
have reference to matters of empirical fact;
if they did not, they could have no claim to be called scientific'
(Parsons, 1949, p. 7)

The following six sections assess the sub-question 'How are PA and sport spoken about in strategies for the health-orientated promotion of PA?' through the inquiry of the whole analysis unit. The selected documents have first been explored through the use of key words. In detail, the selected list of terms has been used to find the sections which assess the topics inquired within the documents. The distribution of the key words is summarised in the table below:

Key Word \ Country	France	Germany	Italy	Total
Movement	35	498	28	561
Physical Activity	435	91	70	596
Sport	116	186	36	338
Total	586	775	134	1495

Figure 14 Key Words in the Case Studies

The contents of the sections identified have been investigated for assessing the following queries[198]:

[198] Even if the formulation of a research question is one of the first methodological steps when undertaking research, its final form and especially the sub-questions and queries it raises have been revised and modified up to the final steps of the research process. In fact, the operationalisation of a research question implies an advanced status of the research, particularly if the sub-questions and queries are preliminary and/or connected to each other or to the results of the empirical analysis. As a result of these facts, not every following query has been established *a priori* but they have instead been developed as a result of the cyclic research process. In particular: categories 1, 2 and 5 have been con-

1. What is the recommended dose of PA?
2. What role do the sport organisations have?
3. Why is sport being delegitimised as a medium of health promotion?
4. How sound are the key concepts?

For each query a category (Lamnek, 1995, p. 192) has been developed for guiding the process of content analysis. In this way, the chosen topics have been filtered from the texts and a cross-section from the material has been created in order to allow for their evaluation (Mayring, 2003, p. 89). This naturally developed in a system of wider sub-categories established during the coding procedures for the meaningful organisation of the information retrieved in the documents.

These category systems are each explained separately in the following four sections by furnishing: insights on their logic and coding rules; anchor examples of the recording units; reductions and classifications of the elements found within the documents; and, finally, a brief comment on the results obtained. Because the four categories do not contain any insight into the differences between the case studies, these are analytically compared in a separate section. The comparison of the case studies has not been considered as a fifth category because its proceeding is different: it does not analyse the documents but simply compares already collected data. Because of their contents, these sections are characterised by a 'dry' register. Its aim is to clearly and synthetically illustrate the procedures adopted and the results obtained. Instead, the discursive and extensive interpretation of the data in the light of the theoretical framework has been kept separate from this chapter and will be discussed in the conclusions. This will extensively assess the main research question by generating advancements in both the theoretical and empirical dimensions. The description and the explanation of the social phenomenon will instead not constitute a theoretical model for the normative optimal governance in PA promotion

5.1 'What is the Recommended Dose of PA?'

This section addresses the topic of the dose of PA recommended in the selected health-strategies. This category has been created *a priori*, by reading primary and secondary literature and in light of the theoretical framework. For a proper understanding of this section, the operative distinction between sport and PA within this dissertation is fundamental: PA is a broad concept defined as 'any body movement produced by the skeletal muscles that results in a substantial increase

ceived *a priori* and in the light of the theoretical framework; whereby categories 3 and 4 emerged as relevant *a posteriori* during the document analysis procedures.

over the resting energy expenditure' (Bouchard & Shephard, 1994, p. 77); Sport[199] is a mode of physical activity branded by being recreational, governed by rules and orientated towards performance (modified version of Heinemann, 2007, p. 56). This characterisation points out some practical characteristics of sport activities which differentiate them from PA: they normally require planned (leisure) time, special fields, equipment, and/or partners and their intensity is unpredictable, often fluctuate and tend to be high.

This section categorises and analyses pieces of text that give advices on the characteristics of the dose of PA. Only the segments which respect the following requirements have been considered as a recording unit:

- Clarity: the segments need to be explicit and clearly expressed without either possible misunderstandings or the need for interpreting the concepts;
- Comprehensiveness: the segments need to assess at least three of the five[200] characteristics of PA. This choice has been taken *a posteriori* after the explorative step. The reason is that recommendations containing two characteristics of PA were far too vague to constitute a base for the analysis of the recommended doses of PA, but recommendations containing four or five characteristics of PA were too few to embody the documents trend.

These guidelines are exemplified in the two recording units below:

1. Positive example of recording unit (German Ministry of Health, 2010a, p. 34):
   'Schon mit einem 30-minütigen flotten Spaziergang fünf- bis sechsmal pro Woche lässt sich ein Maß an körperlicher Leistungsfähigkeit erzielen, die das Sterberisiko halbiert.'
   Translation (EM):
   'Already a 30-minute brisk walk five to six times per week can achieve a level of physical performance that halves the risk of death.'

2. Negative example of recording unit (French Ministry of Health, 2004, p. 2):
   'Quel que soit notre âge, une activité physique régulière, si possible quotidienne, est bénéfique.'
   Translation (EM):
   'Whatever our age is, regular physical activity, daily if possible, is beneficial.'

199 This dissertation refers in particular to the amateur and broad manifestations of organised sport.

200 PA can be specified on the basis of their mode, intensity, duration, frequency and continuity (Ainsworth et al., 2000; Caspersen et al., 1986; Dishman et al., 1985; Evenson et al., 2002; Hagströmer, 2007; King, 2001).

The first example provides information about the typology (a brisk walk), the duration (30 minutes) and the frequency (5-6 times a week) of PA. Even if it does not furnish information on the intensity (the adjective brisk has not been considered a sufficient clue) and continuity, it respects the guidelines explained above and has been accepted as a valid recording unit. Instead, the second example only provides information on frequency (daily) and continuity (regularly), but no clues about typology, intensity or duration. For this reason it is not considered to have satisfied the guideline of this category and has therefore been discarded.

5.1.1 Distribution of the Recording Units

By following the guidelines above, 53 recommendations on the dose of PA have been found. These recording units are distributed as in the following table:

Nation	Document	Recording unit
France	PNNS1 2001-2005	1
	PNNS2 2006-2010	3
	PNNS3 2011-2015	2
	Health comes by moving	12
	Physical Activity and Health	16
Germany	Mentally Fit in Old Age	3
	INFORM	0
	Active for Myself	3
	Advisor on Health Care	5
	National Health Objective	1
Italy	PSN 2006-2008	0
	PSN 2011-2013	0
	Pages of Health	3
	Make Gains in Health	2
	Gaining Health in 4 moves	2
Total		53

Figure 15 Distribution of Recommendations on the Dose of PA

It can be observed that three documents do not contain any recommendations at all on the dose of PA, even if one of their aims (or, in the case of the strategy ‘IN FORM’, its principal aim) is the promotion of PA. Almost all the rest of the documents (9) contain one to three suggestions on the dose of PA. In three cases more recommendations are contained (5, 12, and 16).

5.1.2 Results per Population Segment

For the purpose of this dissertation, it is useful to separate the advice on the dose of PA upon the base of the age segments of the population targeted by the recommendation. In fact, during the analysis, numerous recommendations were detected that are directed to particular age groups. The creation of separate categories has been considered necessary for correctly summarising the meanings of the documents. A summary of the characteristics of the PA suggested for each of these segments will now be separately commented upon:

- *Children and youth*: within the documents, four recommendations for children and teenagers have been found. The duration of the suggested PA is of 60 minutes or more (just one recommendation refers to a smaller amount of time) with a moderate or high intensity and a frequency between three and seven times a week. The typology of the activities entails a mix of sport-orientated activities (2) and PA in general (2). Collective team sports are advised once, but just for 20 minutes three or more times a week. There are no accounts on continuity.
- *Adults*: the ten recommendations for adults are characterised by an averagely lower intensity and a shorter length than the one for children and teenagers. Regarding the frequency, the most fragments advise PA seven times a week. The typology of activities varies from PA in general (2) to exercise and sport (7). In five cases the recommendations refer to endurance sport activities like running, swimming or cycling. However, team sports are never mentioned and there is no reference to traditional-competitive sport activities. A regular continuity is mentioned three times.
- *The elderly*: the frequency, duration, and intensity recommended to the elderly are reduced when compared to the previous two groups. The activities contained in the seven recommendations are in four cases sport-orientated activities and in three cases everyday activities. Also in this category there are no indications of continuity.
- *Everyone*: within the strategies, most of the recommendations (32) are not directed at a particular population segment but simply to everyone. These recommendations are characterised by usually recommending moderate intensity, a duration of 30 minutes or more and an every day frequency. In this sense they are very similar to the WHO's standard.[201] The typologies of recommended activities are PA in general (12), walking (9), and mixed activities entailing sport and exercise (11). Here there is also less advice (1) on continuity.

---

[201] 'At least 30 minutes of regular, moderate-intensity physical activity on most days' (WHO, 2004, p. 4).

5.1.3 Results per Characteristic of PA

An analysis of the date obtained on every single characteristic of the dose of PA has been considered useful in obtaining a focused overview of them. The following observations can be made:

- For the mode of PA, many recommendations (15) don't specify the mode of PA to be carried out at all. Walking is recommended most frequently (11 times) and, in general, the examples of mode furnished often regard everyday activities (20) like climbing stairs or cycling to the workplace. Sport is recommended alone (3) or together with a broader set of physical activities (12). However, collective sport games are mentioned only twice: in the other cases endurance sport activities like swimming, cycling, or jogging are referred to. In summary, the majority of the recommendations refer to PA in general or everyday PA but sometimes leisure activities are specifically referred to or of a mix of both.
- Continuity is, even if the international guidelines underline the importance of a 'life-course' approach (WHO, 2004, p. 4) very rarely spoken about. In fact, a vague reference to this topic has been found three times in the 53 recording units about the dose of PA.
- For the purposes of frequency, the recording units almost always offer a reference to the frequency of the activities (46). Most recommended (33 times) is the practicing of PA on a daily basis. A lower frequency is advised 14 times and in most of these cases, a leisure activity is recommended (8) or the recommendations are directed towards the elderly (6). In summary, the majority of the recommendations recommend PA being practised every day and other suggestions refer to special cases.
- Regarding duration, the recording units almost always offer a reference to the length of the activities (46). The most common recommendation is to do PA 'for at least 30 minutes' (17 times) or 'for 30 minutes' (15 times). Exceptions to this tendency are seven recommendations of a higher length and nine recommendations of a shorter duration.
- The intensity is assessed 29 times in the coded segments. The most recommendations refer to moderate intensity (17). A higher intensity is recommended sometimes (5) for children and teenagers (2) or for a shorter length than the normally advised 30 min (3). A lower intensity is sometimes (4) recommended to the elderly (1) or for a longer duration than the normally advised 30 min (3).

5.1.4 *Reflection on the Results*

In addition to explanations regarding the health effects of PA or the risks connected to PI, indications of the dose of PA are extremely relevant within the discussion on PA promotion because they assess what people concretely should do to keep themselves fit through PA. Furthermore, the scientific literature and the documents analysed often state that simple and concrete recommendations regarding the form and quantity of PA to be carried out should be provided through strategies for the promotion of PA (Bauman & Craig, 2005, p. 3; German Ministry of Health & German Ministry of Nutrition, 2008, p. 21; WHO, 2004, p. 8).

However, the treatment of this topic within the analysed documents is not obvious and the modern discussion on the dose of PA entails instead different and contradictions. Indeed, the health system is naturally orientated towards illness and the core of its rhetoric is the idea that daily moderate physical activity is sufficient for preventing NCDs (Oja, 2004, p. 169). For this reasons, the role of sport activities is becoming increasingly ambiguous in the health-related promotion of PA (Michelini & Thiel, 2013). Nevertheless, sport has been (and often is still) the backbone of the discussion of PA promotion. Last but not least, the double ambiguity concerning the key terms of 'PA', 'health' and their interaction detected in the discourse concerning the effects of PA on health makes an in depth analysis of the characteristics of PA discussed in the documents mandatory. In fact, the analysis of the recommended dose of PA overwhelms the vagueness of the indications, which only generally characterise the amount and typology of PA.[202]

In summary, most of the documents (12/15) analysed contain recommendations regarding the dose of PA to be carried out. By observing the advice and comparing it between the segments of population, one can see that the recommended dose of PA has a longer duration and a higher intensity for children and teenagers and decreases for adults or for everyone and is even further reduced for the elderly. However, the recording units analysed demonstrate imprecision and ambiguity with regards to certain topics and an almost total lack of indication about continuity. Furthermore, the recommendations are often not connected with each other so that it is difficult to understand whether the activities should substitute each other, or whether they could be mixed and if so, how.

Often the recommendations embody the WHO's standard '30 minutes of moderate activity every day' (WHO, 2004, p. 4). As previously affirmed, this format does not offer a clear point of connection for the cooperation of the sport system because it is not compatible with intensity, duration and frequency of

[202] For example the extensively used statement: 'People should do more PA.'

most sport activities, for example those carried out in sport clubs. Nevertheless, 'sport' and sport activities are often mentioned alone or with other activities as mode of PA (18) within the recommendations. However, by reviewing the 13 recommendations, which contain concrete examples of the typology of sport to be practiced, team sport is only recommended twice together with other activities. Instead, the other cases (11 times) all refer to endurance activities like cycling, swimming, or jogging. Furthermore, the recommended duration for collective sport disciplines is very short: only 20 minutes. Again, this is extraneous to the format traditionally offered by sport organisations for these disciplines. This contradiction can be explained by assuming that sport is still - as an abstract term - semantically connected with health; on the other hand it is - in its traditional-competitive form - increasingly marginalised as a medium of health (Michelini & Thiel, 2013). The documents analysed are a vivid example of this trend: even if the term 'sport' is constantly mentioned, the analysis shows that the practices recommended are never commensurable with classical sport format or practicable in sport organisations. For this reason, a further analysis focused on the role of sport organisations in health-orientated strategies for the promotion of PA has been considered necessary.

5.2 'What Role Do the Sport Organisations Have?'

For the implementation of effective PA promotion, the health system explicitly states the need of broader cooperation, in particular with the sport system. At the same time, its health-orientated logic and the recommendation of activities in commensurable with sport raise doubts regarding the capacity of the health-strategies to constitute an understandable message for the sport system. The analysis of the roles of sport organisations in the documents is, for these reasons, relevant for the assessment of the main research question 'What role does sport play in health-orientated promotion of PA?' This category has been created *a priori* and is considered to be fundamental for understanding the health system's perspective on the role of the sport system in the promotion of health-related PA.

As stated in the theoretical framework, function systems each perform a special task for society and implement their logics through organisations (Krause, 2005, p. 60). For the purpose of this section, the categorisation of the sentences on the role of sport organisations on the basis of the typologies of organisations and roles retrieved in the documents emerged as the best strategy to analyse the topic at hand. By referring to Luhmann's systems theoretical framework (Luhmann, 1975, 1981b, 2006), the organisations and roles of the sport system have been sorted into five categories from a macro-level to a micro-level as seen in the table below:

Level	Description	Example
System	Sport system's organisations in general	The sport system
Organisations	Sport governing bodies with regulatory or sanctioning functions	Federations and NOC
	Organisations which represent sport in politics	Sport Ministries
	Sport clubs as typical sport implementing organisations	Gyms and associations
Roles	Sporting professionals within sport organisations	Sport scientists and trainers

Figure 16 Sport System's Organisations and Roles

All recording units containing references to one of the sport organisations or roles listed above and specifying their roles in the strategies have been accepted for this category. The anchor example presented below will represent a piece of text considered valid for this category:

1. Positive example of recording unit (INFORM, 2008, p. 30):

   'Gleichzeitig kann auch gemeinsames sportliches Miteinander einen Beitrag zur Integration leisten. Dieses Ziel verfolgt u.a. der Deutsche Olympische Sportbund (DOSB) in seinem Programm „Integration durch Sport", das von der Bundesregierung unterstützt wird.'

   Translation (EM):

   'At the same time, playing sport together can contribute to integration. This is one of the aims of The German Olympic Sports Federation (DOSB) in its programme "Integration through Sport", which is supported by the federal government.'

In this example, the sentence furnishes an identifiable task (a contribution to integration) of a sport system's organisation (DOSB) and has been considered valid.

5.2.1 Distribution of the Recording Units

By following these guidelines, 104 sentences regarding the role of sport organisations in health-related promotion of PA have been found.

Nation	Document	Recording Unit
France	PNNS 2001-2005	2
	PNNS 2006-2010	18
	PNNS 2011-2015	12
	Health Comes by Moving	3
	Physical Activity and Health	11
Germany	Mentally Fit in Old Age	3
	INFORM	24
	Active for Myself	2
	Advisor on Health Care	9
	National Health Objective	7
Italy	PSN 2006-2008	2
	PSN 2011-2013	1
	Pages of Health	0
	Make Gains in Health	10
	Gaining Health in 4 moves	0
Total		104

Figure 17 Distribution of Sentences on the Role of Sport Organisations

The distribution of the recording shows that 2 documents do not contain any sentences on the function of the sport organisations. Many documents (8) contain 1 to 10 retrieved segments and the rest (5) more than 10.

5.2.2 *Results of the Analysis*

By analysing the recording units, nine different functions entrusted to sport organisations have been identified:

1. The implementation of adapted physical activity (APA) (12 hits);
2. The promotion of both healthy diet and PA (19 hits);
3. The promotion of a healthy diet (5 hits);
4. The prevention of doping (2 hits);
5. The promotion of health (13 hits);
6. The implementation of PA (29 hits);
7. The implementation of PA and sport (PSA) (14 hits);
8. Socially-orientated tasks (2 hits);[203]
9. The implementation of sport activities (8 hits).

These categories have been established *a posteriori* after having examined all the recoding units identified. For establishing a manageable number of examples without oversimplifying the retrieved information, these functions have purposefully not been regrouped into broader categories. In the following

[203] These tasks include for example social inclusion and psychological help.

table the functions listed above have been crossed with the typology of sport organisations in order to gain a deeper and differentiated understanding of the organisations' roles in the perspective of the health system.

Function Ascribed \ Sport Organisation	In the Broad Sense	Governing Body	Ministry	Clubs	Professionals	Tot
Implementation of Adapted PA	1	3	1	4	3	12
Promotion of Healthy Diet and PA	3	0	9	6	1	19
Promotion of a Healthy Diet	0	0	2	1	2	5
Prevention of Doping	2	0	0	0	0	2
Promotion of Health	1	1	3	8	0	13
Implementation of PA	1	2	3	20	3	29
Implementation of PA and Sport	0	3	0	11	0	14
Socially-Orientated Functions	0	1	0	1	0	2
Implementation of Sport	0	1	0	5	2	8
Total	8	11	18	56	11	104

Figure 18 Distribution of Functions of the Sport System

The detail of the distribution of the functions for each organisation typology within the documents is represented in the tab below:

- Sport system organisations are mentioned eight times in general. The most quoted function within the strategies is the promotion of healthy diet and PA (3 times). The prevention of doping is mentioned twice. Health promotion and PA implementation are each mentioned once.
- Sport governing bodies are mentioned 11 times. The most quoted function for these organisations is the implementation of APA (3 times) and of PSA (3). Other functions mentioned are PA implementation (2), the promotion of health (1), social help (1) and sport implementation (1).
- The National Sport Ministry is mentioned 18 times. The most quoted function is the promotion of healthy diet and PA (9 times). The promotion of health (3), the implementation of PA (3), the promotion of healthy diet (2) and the implementation of APA (1) are mentioned, too.
- Sport clubs are by far the most mentioned organisations within the strategies for the promotion of PA (56 times). The roles ascribed to sport clubs are: the implementation of PA (20), the implementation of APS (11), the promotion of health (8), the promotion of a healthy diet and of PA (6), the implementation of sport (5), social help (1), and the promotion of a healthy diet (1).

- Sporting professionals are mentioned 11 times. The most quoted functions for these are the implementation of APA (3 times) and the implementation of PA (3). The promotion of a healthy diet (2), the implementation of sport, and the promotion of a healthy diet and PA (1) are mentioned, too.

5.2.3 Reflections on the Results

In summary, in 13 of the 15 analysed strategies for the health-related promotion of PA the following sport system's organizations are mentioned: sport clubs (56 hits), sport governing bodies (11 hits), the Sport Ministry (18 hits), professionals of sport (11 hits) and sport system's organisations in general (8 hits). These organisations have been entrusted with 9 functions: the implementation of adapted physical activity (12 hits); the promotion of a healthy diet and PA (19 hits); the promotion of a healthy diet (5 hits); the prevention of doping (2 hits); the promotion of health (13 hits); the implementation of PA (29 hits); the implementation of PA and sport (14 hits); social tasks (2 hits); the implementation of sport activities (8 hits). This could lead to the conclusion that sport organisations are, at least at an abstract level, widely involved in health system's strategies for the promotion of PA.

However, a closer look to the functions mentioned reveals some contradictions within the health system's perspective on the function of sport in these strategies. For example, basic operations of sport organisations like the one of implementing sport alone (8 hits) or together with PA (14) are mentioned a few times within the strategies. Indeed, they are mentioned almost as often as operations much more extraneous to sport, like the promotion of health (13) and of a healthy diet (5). Furthermore, in 19 segments the promotion of PA is assessed together with the one of a healthy diet. This phenomenon has been detected also in the pilot analysis of the WHO's 'Global Strategies on Diet, Physical Activity and Health' (2004) and it is in general one of the distinguishing features of the political rhetoric of the promotion of PA. Even if the health consequences related with poor diet and physical inactivity largely overlap, this joined assessing of the two distinct topics is technically questionable. For instance, programmes for the promotion of physical activity and healthy diet as well as their strategic implementation rely on dissimilar approaches (Bauman & Craig, 2005, p. 3). Certainly, sport organisations mainly offer solutions only suitable for the problem of physical inactivity. Another criticisable tendency is the one of avoiding the word 'sport' (22) and of substituting it with other softer concepts like 'PA' or its synonyms (60) in the context of the promotion of PA implemented by sport system's organisations. Against the background of a general ambiguity of words describing PA, this enhances the abstraction of the message.

All together, these phenomena in turn confirm the tendency of the health system to entrust sport system's organisations with tasks extraneous to their logic and orientated toward the logic 'promoting/hindering health' (Bauch, 1996). The health system's vagueness and its exclusive reference toward a logic, which is 'sport-hostile', make the role of sport organisations increasingly vague. Indeed, these tendencies endanger the legitimisation of sport organisations and traditional sport disciplines in the context of health promotion. However, in some countries they are still the most relevant providers of programmes for the promotion of health and are one of the most fertile organisations for structural coupling between the sport and health systems.

5.3 'For Which Reasons is Sport Delegitimised as a Medium of Health?'

The topic of the deligitimisation of sport as a medium of health has been created *a posteriori* because, when examining the documents for the promotion of PA, an unexpected tendency to disqualify the health-related role of sport was detected. Their frequency, their pejorative formulation and the richness of diversified argumentation is more surprising than the simple presence of such arguments. Given the main theme and scope of this dissertation, once this trend has been identified, the modification of the category system was immediately seen to be highly relevant in order to include this topic. For examining it, an ad-hoc category and a structured and standardised set of coding rules have been created. Then, the documents were re-examined in light of this perspective for finding the necessary recording units. Within the selected documents for the promotion of PA, all explicit[204] deligitimisations of sport as a medium of health have been identified as being contained within this category. An example of such a recording unit is offered below:

Positive example of recording unit (French Ministry of Health, 2004, p. 5):

> *'Mais rassurez-vous: se dépenser ne veut pas forcément dire faire du sport intensif ! Il est tout à fait possible d'intégrer une activité physique protectrice pour la santé dans notre vie quotidienne.'*
>
> Translation (EM):

[204] 'Explicit' here means that the disqualifications are expressed without possible misunderstanding or ambiguous interpretation.

> 'But be reassured: PA does not necessarily mean doing intensive sport! Integrating a kind of PA that is protective for health in our daily lives is absolutely possible.'

In this example, sport is represented as something undesirable (like a bad tasting medicine) and unnecessary. The negative formulation of the sentence and not its meaning delegitimises sport. In fact, a milder and more positive formulation of the same concept such as '*along with intensive sport, a less structured form of PA can be a chance to reach the recommended dose of PA*'[205] would not have been considered within this category.

5.3.1 Distribution of the Recording Units

Although it is impossible to make reliable inferences regarding the frequency of the recording units within the strategies, to respect the transparency of the procedures of the document analysis, the distribution of the sentences classified as deligitimisation of sport has been reported in the table below:

Nation	Document	Recording Unit
France	PNNS 2001-2005	0
	PNNS 2006-2010	0
	PNNS 2011-2015	0
	Health Comes by Moving	8
	Physical Activity and Health	12
Germany	Mentally Fit in Old Age	4
	IN FORM	2
	Active for Myself	0
	Advisor on Health Care	4
	National Health Objective	1
Italy	PSN 2006-2008	0
	PSN 2011-2013	0
	Pages of Health	1
	Make Gains in Health	1
	Gaining Health in 4 Moves	1
Total		34

Figure 19 Distribution of the Deligitimisation of Sport

By analysing the documents, 34 sentences that devaluate classical sport as a medium of health promotion have been found. One can observe that six documents do not contain any sentences delegitimising sport. Instead, seven

[205] This quotation has been conceived by the author.

documents contain one to four recording units and two documents contain even more segments (8 and 12) delegitimising sport as a medium of health.

5.3.2 Results of the Analysis

In order to achieve the goal of this research sub-question and a meaningful reduction of the complexity of this topic, it is fruitful to categorise the recording units found according to five different lines of reasoning, which emerged by analysing the arguments of the retrieved segments. This grouping has been established after having examined all the recording units identified. In the following, these sub-categories will be separately explained, commented and exemplified:

- *Advice suggesting a medical examination before beginning a PA*: this sub-category collects the sentences (7), which advise a medical examination as a prerequisite for doing or starting a sport activity. In fact, this concept is only formally and legally legitimate in the case of traditional-competitive sports carried out within the context of sport system's leagues and championships or for particular segment of population like ill or elderly people. Instead, the extension of the health check-up to general sport activities or even to high-intensity PA not related to illnesses or specific population segments[206] must be considered as a form of deligitimisation of sport for 3 reasons: (1) it demonstrates the health system's claim to be the mandatory control-body on PA; (2) it exemplifies the health system's tendency towards the medicalisation of sport; (3) the advice constitutes a 'barrier to entry' for sport, which can discourage people from practicing sport activities in order to avoid the medical check-up and/or its implicit dangers.

  Positive example of a recording unit (Italian Ministry of Employment, Health and Social Policies 2009, p. 5):

  > *'Prima di intraprendere un'attività fisica impegnativa, è bene parlarne con il proprio medico.'*
  > Translation (EM):
  > 'Before starting an intense physical activity, it's a good idea to speak to your doctor.'

- *Praise of the de-sportification of sport*: this sub-category entails sentences (7), which advise sport as a general concept on the one hand and on the other

[206] This tendency is also one of the consequences of the hypostatisation and augmented inclusion power of the health system theorised for example by Illich (2003), Bauch (1996) and Luhmann (1983a).

hand specify that sport activities should be practiced without one or more of the typical components of sport (Heinemann, 2007, p. 56): bodily performance, competition, rules and non-productivity. Mostly, these sentences refer to the avoidance of sport's competitive orientation or to its high intensity.

Positive example of recording unit (Italian Ministry of Health, 2007, p. 22):

> *'Tale obiettivo richiede interventi volti ad affermare una concezione dell'attività sportiva che va al di là della mera attività fisica agonistica, divenendo invece un momento di benessere fisico e psicologico che coinvolge tutti i cittadini, giovani e meno giovani.'*
> Translation (EM):
> 'This objective requires actions to promote a conception of sport that goes beyond the mere competitive physical activity and instead become a moment of physical and psychological well-being involving all citizens, young and old.'

- *Non-necessity of sport*: this sub-category collects sentences (16), which portray sport as being unnecessary for health or underline in a pejorative way that sport is just one of the possible modes of PA that can be performed in order to remain fit. Although the concept is formally correct, the reiteration of this notion and the dissuasive register used for sport activities clearly goes against the purpose of the documents analysed, which should promote every kind of PA for combating the spread of sedentary lifestyles.

  Positive example of recording unit (German Ministry of Health, 2010a, p. 24):

  > *'Mehr Bewegung in den Alltag zu integrieren bedeutet nicht, von heute auf morgen Leistungssport zu betreiben. Das fordert unser Körper gar nicht. Er ist dankbar für jede kleine Aktivität, die wir ihm gönnen.'*
  > Translation (EM):
  > 'Integrating more physical activity into everyday life does not mean starting a competitive sport activity overnight. This is not required at all by our body. It is grateful for every little activity that we treat it to.'

- *Danger of sport activity*: this category comprehends sentences (3), which warn against sport because of its possible bad influence on health. In particular the abstract description of the activities and of the related health-risks could broaden the sense of danger to sports, which are as risky as every day

PAs. Given the aim of the strategies, it is also in this case counterproductive to stress the dangers of sport instead of promoting every form of PA.

Positive example of recording unit (French Ministry of Health, 2004, p. 32):

> *'L'activité physique ne doit pas induire de fatigue excessive. Une activité physique trop intense, surtout chez des personnes non entraînées, peut être à l'origine de tendinites, de problèmes articulaires ou d'accidents cardiaques'*
> Translation (EM):
> 'Physical activity should not induce excessive fatigue. If the physical activity is too intense, especially for untrained subjects, it can be the source of tendinitis, aerterial problems and heart attacks.'

- *Unease of sport activity*: this category has been created for a single sentence,[207] which underline that sport is not the most practical or the easiest form of PA to perform. Again, although the concept might be formally correct, its reiteration is unfitting given the objective of promoting every kind of PA in order to combat the spread of sedentary lifestyles.

Positive example of recording unit (French Ministry of Health, 2004, p. 21):

> *'Quand on est très occupé, il n'est pas toujours facile ou possible d'aller dans une salle de sport ou de danse, à la piscine ou au stade ou de faire du jogging.'*
> Translation (EM):
> 'When you're too busy, it is not easy to go to a gym every day, a dance studio, a swimming pool, a sport or jogging field.'

5.3.3 Reflection on the Results

In summary, nine of the 15 analysed strategies contain sentences, which delegitimise sport even though the aim of the strategy should be the promotion of PA in every form and on all occasions. For the deligitimisation of sport, five different reasons have brought up: the need of a medical examination before doing sport (7); the praise of a de-sportification of sport (7), particularly regarding its competitive orientations or its high intensity; the non-necessity of sport (16) for being healthy; the unease of sport when compared with everyday PA (1); and the dangers (3) connected with the practice of sport activities. It can be observed that

[207] However, the analysis of further documents not contained in the present dissertation evidenced the reiteration of this reasoning in other health-strategies issued by the French health ministry.

the subcategories 'medical examination', 'de-sportification' and 'non-necessity of sport' are contained in all three case studies and are quantitatively the most frequent reasoning for the deligitimisation of sport. For the purpose of clarity, it must once again be stressed that the scientific truthfulness of these sentences, although questionable, has never been *per se* disputed. Instead, the frequent presence of such arguments and their pejorative register raise questions about the adequacy of their occurrence given the scope of the analysed documents for the promotion of PA. With this 'sport-hostile' attitude, the health system limits the range of PAs to the ones directly established for the improvement of health and excludes some sport activities which, even with a different orientation, can also contribute to the betterment of people's health. Furthermore, this approach contradicts not only the aims of the strategies promoting PA but also the main mission of the health system which is 'the attainment by all people of the highest possible level of health' understood as 'a state of complete physical, mental and social well-being and not merely the absence of disease or infirmity' (WHO, 1946, pp. 1-2) In fact the communications of the strategies are clearly orientated toward the scope of preventing 'merely the absence of disease or infirmity' (WHO, 1946, p. 1).

In this section as well as in the previous ones, at the side of these central social phenomena, a considerable ambiguity has been detected in the key concepts of the health-strategies. This ambiguity will be systematically analysed in the following section.

5.4 'How Sound are the Key Concepts?'

As anticipated in the theoretical framework, there is a high level of ambiguity concerning the use of keywords and concepts regarding health on the one hand and sport and PA on the other hand. When speculating about the influence of sport on health, the intersection of these two often vague discussions further enhances the ambiguity. Additionally, the rhetoric of the promotion of health through PA and the ascription of expectations related to sport and PA add vagueness to the discourse of the strategies. This section analyses the documents, searching for clear concept definitions, ambiguous uses of terms and furnishes a systematic categorisation of them. These categories have been created *a posteriori*. In particular, whenever a problem of clarity was found during the coding process, this was coded under the category 'ambiguity', from which subcategories then emerged by reviewing and grouping the recording units.

At the end of this process the following two main categories emerged:

- Definition and uses of key concepts regarding sport and PA

– Ambiguity related to the dose of PA

In the following sections, the results of each one of these topics will be listed and accompanied by anchor examples.

5.4.1 *Definitions and Uses of Key Concepts*

For the creation of this category, the documents have been analysed in order to find clear definitions and explanations regarding the differences of the terms used. As anticipated in the theoretical framework, the exact meaning of words referring to PA are ambiguous, even within the sport science, and they normally need to be defined for avoiding ambiguity from the beginnings of the discussion. Regarding the definitions of terms and use of key concepts, the following two trends have been identified:

– Exchange of Terms

Within the documents, the words 'sport', 'PA' and their synonyms are used 1495 times. Even if they are clearly definable, the strategies very often use these terms interchangeably as if they were synonyms. In detail, the two terms are used in different word clusters containing both the concepts of sport and PA 95 times and are used five times in an erroneous way by exchanging them, even if the discourse clearly requires the use of the opposite concept as in the following example:

> Positive example of recording unit (French Ministry for Employment and Welfare & French Ministry of Health, 2011, p. 26)
>
> *'Porteuse de valeurs sociales et éducatives, l'activité physique a un effet bénéfique sur la santé, qu'elle soit pratiquée dans les déplacements et les activités de la vie quotidienne, ou encadrée dans un club sportif.'*
>
> Translation (EM):
>
> 'As carrier of social and educational values, physical activity has a beneficial effect on health if it is practiced as part of the movement and activities of daily living or carried out in a sport club.'

In the case of this example, the word 'PA' is clearly incorrectly exchanged with 'sport.' In fact, PA is not at all 'carrier of social and educational values' and indicates simply 'any bodily movement produced by skeletal muscles that results in energy expenditure above resting level' (Bouchard & Shephard, 1994, p. 77). Sport is instead often considered 'carrier of social and educational values' because it involves the interaction with teammates and/or opponents and informal rules, which involve educational motives like the one of 'fair-play' and the respect of opponents (Grupe & Krüger, 2007, p. 286).

- Presence of clear definitions
  Within the strategies, three definitions distributed in three documents have been found, which clearly assess the difference between PA and sport or which help to distinguish the concepts by furnishing accurate descriptions of the two concepts. Such definitions are exemplified in the anchor example below:

Anchor example (German Ministry of Health, 2010a, p. 110):

'Der Begriff „körperliche Aktivität" sollte eindeutig vom Begriff „Sport" unterschieden werden. Während sich „körperliche Aktivität" als Oberbegriff auf jede körperliche Bewegung bezieht, die durch die Skelettmuskulatur produziert wird und den Energieverbrauch erhöht, ist der Begriff „Sport" enger gefasst und steht für körperliche Leistung, Wettkampf und Spaß an der Bewegung.'

Translation (EM):

'The term "physical activity" should be clearly distinguished from the term "sport". While "physical activity" is a general term referring to every bodily movement that is produced by skeletal muscles and increased energy consumption, the term "sport" is more specific and indicates physical performance, competition and fun in movements themselves.'

Although brief and relatively abstract, this sentence clarifies the boundaries between the two concepts and sets the basis for a clear discussion. The sporadic presence of precise definitions and boundaries between the two terms often limits the power and precision of the message and instead makes it very superficial.

5.4.2 Ambiguity Related to the Dose of PA

The clarity of the indications regarding the dose of PA is analysed in this category. Normally within the documents, PA is described through the characteristics of mode, intensity, duration, frequency and continuity. By reviewing the recording units on these PA characteristics and other pieces of text regarding this topic, three cases of ambiguity have been retrieved:

– The use of the concept of 'regularity'

The word 'regular' is mentioned 88 times without further specifications in connection to the dose of PA. Within the research, this term has been normally classified as a broad measure of continuity. However, this is a very ambiguous concept because it can be differently interpreted as in the following:[208]

1. On a regular weekly basis (frequency):

Anchor example (French Ministry of Health, 2004, p. 16):

' [...] la régularité de l'activité physique est essentielle pour obtenir un bénéfice sur la santé. L'idéal est de faire de l'activité physique chaque jour de la semaine.'

Translation (EM):

'[...] regular physical activity is essential for health benefits. What is best is to engage in physical activity every day of the week.'

2. With a regular rhythm (intensity):

Anchor example (German Ministry of Health, 2010b, p. 44):

'Bereits regelmäßiges Gehen wird als moderate, gesundheitswirksame körperliche Aktivität eingestuft.'

Translation (EM):

'Even regular walking is considered a moderate physical activity with positive effects on one's health.'

3. On a macro period or on a life basis (duration):

Anchor example (French Ministry of Health, 2004, p. 32):

'Vous vous entraînez régulièrement chaque week-end.'

Translation (EM):

'You train regularly, every weekend.'

The multiple meanings of this term, the complete lack of its definition and its abundant usage constitute one of the most ambiguous points of the rhetoric of PA promotion within the documents analysed.

– Imprecise quantifications of PA

Within the recommendation on the dose of PA within the documents, the intensive use of words (105 hits) referring in an imprecise and/or ambiguous way of dosing recommended has been detected. These imprecise indi-

[208] However the term 'regular' is so ambiguous that even in the anchor examples identified, it has not been possible to ascribe meaning to the word with absolute precision.

cations could not be classified into the categories created for the dose of PA (frequency, intensity, duration, continuity, and typology) and have been resumed in the table below:

People should do ... PA	
at least a little quantity of	5
abundant	2
an healthy quantity of	1
as more as possible	2
a good quantity of	3
more	55
much	3
a proper quantity of	3
recommended quantity of	5
a sufficient quantity of	26
Tot	105

Figure 20 Distribution of Imprecise Quantification of PA

Because the dose of PA is neither precisely nor univocally expressed in the most documents, these indications are often too vague to constitute a profitable indication on the dose of PA and instead contribute to the creation of an ambiguous message. In particular, 'more' is the most recurrent imprecise quantification and also the most questionable. For instance, saying that '*people should do more physical activity*' not only is a vague indication, but also classifies automatically every PAs already carried out by the reader as insufficient. This is a peculiar characteristic especially of the French document 'Health comes by moving' (French Ministry of Health, 2004) whose *leitmotif* is 'A little [physical activity] is good, more is better.'

– The use of the concept of 'everyday'

Within the research the term 'everyday' has been classified as a measure of frequency for the recommendation of the dose of PA. However, the word 'everyday' and its synonyms are mentioned 116 times and sometimes have different meanings, which create ambiguities as in the following:

1. Every day (frequency):

Anchor example (French Ministry for Employment and Welfare & French Ministry of Health, 2011, p. 26):

'L'activité physique au quotidien pour tous, durant les temps de trajets, de loisirs et de travail, complétée par une activité physique encadrée régulière.'

Translation (EM):

'Daily physical activity for all, during the time of trips, leisure and work, supplemented by a regular structured physical activity.'

2. During everyday life (in contrast with free time, work or school):
Anchor example (German Ministry of Health & German Ministry of Nutrition, 2008, p. 29):

'Überall dort, wo Menschen sich bewegen können, gilt es, Motivation und Anreize für Bewegung im Alltag zu schaffen. Dabei geht es zum einen um Bewegung im Alltag an sich (z.B. Rad fahren oder Treppe steigen) und deren gesundheitsförderliche Effekte, [...].'

Translation (EM):

'It is necessary to create motivation and incentives for daily exercise everywhere where people can move. On the one hand this involves everyday movements (ex. bicycle riding or climbing stairs) and their health-promoting effects, [...].'

Even if this term is clearer than the term 'regularly,' 'everyday' also entails a high degree of ambiguity which contributes to confusion in the rhetoric of PA promotion.

– The use of different measures of the dose of PA

The last problem is the sporadic (8 hits) use of different units of measurement to speak about the dose of PA. For example, the description through mode, intensity, duration, frequency, and continuity, the dose of PA through burned Kcal, VO_{2max} and other measures make its description heterogeneous.

Anchor example (French Ministry for Employment and Welfare & French Ministry of Health, 2011, p. 26)

'augmenter chez les adultes, en 5 ans, la proportion de personnes située dans la classe d'activité physique :*

- « élevée » de 20 % au moins chez les hommes et de 25 % au moins chez les femmes ;

- « moyenne » de 20 % au moins.

** : selon le questionnaire IPAQ (International Physical Activity Questionnaire)'*

Translation (EM):

'in 5 years increase the number of adults placed in the following class of physical activity *:

- "High" at least 20% of men and at least 25% of women;

- "Average" at least 20%.
*: based upon the questionnaire IPAQ (International Physical Activity Questionnaire)'

In the anchor example above, a measurement of PA is based upon the IPAQ (International Physical Activity Questionnaire), which is not further explained within the strategy.[209] More than furnishing a differentiated viewpoint, the use of different unit of measures for the dose of PA unnecessarily complicates the discourse and goes against the global guidelines regarding the clarity of the message (Bauman & Craig, 2005, p. 3; WHO, 2004, p. 9) in strategies for the promotion of PA.

5.4.3 Reflections on the Results

This section reveals a lack of clarity in the discourse on the promotion of PA in health-strategies issued by the health system. This particularly regards the lack of distinctions between the concepts of PA and sport and the imprecise description of the recommended dose of PA. This ambiguity can be attributed to:

- the incapacity of the health system of thematising the topic of PA since it does not represent one of its core operations and it is a relatively new area of health promotion.
- the difficulty faced by the health system in developing a new rhetoric of health promotion[210] free from the previous tradition, which had sport as the embodiment of healthy PA.

Together with the main thesis of this dissertation, namely that the health system tends to be orientated towards a health/illness code in which PA is medicalised and sport is sceptically accepted when not clearly directed towards health, the assumptions above lead to a further hypothesis: specifically that the ambiguity in the rhetoric detected in the strategies could be a mirror of a changing phase in the promotion of PA in which the health system is still consolidating its own discussion and lead position. While refusing the performance-orientated perspective of the sport system, the health system has not already developed a complete description of PA out of the pathogenetic perspective.

In other cases the ambiguity detected in the health system's statements looks like a strictly semantic problem. This could be originated by the imprecise

[209] Furthermore, five of these segments contain the adjectives 'moderate,' 'light,' and 'heavy.' This creates ambiguity because the same words are normally used for specifying the intensity of PA.

[210] For example, one of the *piece de resistances* of this development of a new rhetoric regarding the concept of health-enhancing-PA (HEPA) is surprisingly never mentioned within the units of analysis.

translation of English terms contained in international guidelines into other languages.[211] This could happen, for example, in the case of communications between the WHO and the national health ministries. For example, in German speaking countries the word 'sport' is not necessarily connected with its traditional-competitive meaning. For this reason, German sport organisations and clinics use traditionally the word 'sport' in many health-orientated programmes like 'heart-sport,' 'coronary-sport,' and 'back-sport.' However, also in Germany the word 'sport' is disappearing by the strategies and is often substituted by the term 'movement'. This issue has not been raised before within the scientific community. Nevertheless, the context of the messages analysed is characterised by the rising international relevance of the fight of physical inactivity and the increasing globalisation of health governance. In such a scenario, international policies are gaining relevance at national and local levels and the correct translation of the terms and meanings contained in the original documents into the national languages is crucial for their correct implementation.

5.5 Comparison of the Case Studies

Until now, the results of the document analysis for each case study have been kept together and the national differences have not been assessed. In order to profit from the comparison of the case studies, this section compares the results obtained in each one of the categories assessed in the past four sections by focusing on the national differences detected between France, Germany and Italy. The comparison of the case studies has been planned *a priori*: it has been considered relevant for answering to the main research question: 'What role does sport play in the health-orientated promotion of PA?' from the beginning. In particular, this section compares the communications of three health ministries of countries, which have very different sport systems:[212]

- The French sport system is highly politicised and extremely centralised.
- The German sport system is formally highly independent, but in practice influenced by regional policies.
- In the Italian sport system, the Comitato Olimpico Nazionale (CONI) has both the functions of National Olympic Committee and of an umbrella organisation for sport federations.

---

[211] This phenomenon is detectable also in other contexts and communications media. For example, in the internet the terms 'sport' and 'physical activity' are in some contexts mistakenly exchanged by Wikipedia and Google Translator.

[212] This topic has been deeper assessed in the chapter 'Comparison and Sampling.'

Relevant differences in the three units of comparison can be connected, among other factors, with these structural dissimilarities of the national sport structure.

In contrast with the previous sections, this section has a different outlook. In fact, it consists of four parts, which re-analyse the categories of the previous sections by focusing on the differences between case studies, which until now have been intentionally ignored.[213] For purpose of synthesis, an exhaustive description of each category and the belonging anchor examples have not been repeated below. If necessary, they can instead be founded in the previous sections.

5.5.1 Results of the analysis

- What is the recommended dose of PA?

  The majority of recommendations are contained in the French (34) documents. Fewer recommendations are contained in the German (12) and the Italian (7) cases.

  In the following, the characteristics peculiar for each case study regarding the advice on PA will be summarised in a table containing the most frequent advice for each characteristic of recommended PA and briefly commented afterwards:

[213] The documents which constitute the analysis unit have been considered until now as a whole, regardless of their national origin.

Nation / Dose	France		Germany		Italy	
Typology	Mixed activities	11	Sport or exercise	6	Mixed activities	3
	Other	12	Other	4	Other	4
	No entry	11	No entry	2	No entry	0
Frequency	7 / week	24	4-6 / week	4	7 / week	5
	Other	4	Other	7	Other	2
	No entry	6	No entry	1	No entry	0
Intensity	Moderate	14	Moderate	2	Moderate	2
	Other	8	Other	3	Other	1
	No entry	12	No entry	7	No entry	4
Duration	30 min	23	30 min	9	30 min	3
	Other	8	Other	1	Other	3
	No entry	3	No entry	2	No entry	1
Continuity	Regular	3	Regular	0	Regular	2
	Other	0	Other	0	Other	0
	No entry	31	No entry	12	No entry	5

Figure 21 Distribution of Recommendations on the Dose of PA in the Documents

- In the French case study, from a total of 34 retrieved segments, the most recommendations refer to: a varied range of typologies of PA such as a mixture of sport and daily activities (11), sport (2), everyday activities (10); a daily frequency (24); a duration of 30 minutes or more (23); and moderate (14), light (3) or high (5) intensity. As an indication for continuity, 'regularly' is advised three times.
- In the German case study, from a total of 12 retrieved segments, the greater part of the recommendations refer to: typologies of activities like sport and exercise (6) or everyday life activities (4); a frequency of 6-4 (4), less than 4 (4), or 7 times a week (2); a duration of 30 minutes or more (9); moderate intensity (2) or light (1) or variable intensity (2); no advice on continuity has been found.
- In the Italian case study, from a total of seven retrieved segments the greatest number of recommendations refers to: activities mixed of sport and everyday activities (3), everyday life activities (2), sport (1), exercise (1); a frequency of 7 times a week (5); a duration of 30 min (3); moderate intensity (2); and regular continuity (2).

- What role does the sport system have?

  The distribution of the recording units shows that a majority of recommendations are contained in the French (46) and in the German (45) documents. Fewer segments have been identified in the Italian (13) case study.

Below, the organisations and the functions mentioned in each case study will be commented upon and summarised in a table, which combines the data on the organisation with their functions:

- In the French case study, the most quoted organisations are sport clubs (25) followed by the ministry of sport (13), sport professionals (6) and governing bodies (2). The functions mentioned are: implementation of PA (18), promotion of diet and PA (11), implementation of adapted physical activity (9), promotion of a healthy diet (4), of physical activity and sport (3) and of sport (1).

Sport Organisation / Function Ascribed	Organisations	Governing Body	Ministry	Clubs	Professionals	Total
Implementation of Adapted PA	0	2	1	5	1	9
Promotion of Healthy Diet and PA	0	0	9	2	0	11
Promotion of a Healthy Diet	0	0	2	0	2	4
Prevention of Doping	0	0	0	0	0	0
Promotion of Health	0	0	0	0	0	0
Implementation of PA	0	0	1	14	3	18
Implementation of PA and Sport	0	0	0	3	0	3
Socially-Orientated Functions	0	0	0	0	0	0
Implementation of Sport	0	0	0	1	0	1
Total	0	2	13	25	6	46

Figure 22 Distribution of Functions of the Sport System in French Documents

- In the German case study, the most quoted organisations are sport clubs (26) followed by governing bodies (9), the ministry of sport (2), sport organisations in general (5) and sport professionals (3). The functions mentioned are: implementation of PA (16), promotion of diet and PA (11), implementation of adapted physical activity (3), promotion of a healthy diet (1) of health (5), social function (2) and of sport (7).

Function Ascribed \ Sport Organisation	Organisations	Governing Body	Ministry	Clubs	Professionals	Total
Implementation of Adapted PA	0	1	0	2	0	3
Promotion of Healthy Diet and PA	5	0	0	5	1	11
Promotion of a Healthy Diet	0	0	0	1	0	1
Prevention of Doping	0	0	0	0	0	0
Promotion of Health	0	2	0	3	0	5
Implementation of PA	0	4	2	9	1	16
Implementation of PA and Sport	0	0	0	0	0	0
Socially-Orientated Functions	0	1	0	1	0	2
Implementation of Sport	0	1	0	5	1	7
Total	5	9	2	26	3	45

Figure 23 Distribution of Functions of the Sport System in German Documents

- In the Italian case study, the most quoted organisations are sport clubs (4) followed by governing bodies (1), the ministry of sport (3), sport organisations in general (3) and sport professionals (2). The functions mentioned are: implementation of PA (2), of sport (2), implementation of adapted physical activity (3), promotion of health (4) and doping prevention (2).

Function Ascribed \ Sport Organisation	Organisations	Governing Body	Ministry	Clubs	Professionals	Total
Implementation of Adapted PA	1	1	0	0	1	3
Promotion of Healthy Diet and PA	0	0	0	0	0	0
Promotion of a Healthy Diet	0	0	0	0	0	0
Prevention of Doping	2	0	0	0	0	2
Promotion of Health	0	0	2	2	0	4
Implementation of PA	0	0	1	1	0	2
Implementation of PA and Sport	0	0	0	0	0	0
Socially-Orientated Functions	0	0	0	0	0	0
Implementation of Sport	0	0	0	1	1	2
Total	3	1	3	4	2	13

Figure 24 Distribution of Functions of the Sport System in Italian Documents

– Why is sport being delegitimised as a medium of health promotion?

Regarding the distribution of segments within this category, it can be stated that the most recommendations are contained in the French (20) documents, than in the German (11) and finally in the Italian (3).

The reasons for delegitimising sport as a medium of health presented in each case study will be summarised in the following table and commented upon below:

Nation	Document	Medical examination	De-sportification	Non-necessity of sport	Unease of sport	Dangers of sport	Tot.
Germany	Mentally Fit in Old Age	2	2				11
	INFORM		1	1			
	Being Active for Myself						
	Advisor on Health Care		1	3			
	National Health Objective		1				
France	Health comes by moving	2		4	1	1	20
	Physical Activity and Health	2	1	7		2	
	PNNS 2001-2005						
	PNNS 2006-2010						
	PNNS 2011-2015						
Italy	Pages of Health	1					3
	Make Gains in Health		1				
	Gaining Health in 4 moves			1			
	National health plan 2006-2008						
	National health plan 2011-2013						
Total		7	7	16	1	3	34

Figure 25 Distribution of Deligitimisations of the Sport System in the Case Studies

- In the French case study, the most frequently used reasoning is the non-necessity of sport (11) followed by the necessity of a medical examination for doing sport (4), the dangers of sport (3), praise of a de-sportification of sport (1) and unease of sport (1). France is the only case study containing sentences about dangers of sport (3) and unease of sport (1).
- In the German case study, the most frequently used reasoning is the praise of a de-sportification of sport (5), followed by the non-necessity of sport (4) and the necessity of a medical examination for doing sport (2).

- In the Italian case study, few sections delegitimising sport as a medium of health have been found. The three segments identified contain the following reasons: praise of a de-sportification of sport (1), non-necessity of sport (1) and the necessity of a medical examination for doing sport (1).

- How sound are the key concepts?

  In the following, a comparison between the case studies for each subcategory of the section dealing with the clarity of the documents will be furnished. An accompanying table summarising the results will follow.
  - The term 'PA' is used instead of 'sport' five times in the documents: four times in the Italian case study and once in the French case study.
  - Definitions and explanations regarding the differences between sport and other forms of PA are almost absent from the case studies. Such definitions are contained twice in French documents and once in German documents.
  - The term 'regular' is used 49 times in French documents, 31 times in German documents and eight times in Italian documents. As explained in the previous section, it is one of the most ambiguous terms in the rhetoric of the promotion of PA because it can be interpreted as a measure of frequency, continuity or intensity of PA.
  - The ambiguous quantification of the dose of PA is a phenomenon transversal to the three case studies, but particularly present in the German documents. In all three case studies, 'more PA' is the most recurrent imprecise quantification of the dose of PA. The distribution of all the terms used in this category has been summarised in the table below:

People should do ... PA	France	Germany	Italy	Tot.
at least a little quantity of	5	0	0	5
abundant	0	2	0	2
an healthy quantity of	0	1	0	1
as more as possible	1	0	1	2
a good quantity of	1	0	2	3
more	15	37	3	55
much	0	3	0	3
a proper quantity of	0	1	2	3
recommended quantity of	2	0	3	5
a sufficient quantity of	2	24	0	26
Tot.	26	68	11	105

Figure 26 Distribution of Ambiguous Quantification of Sport in the Case Studies

- As clarified in the previous section, the term 'everyday' has a double meaning: it can be used as a measure of frequency or for specifying the time in which the PA should be practiced. In turn, this creates imprecise messages within the strategies. This term is distributed as in the following among the case studies:

Nation	When	How Often	Total
France	11	48	59
Germany	42	5	47
Italy	2	8	10
Tot	55	61	116

Figure 27 Distribution of the Term'Everyday' in the Case Studies

- Different measures of the dose of PA are contained in French (6) and German (2) documents. On the other hand, they are the case studies, which put the most efforts into clarifying and giving examples on the dose of PA. This justifies the sporadic use of different measurements within the strategies.

5.5.2 Reflections on the Results

By reviewing and comparing the results obtained in each sub-category among the case studies French, Germany and Italy, it can be stated that:

- The unit of analysis is, in general, highly heterogeneous and the documents differentiate highly between and within the case studies. Only when the documents belong to a thematic series (like the National Health Plans of Italy and the French National Plans on Nutrition and Health), they show a higher rate of common features and similar rhetorics.
- As a general tendency for the distribution of the retrieved segments it can be stated that the French documents are characterised in almost each category by a great abundance of retrieved segments, sometimes at the expense of synthesis and clarity; the German documents are more equilibrate and are normally clear in their discourse on PA, but lack of examples, and in the Italian documents, very few segments and descriptions of PA have been found.
- A similar tendency regarding many of the categories analysed in further sections has been found. In fact, in all case studies: the average time of PA recommended is normally 30 minutes of moderate PA; the most frequently mentioned organisation is the sport club; and sentences which delegitimise

sport as a medium of health by underlining its dangers by recommending a medical analysis before starting a sport activity or by praising for its de-sportification have been found. Even more surprising is the horizontal use of some ambiguous description of PA like the use of the terms like 'regularly' 'everyday', 'more' and other vague rhetorical constructions that seem to overcome language and territorial borders.

– The most relevant differences peculiar to a single case study found are: Germany is the only case study in which sport and exercise are recommended more than mixed activities and in which the most recommendations refer to a lower frequency than daily PA. In the German case study, imprecise quantifications of the dose of PA occur the most. Italy is the only case study in which the most frequently mentioned function of sport organisations is the promotion of health. The French case study contains plenty of sentences underlining the lack of necessity of sport for being healthy.

In summary, even by differing in many other characteristics the case studies show many similarities in the topic analysed. This suggests the development and influence of a world discourse on the promotion of PA, which is transversal to nations and languages. In fact, the case studies often share not only similar contents, but also common ambiguous rhetorical constructions and identical rhetoric concerning the promotion of PA and the role of sport in this context. Indeed, some relevant differences have been found within the case studies. These seem to be justifiable with the different languages of the three case studies, path dependencies regarding the sport and welfare tradition of the countries and the different styles in the publication of policy documents of the health ministries. However, the comparison does not suggest that the phenomenon differentiates in its core in the three analysed countries and for this reason it can be stated that different sport systems do not influence the perspective of the health system on the function of sport in health-related promotion of PA.

A further point which needs to be stressed regards the advisability of homogenising the messages for the promotion of PA. At least regarding the topic taken into account, the messages of the document analysed are very similar. Without denying the importance of international impulses in the promotion of PA, the national contexts are still displaying disparities regarding not only the sport and the health system, but also regarding cultural-historical patterns which influence the PA-related behaviours of the citizens (European Commission, 2010). For these reasons, the spreading of a similar message toward different countries could fail to meet specific national objectives.

5.6 Summary of the Empirical Results and Discussion

Even if the vagueness of the terms referred to, PA and health determine a high interpretability of the messages, the empirical analyses conducted in this dissertation demonstrate visibly that sport is fundamentally disqualified in the communication for the promotion of PA issued by the health system. In particular:

- The physical activity recommended by the health system is to be carried out in everyday life, is moderate and health-orientated. The format which embodies this approach is '30 min of regular and moderate activity everyday' WHO (2004, p. 4). This standard is not compatible with the format of many sport activities in sport organisations, which are specific, have a variable intensity, an average longer duration and a lower frequency. Even if 'sport' is constantly mentioned, sport disciplines are very rarely directly recommended or have formats incommensurable with activities offered by sport organisations.
- The sport system is regularly mentioned within the documents. However, it is frequently entrusted with health-orientated tasks that are very abstract and extraneous to sport's logic. Sport roles are mostly mentioned for the protection of the health of sport practitioners. The abstract and imprecise approach to the topic of cooperation with sport organisations demonstrates their marginal role for the promotion of healthy PA in the perspective of the health system.
- Sometimes the documents advise against sport within the forms of physical activities recommendable in the context of health related PA. Specifically, the health system puts forth five different reasons for devaluating sport as a medium of health: 1) the advice of a medical examination as a prerequisite for doing or starting a sport activity; 2) the praise of a de-sportification of sport, particularly regarding its competitive and performance orientation; 3) the non-necessity of sport for being healthy; 4) the danger of sport activity; 5) the unease of sport activity.
- The strategies use ambiguous terms, lack definitions and contain discrepant and contradictory recommendations. The double ambiguity detected in the scientific discourse also widely affects the rhetoric of the strategies. Furthermore, the tension between the old rhetoric of PA promotion based upon sport and the new standards based on the moderate turn in the recommendation of physical activity additionally confuse the message. These issues weaken the power and precision of the messages.
- Even if the unit of analysis has a very heterogeneous style and minor differences have been found between case studies, the main characteristics regarding the rhetoric of the health-strategies and the deligitimisation of sport rep-

resent a common and cross-country tendency independent from the national sport system.

In brief, the discourse produced by the health system is imprecise, abstract, contradictory and sometimes sport-hostile. Nevertheless, the aim of the strategies analysed is to promote PAs on every possible occasion and in every possible way for combating the epidemic spread of chronic illnesses and to stimulate the cooperation with other function systems. By its own admission, the health system needs particularly the cooperation of the sport system for implementing effectively strategies for the promotion of PA. For instance, sport organisations are in many countries still within the most relevant providers of health promotion and are the places of implementation of many activities directly orientated towards health. For this reason, the health system's approach is instead openly in contrast to its leading coordinative function assumed in the area of the promotion of physical activity in the last decades. A lack of cooperation between these two systems could create an obstacle for the successful implementation of PA promotion.

6. Concluding Remarks

'If the end is good, everything will be good'[214]
(Unknown, 1872, p. 379)

For exploring the question 'What role does sport play in the health-orientated promotion of PA?' the health system has been identified as being the most relevant system involved in the dissemination of communications regarding the promotion of PA. The analysis of health system's organisational structure, based on Luhmann's systems theory, identified the health ministries as issuing bodies of documents particularly relevant for investigating the social phenomenon at hand. In particular, 15 strategies for the health-related promotion of PA issued by the health ministries of France, Germany, and Italy have been chosen to analyse the attitude of the health system regarding the function of sport in this area. The interpretation of the empirical analysis in light of the theoretical framework has allowed the overall evaluation of the dissertation's main topic and has been used to create inferences regarding the message. This chapter furnishes further conclusive reflections on the phenomenon, on the relevance of the results, and on the possible extensions of the present research.

In brief, the analysis testifies a highly ambiguous, biased and fundamentally sport-hostile attitude of the health system in the context of communications for the health promotion. Given the epidemic spread of noncommunicable diseases provoked by physical inactivity and the health system's engagement as a super-expert for assessing this health issue, this is at least a surprising characteristic of the documents analysed. For instance, sport organisations occupy at least in some countries the most relevant role in the context of health promotion through PA and recent studies are revaluing the effects of traditional sport on health. In fact, recent studies are revaluing the effects of traditional sport on health. For example, the high-intensity interval training (HIIT) relies at the basis of athletic training in many sport disciplines. In a non-systematic review of the MEDLINE database, Guiraud et al. (2012) analysed the effects of HIIT in patients with coronary artery disease, heart failure, and persons with high cardiovascular risk. The literature review shows that HIIT is a safe and effective alter-

[214] Original quotation: *'Si finis bonus erit, totum bonum erit'* (Unknown, 1872).

native for the rehabilitation of patients with coronary artery disease and heart failure. The authors even come to the conclusion that HIIT is better tolerated by patients than moderate-intensity continuous exercise. Even if these conclusions need to be confirmed by larger randomized interventional studies, this demonstrates that the refusal of sport as a form of health-medium relies sometimes on non-scientific bases. To create a message which is understandable and which stimulates the cooperation of the sport system, the health system should instead produce communications also commensurable with the logic of sport. In fact, from the perspective of the systems theory, a super-expert has to act impartially and through understandable communications, which can stimulate reaction in the diverse function systems involved in the context of the promotion of health through PA. Instead, in the selected strategies for the promotion of PA, sport is often underrepresented and the attitude towards the role of sport as a medium of health in such documents is highly sceptical.

To explain this contradictory attitude, the major results of the document analysis will be reviewed in light of the theoretical framework for producing further inferences on the social phenomenon at hand. This is possible because, as whole, the entirety of the results of the conducted analysis is more valuable and capable of explanation than its single elements. Their totality allows for the assessment of further issues emerged from within the theoretical framework. In particular, White & Marsh (2006, p. 27) suggest that a document analysis can furnish insights not only into the message, but also into the communicator and the effect of the message.[215] These two topics will be discussed in the following.

The distrust of the health system about the role of sport in the context of health-orientated promotion of PA might have two distinct reasons. The first explanation is that the health system, even by promoting PA as a medium of health, is still evaluating the results of its programmes through its autopoietic viewpoint (Bauch, 1996, p. 130). The operational closure and the reference to a peculiar logic is the main feature of modern function systems. The logic of the health system is orientated towards the codes 'health/illness' (Luhmann, 1983a, p. 31; 1990d, p. 186) and 'promoting/hindering health' (Bauch, 2004, p. 66). These codes are naturally incommensurable with the sport codes 'victory/defeat' (Schimank, 1988, p. 185) and 'perform/not perform' (Stichweh, 1990, p. 387). For example, training principles[216] as well as the concept of fitness as a goal of PA are totally absent from the communications because they are not directly re-

[215] Instead, the situation surrounding the creation of the documents, including the socio-cultural background of communication, has been already analysed within the theoretical framework.

[216] For example the metabolic training principles of specificity, overload, adaptation, progression, individualisation, maintenance, regression, plateau, warm -up and cool-down (Plowman & Smith, 2007, pp. 154-170).

lated to health. Physical activity is in this viewpoint a medium of health only if it contributes to the reduction of dangers connected to the genesis of chronic illnesses. Furthermore, sport is mostly considered by the health system as a sub category of PA and the psychosocial aspects of it are rarely taken into account. This demonstrates that in the discourse on PA promotion, the health system does not refer to a broad definition of health but clearly toward a health/illness model. This logic excludes from its rhetoric different approaches to the fight against physical inactivity.

The second reason is that the health system has not yet developed its own rhetoric on PA. The process of hypostatisation brought the interests of the health system to the promotion of PA, but this process is still on-going and not precisely defined. Within the documents, this causes a clash of rhetorics: on one side the continuous reference to the old tradition of PA promotion relying on sport as a fundamental health-medium; on the other side this perspective is contradicted by the description of the characteristic of PA and by the disqualification of sport as a medium of health. Furthermore, the double ambiguity regarding the definitions of health, sport and their relationship acknowledged in the scientific discussion is also largely detectable in the strategies for the promotion of PA.

Coming to the effect of the message, the analyses do not take into account the reactions of minor national health organisations, the population or the sport system. For this reason, it can be only speculated about the consequences raised by the strategies. They certainly do not constitute an optimal message for reaching the whished cooperation of the sport system in the promotion of health-related PA. In fact, in the documents analysed the role of the sport is marginal and ambiguous. In general, sport organisations tend to resist to external experts' call for structural change and have a particular learning ability in fending off any hazards that could harm the organization as it is (Thiel & Meier, 2004, pp. 120-121). For this reason, sport organisations generally do not react uniformly or appropriately when pressured to change by their environment. Given the messages analysed and the characteristics of sport organisations, the chance of a positive cooperation[217] between the health and the sport systems in the fight against physical inactivity is very low.

At the level of organisations, this disqualification of sport as a medium of health constitutes a further step in the process of exclusion of sport professionals from health organisations chart (Cachay & Thiel, 1999b). Another possible implication of this process at the level of organisations regards the networks

[217] A situation in which the sport and the health systems develop a recursive interaction system which allows the successful cooperative promotion of PA and constitutes for both a win situation. Furthermore, the operations which arise from this cooperation need to be fair and do not have to damage other systems (Willke, 2001b, p. 101).

between sport clubs and health practices. For Bommes and Tacke (2006, p. 40) social addresses[218] play the key role in the creation of multi-contextual networks. Social addresses are constituted of features like name, address, telephone number, email, etc. These features rely on the successful social inclusion of an individual into working and social environments. Normally, a social address allows *ego* to communicate to an unknown *alter* (as individual or as a worker in an organisation) which performs regulated and expected tasks (Bommes & Tacke, 2006, p. 43). However, social addresses have the chance of fulfilling tasks and expectations different to their formal functions. For example, family doctors use to recommend PA as a medium of health to their patients (A. L. Marshall, Smith, Bauman, & Kaur, 2005). With reference to the promoter model of Witte (1973) and to its extensions (Gemünden & Walter, 1998; Hauschildt & Chakrabarti, 1988), family doctors could in this case facilitate the inclusion of people into the sport system. However, the analysis of central communications of health system underlines the sceptical acceptance of traditional-competitive sport and the recommendation of PAs which are moderate and practiced outside sport organisations. This could endanger the social network between medical practices and sport organisations.

On the background of the analysed context, the relationship between the health and the sport systems in the promotion of health-related PA is likely to develop into a conflictual relationship (Willke, 2001b, p. 106). In this case, the structural coupling between sport and the health systems develops as a struggle in which the experts and the organisations of the respective systems concur for the promotion of health related PA. This situation could give birth to both positive and negative situations. In the best case, the competition between the sport and the health systems for the promotion of health-related PA could stimulate both systems to multiply their health-orientated programmes and could have good consequences on people's health. In the worst situation, the sport system will be excluded from the promotion of PA and be relegated to the professional, spectator and competitive aspects of sport. This would represent an issue not only for the sport system itself, but also for the health system and the entire society. However, at least in a short time, a scenario in which the sport system is completely excluded from the health-orientated promotion of PA is improbable. In fact, society and the sport system are not to be manipulated by the communication of a single function system, even one as relevant as the health system. This means that the health system's disqualifying message will be in many social contexts simply ignored (Willke, 2006b, p. 18). In this scenario, the sport system will continue to offer both traditional-competitive and health-orientated programmes through its organisations and most of the people will continue to do

[218] The concept of adressability has been introduced in the systems theory by P. Fuchs (1997).

sport for being healthy. Also at the societal level, crystallised communications connecting sport and health will continue to be reproduced. Nevertheless, the relevance and difficult manageability of the problem of physical inactivity would require a high level of cooperation which cannot be expected to be obtained through the analysed communication of the health system.

This dissertation covers an original, relevant area and has a practical as well as a theoretical relevance. In particular, the disqualification of sport in the health-related promotion of physical activity and the reappropriation of the promotion of PA by the health system is highly significant and less addressed in sociological literature. The reshaping of the boundaries of the two systems is particularly relevant on many levels, because it implies a renegotiation of the formal role of sport in the battle against physical inactivity: on a societal level the topic of healthy physical activity will be increasingly assessed by communications of the health system instead of those of the sport system; on an organisational level such paradigmatic change could deeply influence the contents of programmes of sport and health organisations; at the academic level this phenomenon poses an almost existential question for some fields of sport science and creates turning points in the content of the health and sport-related academic disciplines and in the career opportunities of graduates in these fields (Cachay & Thiel, 1999b, p. 153).

The acknowledgment of the '*double ambiguity*' within the scientific discussion on the effect of PA on health and its repercussions on the analysed strategies raises further important questions about the value of the discourse. Although this dissertation has a descriptive aim and does not aspire to assess a normative task, it has been demonstrated that a refinement in this scientific discourse at both rhetorical and theoretical level is urgently needed. In particular, more attention to the basic definitions regarding health, PA and their relationship should be paid. Also the multidimensionality of health and sport should be always analytically taken into account: their relationship at the specific and general levels need to be theoretically reorganised and rethought. This also applies to the rhetoric of the strategies, which furthermore need to be understandable by nonprofessional readers and functional for the societal aim. In particular, a more positive attitude toward sport and a higher acknowledgement of its key role in this area would better mirror the societal situation and would better apply to the aim of the strategies. In many cases, clearly explaining the health benefits of sport, not over-emphasising its injury-related risks and formulating the sentences regarding the role of sport with clear and imperative formulations would be enough to constitute a message which sounds less sport-hostile. Such a typology of statements exemplary presented below is instead totally absent from the strategies:

> 'In their competitive and amateur forms, sport activities contribute to enhance people's fitness and can better social and psychological health. For these reasons, among other forms of PAs they are highly advisable in the context of health promotion and of the prevention of noncommunicable diseases'[219]

As a final contribution, the following paragraphs propose some possible extensions of the analysis performed. These proposals emerged during the research process and rely on wider questions inevitably generated by the production of new knowledge on the research topic and by the scarcity of time and resources to assess them. Because every sampling is imperfect by definition, the research could profit by including and comparing more countries. In particular, the extension to clusters of liberal countries (the United States, Great Britain, Canada, and Australia) and/or the one of Scandinavian countries (Sweden, Finland, Norway) could bring further important information and enhance the power of the comparison. In fact, the contrast to countries with different welfare and sport systems could furnish key information for the assessment of their role on the health system's promotion of PA. However, also the analysis of the situation in developing and poor countries could generate interesting information on the sociological phenomenon at hand in radically different countries. Other possible extensions of the comparison could regard different combinations of regional and/or local strategies for enquiring into diverse forms of multi-level governance, strategies issued by different international organisations for comparing the characteristics of global health communications and the temporal comparison of documents on health-orientated promotion of PA for assessing the dimension of time and the development of the exclusion of sport in this discussions.

Other insights could be furnished by the analysis of strategies for the health-orientated promotion of PA issued by the sport system. This would complete the other side of the governance interaction between the sport and health systems. In particular, it is highly interesting how this turn regarding sport's health effects in the scientific community and within the health system is perceived (or not) by the sport system.

Because of the central role of obesity and nutrition within strategies for the promotion of PA, it would be also interesting to analyse the role of sport and PA in strategies focused on the prevention and treatment of obesity. This topic is extremely fascinating because of the escalating stigmatisation of obesity in society (Latner & Stunkard, 2012; Latner, Stunkard, & Wilson, 2012; Puhl & Brownell, 2012; Thiel, Alizadeh, Giel, & Zipfel, 2008).

---

[219] This quotation has been conceived by the author as an example of positive formulation of the role of sport in health promotion.

Furthermore the integration of other methodological designs could contribute to a deeper analysis, to a differentiation of its sources and to an assessment of additional important dimensions. In particular, through interviews, questionnaires and focus groups, the understanding of non-expert readers of the role of sport in health-strategies, the self-perception of people involved in sport for health and the opinion of experts involved in health promotion through PA could be investigated. Also, statistical designs could be used to expand the quantitative steps of the document analysis, which here have been limited to an explorative aim, to a broader sample of documents.

Finally, the social phenomenon of the health system's extension to the promotion of PA is particularly interesting and proves especially challenging when investigated from a systems theory perspective. In fact, in the function-differentiated society, function systems are not organised hierarchically and there is no top-down or bottom-up flow. Nevertheless, the birth of inequalities between the function systems is something natural. For Luhmann, this phenomenon is normally attributable to different degrees of efficacy in the respective system's communication media, which is the principle factor responsible for generating an advantage for some systems and for bringing about the marginalisation of others (Moeller, 2006, pp. 27-28). However, in the case of the health and sport systems, the reason for different rates and trajectories of evolution is not attributable to the communication medium. Indeed, the health system suffers from a general lack of self-reflection (Bauch, 2004, p. 56) and it has no specific generalised symbiotic means of communication (Luhmann, 1983a, p. 173). In the case of the sport system, it can be stated that its symbolically generalised communication medium is the performance of human bodies (Stichweh, 1990, p. 380) through the use of specific communication instruments such as ranking, records, and disciplines-specific descriptions. This communication medium, even if it is not as developed as for other systems (for example, money in the economic system), is very successful and desirable for mass media channels such as newspaper, television, radio and the internet. For this reason: sport events are within the most watched television broadcasts (FIFA, 2006, 2007), many athletes are world famous; sports is one of the most recurrent topics in common conversations (Anderson & Stone, 1981, p. 14). On the contrary, health-related topics are not similarly socially overexposed. In other words, in the analysed case the most evolutionarily successful function system is the one with the less developed communication medium. This represents a kind of contradiction for systems theory. It seems that the asymmetric evolution of function systems, only marginally theorised in Luhmann's systems theory, is a topic that has wider development potential.

The above-mentioned extensions of the analysis would further enhance the significance of the results obtained.[220] Nevertheless, this dissertation documents, theorises and empirically investigates for the first time the topic of the disqualification of sport from health-related promotion of physical activity. In this sense, it constitutes at least a solid theoretical and empirical starting point for the deeper analysis of this relevant social phenomenon.

[220] As an old Italian proverb puts it: *'the one who is at the end of a walk is just at its beginning'* (Anonymous).

Bibliography

Abele, A., Brehm, W., & Gall, T. (1991). Sportliche Aktivität und Wohlbefinden. [Sport activity and well-being]. In A. Abele & P. Becker (Eds.), *Wohlbefinden. Theorie, Empirie, Diagnostik* (pp. 279-296). Weinheim: Juventa.

Abell, J. E., Hootman, J. M., Zack, M. M., Moriarty, D., & Helmick, C. G. (2005). Physical activity and health related quality of life among people with arthritis. *Journal of epidemiology and community health, 59*(5), 380-385.

Abu-Omar, K., Rütten, A., & Lehtinen, V. (2004). Mental health and physical activity in the European Union. *Sozial- und Präventivmedizin/Social and Preventive Medicine, 49*(5), 301-309. doi: 10.1007/s00038-004-3109-8

Acree, L. S., Longfors, J., Fjeldstad, A. S., Fjeldstad, C., Schank, B., Nickel, K. J., . . . Gardner, A. W. (2006). Physical activity is related to quality of life in older adults. *Health and quality of life outcomes, 4*(1), 37.

ACSM. (1981). The recommended quantity and quality of exercise for developing and maintaining fitness in healthy adults. *Journal of Cardiopulmonary Rehabilitation and Prevention, 1*, 375-384.

ACSM. (1990). The recommended quantity and quality of exercise for developing and maintaining cardiorespiratory and muscular fitness in healthy adults. *Medicine and science in sports and exercise, 22*, 265-274.

ACSM, & AHA. (2007). Physical activity and public health in older adults: Recommendation from the American College of Sports Medicine and the American Heart Association. *Medicine and science in sports and exercise, 39*, 1423-1434.

Ada, L., Dean, C. M., Vargas, J., & Ennis, S. (2010). Mechanically assisted walking with body weight support results in more independent walking than assisted overground walking in non-ambulatory patients early after stroke: a systematic review. *J Physiother, 56*(3), 153-161.

Ainsworth, B. E., Haskell, W., Leon, A., Jacobs, D., Montoye, H., Sallis, J., & Paffenbarger, R. (1993). Compendium of physical activities: classification of energy costs of human physical activities. *Medicine & Science in Sports & Exercise, 25*(1), 71.

Ainsworth, B. E., Haskell, W. L., Whitt, M. C., Irwin, M. L., Swartz, A. M., Strath, S. J., . . . Leon, A. S. (2000). Compendium of physical activities: An update of activity codes and MET intensities. *Medicine & Science in Sports & Exercise, 32*(9 Suppl.), 498-516.

Albert, M. (2004). On the modern systems theory of society and IR. In M. Albert & L. Hilkermeier (Eds.), *Observing international relations. Niklas Luhmann and world politics* (pp. 13-29). London: Routledge.

Alfermann, D., Stoll, O., Wagner, S., & Wagner-Stoll, P. (1995). Auswirkungen des Sporttreibens auf Selbstkonzept und Wohlbefinden: Ergebnisse eines kontrollierten Feldexperiments. [Effects of sport on self-concept and well-being: Results of a controlled field experiment]. In W. Schlicht & P. Schwenkmezger (Eds.), *Gesundheitsverhalten und Bewegung: Grundlagen, Konzepte und empirische Befunde* (pp. 95-111). Schorndorf: Hofmann.

Allensworth, D. D., & Kolbe, L. J. (1987). The Comprehensive School Health Program: Exploring an Expanded Concept. *Journal of School Health, 57*(10), 409-412. doi: 10.1111/j.1746-1561.1987.tb03183.x

Almond, G. A. (1966). Political Theory and Political Science. *The American Political Science Review, 60*(4), 869-879.
Almond, G. A., & Powell, G. B. J. r. (1966). *Comparative Politics. A Developmental Approach.* Boston: Little Brown & Company.
Altrichter, H. (Ed.). (2007). *Educational Governance. Handlungskoordination und Steuerung im Bildungssystem.* [Educational governance. Coordination and management of education system]. (1th ed.). Wiesbaden: VS, Verlag für Sozialwissenschaften.
Anderson, D., & Stone, G. P. (1981). Responses of male and female metropolitans to the commercialization of professional sport 1960 to 1975. *International Review for the Sociology of Sport, 16*(3), 5.
Andriolo, R. B., El Dib, R. P., & Ramos, L. R. (2005). Aerobic exercise training programmes for improving physical and psychosocial health in adults with Down syndrome. *Cochrane Database of Systematic Reviews*(3), CD005176. doi: 10.1002/14651858.CD005176.pub2
Anokye, N., Trueman, P., Green, C., Pavey, T., & Taylor, R. (2012). Physical activity and health related quality of life. *BMC Public Health, 12*(1), 624.
Antonovsky, A. (1979). *Health, stress, and coping.* San Francisco: Jossey Bass.
Antonovsky, A. (1987). *Unraveling the Mystery of Health: How People Manage Stress and Stay Well.* San Francisco: Jossey Bass
Antonovsky, A. (1990). *Studying Health vs. Studying Diseas.* Paper presented at the Congress for Clinical Psychology and Psychotherapy, Berlin. http://www.ensp.unl.pt/saboga/soc/pulic/soc_AAconference_berlim_91.pdf
Antonovsky, A. (1996). The Salutogenic Model as a Theory to Guide Health Promotion. *HEALTH PROMOTION INTERNATIONAL, 11*(1), 11-18.
Antonovsky, A. (1997). *Salutogenese : zur Entmystifizierung der Gesundheit.* [Unraveling the mystery of health]. Tübingen: Deutsche Gesellschaft für Verhaltenstherapie.
Arts, W., & Gelissen, J. (2002). Three worlds of welfare capitalism or more? A state-of-the-art report. *Journal of European social policy, 12*(2), 137-158.
Ashworth, N. L., Chad, K. E., Harrison, E. L., Reeder, B. A., & Marshall, S. C. (2005). Home versus center based physical activity programs in older adults. *Cochrane Database of Systematic Reviews*(1), CD004017. doi: 10.1002/14651858.CD004017.pub2
Astrand, P.-O. (1994). Physical Activity and Fitness: Evolutionary Perspective and Trends for the Future. In C. Bouchard, R. J. Shephard & T. Stephens (Eds.), *Physical Activity, Fitness, and Health: International Proceedings and Consensus Statement* (pp. 98-105). Champaign: Human Kinetics.
Atlantis, E., Barnes, E. H., & Singh, M. A. (2006). Efficacy of exercise for treating overweight in children and adolescents: a systematic review. *International Journal of Obesity, 30*(7), 1027-1040. doi: 10.1038/sj.ijo.0803286
Babatunde, O. O., Forsyth, J. J., & Gidlow, C. J. (2012). A meta-analysis of brief high-impact exercises for enhancing bone health in premenopausal women. *Osteoporosis international, 23*(1), 109-119. doi: 10.1007/s00198-011-1801-0
Babey, S. H., Diamant, A. L., Brown, E. R., & Hastert, T. A. (2005). California Adolescents Increasingly Inactive. *UCLA Center for Health Policy Research.* Retrieved from http://escholarship.org/uc/item/2f0479g1
Badura, B., & Feuerstein, G. (1994). *Systemgestaltung im Gesundheitswesen : zur Versorgungskrise der hochtechnisierten Medizin und den Möglichkeiten ihrer Bewältigung.* [System Management in Healthcare: The Supply Crisis of High-Tech Medicine and the Possibilities of Coping]. Weinheim: Juventa-Verlag.
Baier, H. (1970). Die Wirklichkeit der Industriegesellschaft als Krankheitsfaktor. [The reality of industrial society as a disease factor]. In A. Mitscherlich (Ed.), *Der Kranke in der modernen Gesellschaft* (pp. 37-50). Berlin: Kiepenheuer & Witsch.

Balz, E. (1992). Sport und Gesundheit: Problemorientierte Reflexionen in pädagogischer Absicht. [Sport and Health: Reflections in a problem-oriented pedagogical perspective]. *Sportwissenschaft, 22*(3), 257-282.

Baraldi, C., Corsi, G., & Esposito, E. (1997a). *GLU - Glossar zu Niklas Luhmanns Theorie sozialer Systeme.* [Glossary of Niklas Luhmann's systems theory] (2 nd ed.). Frankfurt am Main: Suhrkamp.

Baraldi, C., Corsi, G., & Esposito, E. (1997b). *Luhmann in glossario. I concetti fondamentali della teoria dei sistemi sociali.* [Glossary of Niklas Luhmann's Systems Theory] (2nd ed.). Milano: Franco Angeli.

Bargar, R. R., & Duncan, J. K. (1982). Cultivating creative endeavor in doctoral research. *The Journal of Higher Education, 53*(1), 1-31.

Bauch, J. (1996). *Gesundheit als sozialer Code: von der Vergesellschaftung des Gesundheitswesens zur Medikalisierung der Gesellschaft.* [Health as a social code: From the socialisation of health care to the medicalisation of society]. Weinheim: Juventa.

Bauch, J. (1997). Was heißt Saluto Correctness? Zur Dialektik von Sozialabbau und Verhaltensdisziplinierung im Gesundheitswesen. [What is Saluto Correctness? The dialectics of social cuts and disciplinary behaviours in healthcare]. In G. Hörnemann (Ed.), *Freiheit und Solidarität im Sozialstaat* (pp. 29-42). Konstanz: Festschrift für Horst Baier.

Bauch, J. (2000). *Medizinsoziologie.* [Sociology of medicine]. München: Oldenbourg.

Bauch, J. (2004). *Krankheit und Gesundheit als gesellschaftliche Konstruktion: Gesundheits- und medizinsoziologische Schriften 1979 - 2003.* [Illness and Health as a Social Construction: Health and Medical Sociological Writings Between 1979 and 2003] (1st ed.). Konstanz: Hartung-Gorre.

Bauman, A., & Craig, C. (2005). The Place of Physical Activity in the WHO Global Strategy on Diet and Physical Activity. *International Journal of Behavioral Nutrition and Physical Activity, 2*(1), 10. Retrieved from http://www.ijbnpa.org/content/2/1/10

Becker, P. (1987). Steigerung und Knappheit. Zur Kontingenzformel des Sportsystems und ihren Folgen. [Increase and shortages. To the contingency of the sports system and its consequences]. In P. Becker (Ed.), *Sport und Höchstleistung* (1 ed., pp. 17-37). Reinbek bei Hamburg: Rowohlt.

Becker, S. (2011). *Sport zur Gesundheitsförderung oder treiben nur Gesunde Sport? Eine empirische Längsschnittanalyse.* [Sport for the promotion of health or do only healthy people practice sport? An empirical analysis of longitudinal data]. Wiesbaden: VS Verlag für Sozialwissenschaften.

Bednarz, J. (1985). Complexity and intersubjectivity: Towards the theory of Niklas Luhmann. *Environmental Geochemistry and Health, 7*(1), 55-69. doi: 10.1007/bf00143312

Begg, D. J., Langley, J. D., Moffitt, T., & Marshall, S. W. (1996). Sport and delinquency: an examination of the deterrence hypothesis in a longitudinal study. *British Journal of Sports Medicine, 30*(4), 335-341.

Benz, A. (2007). Accountable Multilevel Governance by the Open Method of Coordination? *European Law Journal, 13*(4), 505-522. doi: 10.1111/j.1468-0386.2007.00381.x

Benz, A., & Eberlein, B. (1999). The Europeanization of regional policies: patterns of multi-level governance. *Journal of European Public Policy, 6*(2), 329 - 348.

Benz, A., Lütz, S., Schimank, U., & Simonis, G. (Eds.). (2007). *Handbuch Governance : theoretische Grundlagen und empirische Anwendungsfelder.* [Manual of governance: Theoretical foundations and fields of empirical application]. (1th ed.). Wiesbaden: VS Verlag für Sozialwissenschaften.

Berelson, B. (1952). *Content analysis in communication research.* New York: Hafner.

Berghaus, M. (2004). *Luhmann leicht gemacht : eine Einführung in die Systemtheorie.* [Luhmann made easy: An introduction to systems theory] (2nd ed.). Köln: Böhlau.

Bergman, A., & Norlander, T. (2005). "Hay Sacks Anonymous": Living in the Shadow of the Unidentified. Psychological Aspects of Physical Inactivity From a Phenomenological Perspective. *The Qualitative Report, 10*(4), 795-816.

Berk, R. A. (1983). An introduction to sample selection bias in sociological data. *American Sociological Review*, 386-398.

Berlin, J. A., & Colditz, G. A. (1990). A meta-analysis of physical activity in the prevention of coronary heart disease. *American Journal of Epidemiology, 132*, 612 - 628.

Bernard of Chartres. (Unknown). *De expositione Porphyrii.*

Bertalanffy, L. v. (1968). *General system theory.* New York: Braziller.

Bette, K.-H. (1984). *Strukturelle Aspekte des Hochleistungssports in der Bundesrepublik : Ansatzpunkte fuer eine System-Umwelt-Theorie des Hochleistungssports.* (PhD), Deutsche Sporthochschule Köln, Köln. Bibliothekskatalog Tübingen database.

Bette, K.-H. (1987). Wo ist der Körper? [Where is the body?]. In D. Baecker & N. Luhmann (Eds.), *Theorie als Passion: Niklas Luhmann zum 60. Geburtstag* (pp. 600-628). Frankfurt am Main: Suhrkamp.

Bette, K.-H. (1989). *Körperspuren : zur Semantik und Paradoxie moderner Körperlichkeit.* [Body marks: The paradox and semantic of modern physicality] (2nd ed.). Berlin: Walter de Gruyter & Co.

Bette, K.-H. (1995). Sport and individualization. In K.-H. Bette & A. Rütten (Eds.), *International Sociology of Sport: Contemporary Issues* (pp. 33-44). Stuttgart: Naglschmid.

Bette, K.-H. (1999). *Systemtheorie und Sport.* [Systems Theory and Sport]. Frankfurt am Main: Suhrkamp.

Bette, K.-H. (2007). Rezension zu Schulze, Bernd: Sportarten als soziale Systeme. Ansätze einer Systemtheorie der Sportarten am Beispiel des Fußballs. [Review of Schulze, Bernd: sports as social systems. Approaches to systems theory on the example of football]. *Sport und Gesellschaft*(2), 199-205.

Bette, K.-H., Kühnle, F., & Thiel, A. (2012). *Dopingprävention: eine soziologische Expertise.* [Doping prevention: A sociological expertise]. Bielefeld: Transcript.

Bette, K.-H., & Schimank, U. (2006). *Doping im Hochleistungssport : Anpassung durch Abweichung.* [Doping in Competitive Sports: Adaptation Through Deviation] (2nd ed.). Frankfurt am Main: Suhrkamp.

Bevir, M. (2009). *Key concepts in governance.* Los Angeles: Sage.

Biddle, S. J. H., & Mutrie, N. (2008). *Psychology of Physical Activity: Determinants, Well-Being, and Interventions.* (2nd ed.). London and New York: Routledge.

Bize, R., Johnson, J. A., & Plotnikoff, R. C. (2007). Physical activity level and health-related quality of life in the general adult population: A systematic review. *Prev Med, 45*(6), 401-415. http://dx.doi.org/10.1016/j.ypmed.2007.07.017

Blacklock, R. E., Rhodes, R. E., & Brown, S. G. (2007). Relationship between regular walking, physical activity, and health-related quality of life. *JOURNAL OF PHYSICAL ACTIVITY & HEALTH, 4*(2), 138-152.

Blair, S. N., LaMonte, M. J., & Nichaman, M. Z. (2004). The evolution of physical activity recommendations: How much is enough? *The American Journal of Clinical Nutrition, 79*(5), 913-920.

Bommes, M., & Tacke, V. (2006). Das Allgemeine und das Besondere des Netzwerkes. [The general and the particular of the network]. In B. Hollstein & F. Straus (Eds.), *Qualitative Netzwerkanalyse. Konzepte, Methoden, Anwendungen* (pp. 37-62). Wiesbaden: VS Verlag.

Borggrefe, C. (2013). *Spitzensport und Beruf. Eine qualitative Studie zur dualen Karriere in funktional differenzierter Gesellschaft.* [Elite sport and profession. A qualitative study of dual careers in functionally differentiated society]. Schorndorf: Hofmann.

Bös, K., & Brehm, W. (1998). *Gesundheitssport. Ein Handbuch.* [Health sports. A Handbook] (1th ed.). Schorndorf: Hofmann.

Bös, K., & Brehm, W. (1998). Zur Konzeption des Handbuchs: Zugänge zum „Gesundheitssport". [The conception of the manual: Approaches to "health sport"]. In K. Bös & D. Alfermann (Eds.), *Gesundheitssport: ein Handbuch* (pp. 7-14). Schorndorf: Hofmann.

Bös, K., & Brehm, W. (2006). *Handbuch Gesundheitssport.* (2nd ed.). Schorndorf: Hofmann.

Bouchard, C., & Shephard, R. J. (1994). Physical activity, Fitness, and Health: The Model and Key Concepts. In C. Bouchard, R. J. Shephard & T. Stephens (Eds.), *Physical Activity, Fitness, and Health. International Proceedings and Consensus Statement* (pp. 77-88). Champaign: Human Kinetics.

Bouchard, C., Shephard, R. J., & Stephens, T. (Eds.). (1994). *Physical activity, fitness, and health: International proceedings and consensus statement.* Champaign, Illinois: Human Kinetics Publishers.

Brazzelli, M., Saunders, D. H., Greig, C. A., & Mead, G. E. (2011). Physical fitness training for stroke patients. *Cochrane Database of Systematic Reviews*(11). doi: 10.1002/14651858.CD003316.pub4

Breedveld, K., Goossens, R., van Bottenburg, M., Ooijendijk, W., Hildebrandt, V., Stiggelbout, M., . . . van der Poel, H. (2003). *Report on Sport 2003.* The Hague: The Netherlands Institute for Social Research Retrieved from http://www.scp.nl/english/Publications/Summaries_by_year/Summaries_2003/Report_on_Sport_2003

Brehm, W. (1998). Qualitäten und deren Sicherung im Gesundheitssport. [Quality and its assurance in health sport]. In A. Rütten (Ed.), *Public Health und Sport* (pp. 181-202). Stuttgart: Nagelschmid.

Brettschneider, W.-D., & Naul, R. (2004). Study on Young People's Lifestyles and Sedentariness and the Role of Sport in the Context of Education and as a Means of Restoring the Balance. Paderborn: European Commission.

Breuer, C., & Wicker, P. (2008). Gesundheitssport im Verein *Sportentwicklungsbericht.* Köln: Deutsche Sportochschule Köln.

British Medical Association. (1992). *Cycling: Towards Health and Safety.* Oxford: Oxford University Press.

Brown, D. W., Balluz, L. S., Heath, G. W., Moriarty, D. G., Ford, E. S., Giles, W. H., & Mokdad, A. H. (2003). Associations between recommended levels of physical activity and health-related quality of life. Findings from the 2001 Behavioral Risk Factor Surveillance System (BRFSS) survey. *Prev Med, 37*(5), 520-528.

Brown, D. W., Brown, D. R., Heath, G. W., Balluz, L., Giles, W. H., Ford, E. S., & Mokdad, A. H. (2004). Associations between physical activity dose and health-related quality of life. *Medicine and science in sports and exercise, 36*(5), 890.

Bunton, R. (1997). Popular health, advanced liberalism and good housekeeping magazine. In A. Petersen & R. Bunton (Eds.), *Foucault, health and medicine* (pp. 223-248). London: Routledge.

Busch, A. J., Barber, K. A., Overend, T. J., Peloso, P. M., & Schachter, C. L. (2007). Exercise for treating fibromyalgia syndrome. *Cochrane Database of Systematic Reviews*(4), CD003786. doi: 10.1002/14651858.CD003786.pub2

Cachay, K. (1988). *Sport und Gesellschaft: Zur Ausdifferenzierung einer Funktion und ihrer Folgen.* [Sport and Society: On the Differentiation of a Function and its Consequences]. Schorndorf: Hofmann.

Cachay, K. (1990). Versportlichung der Gesellschaft und Entsportung des Sports - Systemtheoretische Anmerkungen zu einem gesellschaftlichen Phänomen. [The Sportification of Society and the de-Sportification of Sport - Systems Theoretical Reflections on a Social Phenomenon]. In H. Gabler & U. Göhner (Eds.), *Für einen besseren Sport* (pp. 97-113). Schorndorf: Hofmann.

Cachay, K., & Kastrup, V. (2006). Professionalisierung und De-Professionalisierung der Sportlehrerrolle. [Professionalisation and de-professionalisation of physical education teacher's role]. *Sport und Gesellschaft, 3*(2).

Cachay, K., & Thiel, A. (1999a). *Ausbildung ins Ungewisse? Beschäftigungschancen für Sportwissenschaftlerinnen und Sportwissenschaftler im Gesundheitssystem.* [Uncertain Education? Employment Opportunities for Sport Scientists in the Health System]. Aachen: Meyer&Meyer.

Cachay, K., & Thiel, A. (1999b). Vom Medizin- zum Gesundheitssystem - Professionalisierungschance für Sportwissenschaftlerinnen und Sportwissenschaftler. [From the Medical System to the Health System - Professionalisation Opportunities for Sport Scientists]. *Sportwissenschaft, 29*(2), 143-157.

Cachay, K., & Thiel, A. (2000). *Soziologie des Sports: Zur Ausdifferenzierung und Entwicklungsdynamik des Sports der modernen Gesellschaft.* [Sociology of Sport: On the Differentiation and Dynamics of the Development of Sport in Modern Society]. Weinheim: Juventa-Verlag.

Cachay, K., Thiel, A., & Kastrup, V. (2010). Professionalisierung des Sportlehrerberufs. [Professionalisation of sport-related employments]. In N. Fessler, A. Hummel & G. Stibbe (Eds.), *Handbuch Schulsport* (pp. 245-255). Schorndorf: Hofmann.

Cannon, G. (2004). Why the Bush administration and the global sugar industry are determined to demolish the 2004 WHO Strategy on diet, physical activity and health. *Public health nutrition, 7*(3), 369 - 380.

Caspersen, C. J., Christenson, G. M., & Pollard, R. A. (1986). Status of the 1990 physical fitness and exercise objectives - Evidence from NHIS 1985. *Public health reports, 101*(6), 587-592.

Caspersen, C. J., Powell, K. E., & Christenson, G. M. (1985). Physical activity, exercise, and physical fitness: Definitions and distinctions for health-related research. *Public health reports, 100*(2), 126-131.

Castles, F. (Ed.). (1993). *Families of nations: Patterns of public policy in western democracies.* London: Dartmouth Publishing Company Ltd.

Castles, F., & Mitchell, D. (1993). Worlds of welfare and families of nations. In F. Castles (Ed.), *Families of nations: Patterns of public policy in Western democracies* (pp. 93-128). London: Dartmouth Publishing Company Ltd.

Caudwell, J. (Ed.). (2006). *Sport, sexualities and queer/theory.* London: Routledge.

Cavill, N., Kahlmeier, S., & Racioppi, F. (2006). *Physical activity and health in Europe: evidence for action.* World Health Organization.

CDC. (1993). Prevalence of Sedentary Lifestyle - Behavioral Risk Factor Surveillance System, United States, 1991. *Morbidity and Mortality Weekly Report, 29*, 576-579. Retrieved from http://www.cdc.gov/mmwr/preview/mmwrhtml/00021313.htm

CDC. (2000). *Measuring Healthy Days: Population Assessment of Health-related Quality of Life.* Atlanta, Georgia: CDC

CDC, & ACSM. (1995). Physical activity and public health. A recommendation from the Centers for Disease Control and Prevention and the American College of Sports Medicine. *Journal of the American Medical Association, 273*, 402-407.

Collin, F. (2008). *Konstruktivismus für Einsteiger.* [Constructivism for beginners] (1st ed.). Stuttgart: UTB GmbH.

Conn, V. S., Hafdahl, A. R., Porock, D. C., McDaniel, R., & Nielsen, P. J. (2006). A meta-analysis of exercise interventions among people treated for cancer. *Support Care Cancer, 14*(7), 699-712. doi: 10.1007/s00520-005-0905-5

Conrad, P. (1992). Medicalization and Social Control. *Annual Review of Sociology, 18*, 209-232.

Conrad, P., & Schneider, J. W. (1980). *Deviance and Medicalization: From Badness to Sickness.* Philadelphia: Temple University Press.

Corbetta, P. (1999). *Metodologia e tecniche della ricerca sociale.* [Methodology and techniques of social research]. Bologna: il Mulino.

Craft, L. L., Vaniterson, E. H., Helenowski, I. B., Rademaker, A. W., & Courneya, K. S. (2012). Exercise effects on depressive symptoms in cancer survivors: a systematic review and meta-analysis. *Cancer epidemiology, biomarkers & prevention, 21*(1), 3-19. doi: 10.1158/1055-9965.epi-11-0634

Crawford, R. (1980). Healthism and the Medicalization of Everyday Life. *International Journal of Health Services, 10*(3), 365-388.

Daley, A., Jolly, K., & MacArthur, C. (2009). The effectiveness of exercise in the management of post-natal depression: systematic review and meta-analysis. *Fam Pract, 26*(2), 154-162. doi: 10.1093/fampra/cmn101

Danzon, M. (2004). WHO - Diet and physical activity : the public health debate. *European Journal of Public Health, 14*(3), 336.

Dauer, V. P., & Pangrazi, R. P. (1975). *Dynamic Physical Education for Elementary School Children.* Minneapolis: Burgess Publishing Company.

Daugbjerg, S. B., Kahlmeier, S., Francesca, R., Martin-Diener, E., Martin, B., Oja, P., & Bull, F. (2009). Promotion of physical activity in the European region: content analysis of 27 national policy documents. *Journal of Physical Activity and Health, 6*(6), 805-817.

Dawber, T. R., Meadors, G. F., & Moore Jr, F. E. (1951). Epidemiological approaches to heart disease: The Framingham Study. *American Journal of Public Health, 41*(3), 279-286.

De Wachter, F. (1983). Spielregeln und ethische Problematik. [Rules of the game and ethical problems]. In H. Lenk (Ed.), *Aktuelle Probleme der Sportphilosophie* (pp. 278-294). Schorndorf: Hofmann.

Defrance, J., & Renard, D. (2003). Sport and the welfare state in France. In K. Heinemann (Ed.), *Sport and welfare policies : 6 European case studies* (pp. 219-252). Schorndorf: Hofmann.

Demetriou, Y. (2012). *Health promotion in physical education.* (PhD), Eberhard-Karls-Universität Tübingen, Tübingen. Retrieved from http://nbn-resolving.de/urn:nbn:de:bsz:21-opus-64271

Department for Culture, Media and Sport, & Strategy Unit. (2002). *Game plan: A strategy for delivering government's sport and physical activity objectives.* DCMS/Strategy Unit, London

Diehl, K., Thiel, A., Zipfel, S., Mayer, J., Litaker, D. G., & Schneider, S. (2012). How healthy is the behavior of young athletes? A systematic literature review and meta-analyses. *Journal of Sports Science and Medicine, 11*, 201-220.

Diehl, K., Thiel, A., Zipfel, S., Mayer, J., & Schneider, S. (2012). Substance use among elite adolescent athletes: Findings from the GOAL Study. *Scandinavian Journal of Medicine & Science in Sports*, n/a-n/a. doi: 10.1111/j.1600-0838.2012.01472.x

Diener, E., Suh, E. M., Lucas, R. E., & Smith, H. L. (1999). Subjective well-being: Three decades of progress. *Psychological bulletin, 125*(2), 276.

Digel, H. (1990). Die Versportlichung unserer Kultur und deren Folgen für den Sport - Ein Beitrag zur Uneigentlichkeit des Sports. [The Sportification of our Culture and its Impact on Sport - An Essay on the Inauthenticity of Sport]. In H. Gabler & U. Göhner (Eds.), *Für einen besseren Sport* (pp. 73-96). Schorndorf: Hofmann.

Digel, H. (1995). Was ist der Gegenstand der Sportwissenschaft? [What is the subject of sport science?]. In H. Digel (Ed.), *Sportwissenschaft heute. Eine Gegenstandsbestimmung* (pp. 1-18). Darmstadt: Wissenschaftlichen Buchgesellschaft.

Digel, H., & Barra, M. (2004). *Hochleistungssport in Italien.* [Professional sport in Italy]. Weilheim/Teck: Bräuer.

Digel, H., & Fahrner, M. (2003). *Hochleistungs Sport in Frankreich.* [Professional sport in France] (Vol. 1). Weilheim/Teck: Bräuer.

Dishman, R. K., Sallis, J. F., & Orenstein, D. R. (1985). The determinants of physical activity and exercise. *Public health reports, 100*(2), 158-171.

Dishman, R. K., Washburn, R. A., & Heath, G. (2004). *Physical activity epidemiology.* Champaign, Illinois: Human Kinetics Publishers.

Dodgson, R., Lee, K., & Drager, N. (2002). Global health governance: a conceptual review. *Key Issues in Global Health Governance, 1*, 1-27.

Drewnowski, A., & Evans, W. J. (2001). Nutrition, physical activity, and quality of life in older adults summary. *The Journals of Gerontology Series A: Biological Sciences and Medical Sciences, 56*(suppl 2), 89-94.

Drexel, G. (2003). Paradigmen in Sport und Sportwissenschaft. [Paradigms in sport and sport science]. *Sportwissenschaft, 33*(4), 488-491.

Dubos, R. J. (1965). *Man adapting.* New Haven: Yale University Press.

Düllings, J. (1993). Die Kostenexpansion des Gesundheitssystems als Risikoprozeß. [The expansion of the costs of the health system as a risk-process]. *Sozial-und Präventivmedizin/Social and Preventive Medicine, 38*(4), 239-244.

Dunning, E. (1995). The civilizing and state-formation processes of western Europe and the early developement of modern sport. In K.-H. Bette & A. Rütten (Eds.), *International sociology of sport: Contemporary issues* (pp. 5-14). Stuttgart: Naglschmid.

Dzurec, L. C., & Abraham, I. L. (1993). The nature of inquiry: Linking quantitative and qualitative research. *Advances in Nursing Science, 16*(1), 73.

Easton, D. (1965). *A systems analysis of political life.* New York: Wiley.

Eckstein, H. (1975). Case study and theory in political science. In F. I. Greenstein & N. W. Polsby (Eds.), *Strategies of Inquiry* (Vol. 7, pp. 79-137). Reading: Addison-Wesley.

Ehlich, K., & Switalla, B. (1976). Transkriptionssysteme - Eine exemplarische Übersicht. [Transcription systems - An exemplary overview]. *Studium Linguistik, 2*(2), 79–105.

Eitle, D., Turner, R. J., & Eitle, T. M. (2003). The deterrence hypothesis reexamined: sports participation and substance use among young adults. *Journal of Drug Issues, 33*(1), 193-221.

Engelhardt, G. H., & Heinemann, K. (2003). Sport and the welfare policy in Germany. In K. Heinemann (Ed.), *Sport and welfare policies : 6 European case studies* (pp. 139-218). Schorndorf: Hofmann.

Ennis, C. D. (1999). A theoretical framework: The central piece of a research plan. *Journal of Teaching in Physical Education, 18*, 129-140.

Esping-Andersen, G. (1990). *The three worlds of welfare capitalism.* Cambridge: Polity Press.

Esping-Andersen, G. (1999). *Social foundations of postindustrial economies.* Oxford: Oxford University Press.

Esposito, E. (1997). Costruttivismo. [Constructivism]. In C. Baraldi, G. Corsi & E. Esposito (Eds.), *Luhmann in glossario. I concetti fondamentali della teoria dei sistemi sociali* (2nd ed., pp. 77-80). Milano: FrancoAngeli.

European Commission (2007). *White paper on sport.* (9279065521). Office for Official Publications of the European Communities

European Commission. (2010). Sport and physical activity *Special Eurobarometer* (Vol. 334).

Evans, J., Davies, B., & Wright, J. (Eds.). (2004). *Body knowledge and control: Studies in the sociology of physical education and health*. London: Routledge.
Evenson, K. R., Rosamond, W. D., Cai, J., Diez-Roux, A. V., & Brancati, F. L. (2002). Influence of retirement on leisure-time physical activity. *American Journal of Epidemiology, 155*(8), 692-699.
Faltermaier, T. (2005). *Gesundheitspsychologie*. [Psychology of health]. Stuttgart: Kohlhammer.
Ferrari, M., Porro, N., & Russo, P. (2003). Sport and the welfare policy in Italy. In K. Heinemann (Ed.), *Sport and welfare policies : 6 European case studies* (pp. 253-294). Schorndorf: Hofmann.
Fidler, D. P. (2007). Architecture amidst anarchy: Global health's quest for governance. *GLOBAL HEALTH, 1*(1), 1-17. Retrieved from http://ghgj.org/Fidler_Architecture.pdf
Fidler, D. P. (2008). After the revolution: Global health politics in a time of economic crisis and threatening future trends. *GLOBAL HEALTH, 2*(2), 1-21. Retrieved from http://ghgj.org/Fidler_After%20the%20Revolution.pdf
FIFA. (2006). Big count. Retrieved 2011-11-21. Retrieved from http://www.fifa.com/worldfootball/bigcount/
FIFA. (2007). *FIFA Big Count 2006*. Information Services Retrieved from http://www.fifa.com/worldfootball/bigcount/
Flick, U. (2011). *Triangulation: Eine Einführung*. [Triangulation: An Introduction] (3rd ed.). Wiesbaden: VS Verlag für Sozialwissenschaften.
Flick, U. (2012). *Qualitative Sozialforschung: eine Einführung*. [An Introduction to Qualitative Research] (5th ed.). Reinbek bei Hamburg: Rowohlt Taschenbuch Verlag.
Flick, U., von Kardorff, E., & Steinke, I. (Eds.). (2000). *Qualitative Forschung: Ein Handbuch*. [Qualitative research: A handbook]. Reinbek bei Hamburg: Rowohlt-Taschenbuch-Verlag.
Foer, F. (2006). The goals of globalization. *Foreign Policy, 153*, 86–87.
Forbes, D., Forbes, S., Morgan, D. G., Markle-Reid, M., Wood, J., & Culum, I. (2008). Physical activity programs for persons with dementia. *Cochrane Database Syst Rev*(3), CD006489. doi: 10.1002/14651858.CD006489.pub2
Foster, C. (2000). *Guidelines for health-enhancing physical activity promotion programmes*. Tampere: UKK Institute.
Foucault, M. (1998). *The will to knowledge*. (R. Hurley, Trans.). London: Penguin.
Fox, R. (2001). Constructivism examined. *Oxford Review of Education, 27*(1), 23-35.
Franke, A. (1993). Die Unschärfe des Begriffs „Gesundheit "und seine gesundheitspolitischen Auswirkungen. [The ambiguity of the term "health" and its impact on health policies]. In A. Franke & B. Michael (Eds.), *Psychosomatische Gesundheit. Versuch einer Abkehr vom Pathogenese-Konzept* (pp. 15-34). Tübingen: DGVT-Verlag.
Franke, A. (Ed.). (2006). *Modelle von Gesundheit und Krankheit* [Models for health and illness]. Bern: Hans Huber Verlag.
French Ministry for Employment and Welfare, & French Ministry of Health. (2011). *National Programme for Nutrition and Health 2011-2015*. Paris: French Ministry for Employment and Welfare, French Ministry of Health Retrieved from http://www.sante.gouv.fr/IMG/pdf/PNNS_2011-2015.pdf
French Ministry of Health. (2001). *National Programme for Nutrition and Health 2001-2005*. Paris: French Ministry of Health Retrieved from http://www.sante.gouv.fr/IMG/pdf/1n1.pdf
French Ministry of Health, Youth, Sports and Community. (2008). *Find your freedom of movement*. Retrieved from http://www.sante.gouv.fr/IMG/pdf/RapPreventionActivite-2008.pdf
French Ministry of Health and Solidarity. (2005). *Physical Activity and Health. Scientific Arguments, Practical Tracks*. Paris: French Ministry of Health and Solidarity Retrieved from

www.sante.gouv.fr/IMG/pdf/actions42_activite.pdf

French Ministry of Health and Solidarity. (2006). *National Programme for Nutrition and Health 2006-2010.* Paris: French Ministry of Health and Solidarity Retrieved from http://www.sante.gouv.fr/IMG/pdf/plan.pdf

French Ministry of Health, Youth, Sports and Community. (2004). *Health Comes by Moving. The Nutrition Guide for All.* Paris: French Ministry of Health, Youth, Sports and Community Retrieved from www.inpes.sante.fr/CFESBases/catalogue/pdf/715.pdf

Früh, W. (2007). *Inhaltsanalyse: Theorie und Praxis.* [Content analysis: Theory and practice] (6th ed.). Konstanz: UVK Verlagsgesellschaft.

Fuchs, P. (1997). Adressabilität als Grundbegriff der soziologischen Systemtheorie : non sunt multiplicanda entia praeter necessitatem. [Adressability as a basic idea of sociological systems theory: Entities must not be multiplied beyond necessity]. *Soziale Systeme : Zeitschrift für soziologische Theorie, 3*(1), 57-79.

Fuchs, R. (1989). *Sportliche Aktivität bei Jugendlichen. Entwicklungsverlauf und sozial-kognitive Determinanten.* (PhD), Universität Berlin, Köln.

Fuchs, R. (1997). *Psychologie und körperliche Bewegung.* [Psychology and Physical Activity]. Göttingen: Hogrefe.

Fuchs, R. (2003). *Sport, Gesundheit und Public Health.* [Sport, Health and Public Health]. Göttingen: Hogrefe.

Fuchs, R. (Ed.). (2007). *Aufbau eines körperlich-aktiven Lebensstils.* [Development of a physically-active lifestyle]. Göttingen: Hogrefe.

Fuchs, R. (Ed.). (2012). *Seelische Gesundheit und sportliche Aktivität.* [Spiritual health and physical activity]. Göttingen: Hogrefe.

Fuchs, S. (1999). Niklas Luhmann. *Sociological Theory, 17*(1), 117-119.

Fuhse, J. (2005). Persönliche Netzwerke in der Systemtheorie. [Personal networks in systems theory]. *SISS, 1*(1), 1-26.

Fuhse, J. (2009). Die kommunikative Konstruktion von Akteuren in netzwerken. [The communicative construction of actors in networks]. *Soziale Systeme, 15*(2), 288-316.

Gemünden, H. G., & Walter, A. (1998). Der Beziehungspromotor: Schlüsselperson für zwischenbetriebliche Innovationsprozesse. [The relationship promoter: The key person for inter-company innovation processes]. In J. Hauschildt & H. G. Gemünden (Eds.), *Promotoren. Champions der Innovation* (pp. 113-132). Wiesbaden: Gabler.

German Ministry of Health. (2008). *Strategy of the government to promote children's health.* Retrieved from http://www.bundesgesundheitsministerium.de/fileadmin/redaktion/pdf_misc/psychische-Gesundheit_01.pdf

German Ministry of Health. (2010a). *Advisor on health care.* Retrieved from http://www.bundesgesundheitsministerium.de/fileadmin/redaktion/pdf_publikationen/BMG-V-09053-Ratgeber-Zur-Gesundheitlichen-Praevention_201005.pdf

German Ministry of Health. (2010b). *Being active for myself.* Retrieved from https://www.bundesgesundheitsministerium.de/fileadmin/redaktion/pdf_publikationen/BMG-V-07008-Aktiv-sein-fuer-mich_201003.pdf

German Ministry of Health. (2010c). *Mentally fit in old age.* Retrieved from http://www.bundesgesundheitsministerium.de/fileadmin/redaktion/pdf_broschueren/geistig-fit-im-alter.pdf

German Ministry of Health. (2010d). *National health objective.* Retrieved from http://www.bundesgesundheitsministerium.de/fileadmin/redaktion/pdf_publikationen/BMG-G-07014-NationalesGesundheitsziel_Internet.pdf

German Ministry of Health, & German Ministry of Nutrition, Agricultur and Consumer Protection. (2008). *IN FORM* Retrieved from

http://www.bmg.bund.de/fileadmin/redaktion/pdf_pressemeldungen/2008/081202_PM_Nationaler-Aktionsplan-In-Form.pdf
Giles-Corti, B., Timperio, A., Bull, F., & Pikora, T. (2005). Understanding physical activity environmental correlates: increased specificity for ecological models. *Exercise and sport sciences reviews, 33*(4), 175-181.
Göckenjahn, G. (1991). Stichwort: Gesundheit. [Keyword: Health]. In H.-U. Deppe, H. Friedrich & R. Muller (Eds.), *Öffentliche Gesundheit: Public Health* (pp. 15-24). Frankfurt: Campus Verlag.
Gourlan, M. J., Trouilloud, D. O., & Sarrazin, P. G. (2011). Interventions promoting physical activity among obese populations: a meta-analysis considering global effect, long-term maintenance, physical activity indicators and dose characteristics. *Obesity reviews, 12*(7), 633-645. doi: 10.1111/j.1467-789X.2011.00874.x
Grad, F. P. (2002). The preamble of the Constitution of the World Health Organization. *Bulletin of the WHO, 80*, 981-981. Retrieved from http://www.scielosp.org/scielo.php?script=sci_arttext&pid=S0042-96862002001200014&lng=en&nrm=iso
Grupe, O. (1988). Menschen im Sport 2000. Von der Verantwortlichkeit der Person und der Verpflichtung der Organisation. [People in sport 2000. Of the individual's responsibility and the organisation's obligation]. In K. Gieseler, O. Grupe & K. Heinemann (Eds.), *Menschen im Sport 2000. Dokumentation des Kongresses "Menschen im Sport 2000"* (pp. 44-67). Schondorf: Hofmann.
Grupe, O., & Baitsch, H. (1972). *The scientific view of sport: Perspectives, aspects, issues*. Berlin: Springer.
Grupe, O., & Krüger, M. (2007). *Einführung in die Sportpädagogik.* [Introduction to Sport Pedagogy] (3rd ed.). Schorndorf: Hofmann.
Guiraud, T., Nigam, A., Gremeaux, V., Meyer, P., Juneau, M., & Bosquet, L. (2012). High-intensity interval training in cardiac rehabilitation. *Sports Medicine, 42*(7), 587-605.
Güldenpfennig, S. (2004). *Olympische Spiele als Weltkulturerbe: zur Neubegründung der Olympischen Idee.* [Olympic Games as a world cultural heritage: On the refounding of the Olympic idea]: St. Augustin: Academia.
Guttmann, A. (1979). *Vom Ritual zum Rekord : das Wesen des modernen Sports.* [From ritual to record]. Schorndorf: Hofmann.
Haag, H., & Haag, G. (2003). *Dictionary Sport, physical education, sport science: with Indices in German, French, Spanish and a CD with indices in twelve languages.* (1 st ed.). Kiel: Institut für Sport und Sportwissenschaften.
Habermas, J. (1986). *Der philosophische Diskurs der Moderne : zwölf Vorlesungen.* [The philosophical discourse of modernity: Twelve lectures] (3rd ed.). Frankfurt am Main: Suhrkamp.
Habermas, J. (1990). *Die Moderne - ein unvollendetes Projekt : philosophisch-politische Aufsätze 1977 - 1990.* [Modernity - an unfinished project: Philosophical and political essays 1977 - 1990] (1th ed.). Leipzig: Reclam-Verlag.
Habermas, J. (1993). The Entry into Postmodernity: Nietzsche as a turning point. In T. Docherty (Ed.), *Postmodernism: a reader* (pp. 51-61). New York: Columbia University Press.
Hagen, R. (2000). Rational solidarity and functional differentiation. *Acta Sociologica, 43*(1), 27-42.
Hagströmer, M. (2007). *Assessment of health-enhancing physical activity at population level.* (PhD), Karolinska Insitute, Stockholm. Retrieved from http://diss.kib.ki.se/2007/978-91-7357-334-4/thesis.pdf
Hague, R., & Harrop, M. (2007). *Comparative government and politics : an introduction.* (7th ed.). Basingstoke: Palgrave Macmillan.

Hamer, M., & Chida, Y. (2008a). Active commuting and cardiovascular risk: a meta-analytic review. *Prev Med, 46*(1), 9-13. doi: 10.1016/j.ypmed.2007.03.006

Hamer, M., & Chida, Y. (2008b). Walking and primary prevention: a meta-analysis of prospective cohort studies. *British Journal of Sports Medicine, 42*(4), 238-243. doi: 10.1136/bjsm.2007.039974

Hardman, K. (2004). An update on the status of physical education in schools worldwide. In WHO (Ed.), *Technical Report for the World Health Organization*. Geneva.

Hardman, K. (2007). Current situation and prospects for physical education in the European Union. Brussels: European Parliament.

Hardman, K. (2011). Recent international initiatives and developments in physical education and related areas of youth sport, physical activity, health and fitness. *International journal of physical education, 48*(3), 15-31.

Harriss, D. J., Atkinson, G., Batterham, A., George, K., Cable, N. T., Reilly, T., . . . Renehan, A. G. (2009). Lifestyle factors and colorectal cancer risk: a systematic review and meta-analysis of associations with leisure-time physical activity. *Colorectal disease, 11*(7), 689-701. doi: 10.1111/j.1463-1318.2009.01767.x

Hart, C. (1999). *Doing a literature review: Releasing the social science research imagination.* London: Sage Publications Limited.

Hartmann-Tews, I. (1996). *Sport für alle!? Strukturwandel europäischer Sportsysteme im Vergleich: Bundesrepublik Deutschland, Frankreich, Großbritannien.* [Sport for All? The structural change of European sport systems in comparison: The Federal Republic of Germany, France and Great Britain]. Schorndorf: Hofmann.

Haskell, W. L. (2004). General Dose Response Issues Concerning Physical Activity and Health. In P. Oja (Ed.), *Health enhancing physical activity* (Vol. 6, pp. 149-168). Adelaide: Meyer & Meyer Sport.

Hauschildt, J., & Chakrabarti, A. K. (1988). Arbeitsteilung im Innovationsmanagement. Forschungsergebnisse, Kriterien und Modelle. [Division of labor in innovationsmanagement. Empirical results, criteria and models]. *Zeitschrift Führung und Organisation, 57*(6), 378-388.

Health and Human Services. (2008). *2008 physical activity guidelines for Americans.* Washington D.C.: Office of Disease Prevention and Health Promotion

Hein, W., Bartsch, S., & Kohlmorgen, L. (2006). *Interfaces between Global and National Politics in Global Health Governance. A Concept for the Analysis of Multi-level Governance.* Paper presented at the Defining and Shaping the Architecture for Global Health Governance. Current Issues and Future Perspectives, Hamburg.

Heinemann, K. (1986). Zum Problem der Einheit des Sports und des Verlusts seiner Autonomie. [To the problem of the unity of sport and the loss of its autonomy]. In K. Heinemann & B. Hartmut (Eds.), *Die Zukunft des Sports: Materialien zum Kongreß „Menschen im Sport 2000"* (pp. 112-128). Schorndorf: Hofmann.

Heinemann, K. (1998). *Einführung in die Soziologie des Sports.* [Introduction to the sociology of sport] (4th ed.). Schorndorf: Hofmann.

Heinemann, K. (2003). *Sport and welfare policies : 6 European case studies.* Schorndorf: Hofmann.

Heinemann, K. (2007). *Einführung in die Soziologie des Sports.* [Introduction to the Sociology of Sport] (5th ed.). Schorndorf: Hofmann.

Hicks, A., & Kenworthy, L. (2003). Varieties of welfare capitalism. *Socio-economic review, 1*(1), 27-61.

Holsti, O. R. (1969). *Content analysis for the social sciences and humanities.* Reading: Addison-Wesley.

Hootman, J. M., Macera, C. A., Ainsworth, B. E., Addy, C. L., Martin, M., & Blair, S. N. (2002). Epidemiology of musculoskeletal injuries among sedentary and physically active adults. *Medicine and science in sports and exercise, 34*(5), 838.

Howe, K. R. (1988). Against the quantitative-qualitative incompatibility thesis, or, dogmas die hard. *Educational researcher, 17*(8), 10-16.

Howe, T. E., Rochester, L., Neil, F., Skelton, D. A., & Ballinger, C. (2011). Exercise for improving balance in older people. *Cochrane Database of Systematic Reviews*(11), CD004963. doi: 10.1002/14651858.CD004963.pub3

Howe, T. E., Shea, B., Dawson, L. J., Downie, F., Murray, A., Ross, C., . . . Creed, G. (2011). Exercise for preventing and treating osteoporosis in postmenopausal women. *Cochrane Database of Systematic Reviews*(7), CD000333. doi: 10.1002/14651858.CD000333.pub2

Hsieh, H.-F., & Shannon, S. E. (2005). Three approaches to qualitative content analysis. *Qualitative Health Research, 15*(9), 1277-1288. doi: 10.1177/1049732305276687

Huber, E., & Stephens, J. D. (2001). *Development and crisis of the welfare state: parties and policies in global markets.* Chicago: University of Chicago Press.

Hurrelmann, K. (2006). *Gesundheitssoziologie : eine Einführung in sozialwissenschaftliche Theorien von Krankheitsprävention und Gesundheitsförderung.* [Health Sociology: An Introduction to Social Science Theories of Disease Prevention and Health Promotion] (6th ed.). Weinheim: Juventa-Verlag.

Illich, I. (2003). Medical nemesis. *Journal of epidemiology and community health, 57*(12), 919-922. doi: 10.1136/jech.57.12.919

Ingham, A. G., & Donnelly, P. (1997). A sociology of north American sociology of sport: Disunity in unity, 1965 to 1996. *Sociology of Sport Journal, 14*(4), 362-418.

Irwin, A., & Scali, E. (2007). Action on the social determinants of health: A historical perspective. *Global Public Health, 2*(3), 235-256.

Ismail, I., Keating, S. E., Baker, M. K., & Johnson, N. A. (2012). A systematic review and meta-analysis of the effect of aerobic vs. resistance exercise training on visceral fat. *Obesity reviews, 13*(1), 68-91. doi: 10.1111/j.1467-789X.2011.00931.x

Italian Health Ministry. (2012). Piano Sanitario Nazionale. Retrieved 2012.11.12. Retrieved from http://www.salute.gov.it/pubblicazioni/ppRisultatiPSN.jsp

Italian Ministry of Employment, Health and Social Policies. (2009). *Pages of Health.* Milan: Pagine Bianche Retrieved from http://www.salute.gov.it/imgs/volume.pdf

Italian Ministry of Health. (2003). *National Health Plan 2003-2005.* Retrieved from http://www.salute.gov.it/resources/static/psn/documenti/psn_2003-2005.PDF

Italian Ministry of Health. (2007). *Make Gains in Health.* Rome: Italian Ministry of Health Retrieved from http://www.salute.gov.it/imgs/C_17_pubblicazioni_605_allegato.pdf

Italian Ministry of Health. (2009). *Gaining Health in 4 Moves.* Rome: Italian Ministry of Health Retrieved from http://www.salute.gov.it/imgs/C_17_opuscoliPoster_68_allegato.pdf

Italian Ministry of Health. (2011). *National Health Plan 2011-2013.* Rome: Italian Ministry of Health Retrieved from http://www.salute.gov.it/imgs/C_17_pubblicazioni_1454_allegato.pdf

Jadad, A. R., & O'Grady, L. (2008). How should health be defined? *Bmj, 337*, 1363-1364. doi: 10.1136/bmj.a2900

Johnson, R. B., & Onwuegbuzie, A. J. (2004). Mixed Methods Research: A Research Paradigm Whose Time has Come. *Educational researcher, 33*(7), 14-26.

Jordan, A., Wurzel, R., & Zito, A. (2005). The rise of 'new' policy instruments in comparative perspective: has governance eclipsed government? *Political Studies, 53*(3), 477-496.

Karns, M. P., & Mingst, K. A. (2004). *International organizations : the politics and processes of global governance.* Boulder: Lynne Rienner.

Kelley, G. A., Kelley, K. S., & Tran, Z. V. (2005). Walking and Non-HDL-C in adults: a meta-analysis of randomized controlled trials. *Prev Cardiol, 8*(2), 102-107.

Kickbusch, I. (1992). Plädoyer für ein neues Denken über Gesundheit: Muster-Chaos-Kontext. Neue Handlungsansätze in der Gesundheitsförderung. In P. Paulus (Ed.), *Prävention und Gesundheitsförderung-Perspektiven für die psychosoziale Praxis* (pp. 23–33). Köln: GwG-Verlag.

King, A. C. (2001). Interventions to promote physical activity by older adults. *The Journals of Gerontology Series A: Biological Sciences and Medical Sciences, 56*(2), 36-46.

King, A. C., Jeffery, R. W., Fridinger, F., Dusenbury, L., Provence, S., Hedlund, S. A., & Spangler, K. (1995). Environmental and policy approaches to cardiovascular disease prevention through physical activity: issues and opportunities. *Health Education & Behavior, 22*(4), 499-511.

King, A. C., Pruitt, L. A., Phillips, W., Oka, R., Rodenburg, A., & Haskell, W. L. (2000). Comparative effects of two physical activity programs on measured and perceived physical functioning and other health-related quality of life outcomes in older adults. *Journal of Gerontology, 55*(2), 74-83.

Kjær, A. M. (2004). *Governance.* Cambridge: Polity Press.

Klavestrand, J., & Vingård, E. (2009 (Retracted)). The relationship between physical activity and health-related quality of life: a systematic review of current evidence. *Scandinavian Journal of Medicine & Science in Sports, 19*(3), 300-312.

Kneer, G., & Nassehi, A. (1994). *Niklas Luhmanns Theorie sozialer Systeme : eine Einführung.* [Niklas Luhmann's social systems theory: An introduction] (2nd ed.). München: Fink.

Knoll, M. (1997). *Sporttreiben und Gesundheit : eine kritische Analyse vorliegender Befunde.* [Sport and health: A critical analysis of available evidences]. Schorndorf: Hofmann.

Kohl, H. W., III, Craig, C. L., Lambert, E. V., Inoue, S., Alkandari, J. R., Leetongin, G., & Kahlmeier, S. (2012). The Pandemic of Physical Inactivity: Global Action for Public Health. *The Lancet, 380*, 294-305.

Kohn, M. L., Naoi, A., Schoenbach, C., Schooler, C., & Slomczynski, K. M. (1990). Position in the class structure and psychological functioning in the United States, Japan, and Poland. *American Journal of Sociology, 95*(4), 964-1008.

Kolb, M. (1995). Gesundheitsförderung und Sport. [Health promotion and sport]. *Sportwissenschaft, 25*, 335-359.

König, E. (1995). Criticism of doping: The nihilistic side of technological sport and the antiquated view of sport ethics. *International Review for the Sociology of Sport, 30*(3-4), 247-260.

Krause, D. (2005). *Luhmann-Lexikon: eine Einführung in das Gesamtwerk von Niklas Luhmann.* [Luhmann Lexicon: An Introduction to the Complete Works of Niklas Luhmann] (4 th ed.). Stuttgart: Lucius & Lucius.

Kretchmar, R. S. (1994). *Practical philosophy of sport.* Champaign, Ill.: Human Kinetics.

Krippendorff, K. (1969). Models of messages: three prototypes. In G. Gerbner, O. R. Holsti, K. Krippendorff, G. J. Paisly & P. J. Stone (Eds.), *The analysis of communication content: developments in scientific theories and computer techniques* (pp. 69-106). New York: Wiley.

Krippendorff, K. (2004). *Content analysis: An introduction to its methodology.* London: Sage Publications.

Kuchler, B. (2006). Bourdieu und Luhmann über den Wohlfahrtsstaat. Die Autonomie gesellschaftlicher Teilbereiche und die Asymmetrie der Gesellschaftstheorie. *Zeitschrift für Soziologie, 35*(1), 5.

Kujala, U. M., Kaprio, J., Sarna, S., & Koskenvuo, M. (1998). Relationship of leisure-time physical activity and mortality: the Finnish twin cohort. *JAMA, 279*(6), 440-444.

Kussau, J., & Brüsemeister, T. (Eds.). (2007). *Governance, Schule und Politik. Zwischen Antagonismus und Kooperation.* [Governance, politics and school. Between antagonism and cooperation]. Wiesbaden: VS Verlag für Sozialwissenschaften.

Laitin, D. D. (2002). *Comparative politics: The state of the subdiscipline.* Paper presented at the Annual Meeting of the American Political Science Association, Washington D.C.

Lamnek, S. (1989). *Qualitative Sozialforschung. Methodologie.* [Qualitative Research. Methodology] (Vol. 1). München: Psychologie-Verlag-Union.

Lamnek, S. (1995). *Qualitative Sozialforschung. Methoden und Techniken* [Qualitative Research. Methods and Techniques] (2nd ed. Vol. 2). München: Psychologie Verlags Union.

Lamnek, S. (2010). *Qualitative Sozialforschung.* [Qualitative Research] (5th ed.). Weinheim: Beltz.

Lampman, R. J. (1984). *Social welfare spending: accounting for changes from 1950 to 1978.* Orlando: Academic Press.

Landman, T. (2002). Comparative politics and human rights. *Human Rights Quarterly, 24*(4), 890-923.

Landman, T. (2003). *Issues and methods in comparative politics: An introduction.* (2nd ed.). London: Routledge.

Lange, S. (2004). *Governance und gesellschaftliche Integration.* (1 ed.). Wiesbaden: VS-Verlag.

Latner, J. D., & Stunkard, A. J. (2012). Getting worse: The stigmatization of obese children. *Obesity Research, 11*(3), 452-456.

Latner, J. D., Stunkard, A. J., & Wilson, G. T. (2012). Stigmatized students: Age, sex, and ethnicity effects in the stigmatization of obesity. *Obesity Research, 13*(7), 1226-1231.

Lee, C. D., Folsom, A. R., & Blair, S. N. (2003). Physical activity and stroke risk: A meta-analysis. *Stroke, 34*(10), 2475-2481. doi: 10.1161/01.str.0000091843.02517.9d

Lee, D. (2000). The society of society: The grand finale of Niklas Luhmann. *Sociological Theory, 18*(2), 320-330.

Lee, K. (2003). *Globalization and health : An introduction.* Basingstoke: Palgrave Macmillan.

Lessenich, S. (1995). *Wohlfahrtsstaat, Arbeitsmarkt und Sozialpolitik in Spanien.* [Welfare state, labor market and social policies in Spain]. Opladen: Leske + Budrich.

Leung, D. P., Chan, C. K., Tsang, H. W., Tsang, W. W., & Jones, A. Y. (2011). Tai chi as an intervention to improve balance and reduce falls in older adults: A systematic and meta-analytical review. *Altern Ther Health Med, 17*(1), 40-48.

Lewin, K. (1952). *Field theory in social science.* London: Tavistock.

Lijphart, A. (1971). Comparative politics and the comparative method. *The American Political Science Review, 65*(3), 682-693.

Lisch, R., & Kriz, J. (1978). *Grundlagen und Modelle der Inhaltsanalyse : Bestandsaufnahme und Kritik.* [Foundations and models of content analysis: Review of the situation and criticism]. Reinbek bei Hamburg: Rowohlt.

Lisha, N. E., & Sussman, S. (2010). Relationship of high school and college sports participation with alcohol, tobacco, and illicit drug use: A review. *Addictive behaviors, 35*(5), 399-407.

Loew, L., Brosseau, L., Wells, G. A., Tugwell, P., Kenny, G. P., Reid, R., . . . Coyle, D. (2012). Ottawa panel evidence-based clinical practice guidelines for aerobic walking programs in the management of osteoarthritis. *Arch Phys Med Rehabil, 93*(7), 1269-1285. doi: 10.1016/j.apmr.2012.01.024

Lowe, W. (2003). *The statistics of text: New methods for content analysis.* Paper presented at the Midwest Political Science Association, Mannheim.

Loy, J. W. (1968). The nature of sport: A definitional effort. *Quest, 10*, 1-15.

Luhmann, N. (1970). *Soziologische Aufklärung: Aufsätze zur Theorie sozialer Systeme.* [Sociological Enlightenment: Essays on the theory of social systems] (1th ed. Vol. 1). Opladen: Westdeutscher Verlag.

Luhmann, N. (1971). Die Weltgesellschaft. [The world society]. *Archiv für Rechts- und Sozialphilosophie, 57*(1), 1-35.

Luhmann, N. (1975). *Soziologische Aufklärung: Aufsätze zur Theorie der Gesellschaft.* [Sociological enlightenment: Essays on the theory of society] (1th ed. Vol. 2). Opladen: Westdeutscher Verlag.

Luhmann, N. (1977). Differentiation of Society. *The Canadian Journal of Sociology, 2*(1), 29-53.

Luhmann, N. (1981a). *Politische Theorie im Wohlfahrtsstaat.* [Political theory in the welfare state] (1th ed.). München: Olzog.

Luhmann, N. (1981b). *Soziologische Aufklärung : Soziales System, Gesellschaft, Organisation.* [Sociological enlightenment: Social system, society, organization]. Opladen: Westdeutscher Verlag.

Luhmann, N. (1982a). *The differentiation of society.* (S. Holmes & C. Larmore, Trans.). New York: Columbia University Press.

Luhmann, N. (1982b). The world society as a social system. *International Journal of General Systems, 8*(3), 131 - 138.

Luhmann, N. (1983a). Anspruchsinflation im Krankheitssystem. Eine Stellungnahme aus gesellschaftstheoretischer Sicht. [Pretence's Inflation of the Medicine System. A Statement in the Perspective of Social Theory]. In P. Herder-Dorneich & A. Schuller (Eds.), *Die Anspruchsspirale: Schicksal oder Systemdefekt?* (Vol. Köllner Kolloquium, pp. 28-49). Stuttgart: Kohlhammer.

Luhmann, N. (1983b). Medizin und Gesellschaftstheorie. [Medicine and Social Theory]. *Medizin, Mensch, Gesellschaft, 8*, 168-175.

Luhmann, N. (1984). *Soziale Systeme: Grundriß einer allgemeinen Theorie.* [Social Systems: Outline of a General Theory] (1st ed.). Frankfurt am Main: Suhrkamp.

Luhmann, N. (1985a). Kultur als historischer Begriff. [Culture as a historical term]. In N. Luhmann (Ed.), *Gesellschaftsstruktur und Semantik: Studien zur Wissenssoziologie der modernen Gesellschaft* (Vol. 4, pp. 31-54). Frankfurt am Main: Suhrkamp Verlag.

Luhmann, N. (1985b). *Soziale Systeme: Grundriß einer allgemeinen Theorie.* [Social Systems: Outline of a General Theory] (2nd ed.). Frankfurt am Main: Suhrkamp.

Luhmann, N. (1986). *Ökologische Kommunikation : kann die moderne Gesellschaft sich auf ökologische Gefährdungen einstellen?* [Ecological communication: Can the modern society stop environmental hazards?]. Opladen: Westdeutscher Verlag.

Luhmann, N. (1987). *Archimedes und wir : Interviews.* Berlin: Merve.

Luhmann, N. (1988). Law as a social system. *Northwestern University Law Review, 83*, 136-150.

Luhmann, N. (1990a). *Die Wissenschaft der Gesellschaft.* [The science of society] (1st ed.). Frankfurt am Main: Suhrkamp.

Luhmann, N. (1990b). *Political Theory in the Welfare State.* [Politische Theorie im Wohlfahrtsstaat]. Berlin: de Gruyter.

Luhmann, N. (1990c). *Sistemi sociali: fondamenti di una teoria generale.* [Social systems: Outline of a general theory] (A. Febbrajo & R. Schmidt, Trans.). Bologna: Il Mulino.

Luhmann, N. (1990d). *Soziologische Aufklärung: Konstruktivistische Perspektiven.* [Sociological Enlightenment: Constructivist Perspectives] (1th ed. Vol. 5). Opladen: Westdeutscher Verlag.

Luhmann, N. (1992). What is Communication? *Communication Theory, 2*(3), 251-259. doi: 10.1111/j.1468-2885.1992.tb00042.x

Luhmann, N. (1993). Deconstruction as Second-Order Observing. *New Literary History, 24*(4), 763-782.

Luhmann, N. (1994a). *Die Wirtschaft der Gesellschaft.* [The economy of society] (1th ed.). Frankfurt am Main: Suhrkamp.

Luhmann, N. (1994b). *Soziale Systeme : Grundriß einer allgemeinen Theorie.* [Social systems: Outline of a general theory] (5th ed.). Frankfurt am Main: Suhrkamp.

Luhmann, N. (1995a). The paradoxy of observing systems. *Cultural Critique*(31), 37-55.

Luhmann, N. (1995b). *Social Systems.* (J. J. Bednarz & D. Baecker, Trans.). Stanford: Stanford University Press.

Luhmann, N. (1995c). *Soziologische Aufklärung: Soziologie und der Mensch.* [Sociological enlightenment: Sociology and human being] (1th ed. Vol. 6). Wiesbaden: VS Verlag.

Luhmann, N. (1995d). Why does society describe itself as postmodern? *Cultural Critique*(30), 171-186.

Luhmann, N. (1997a). *Die Gesellschaft der Gesellschaft.* [Society as a Social System]. Frankfurt am Main: Suhrkamp.

Luhmann, N. (1997b). Globalization or world society: How to conceive of modern society? *International Review of Sociology, 7*, 67-80.

Luhmann, N. (1999). *Funktionen und Folgen formaler Organisation.* [Functions and consequences of formal organization] (5th ed.). Berlin: Duncker & Humblot.

Luhmann, N. (2001). *Aufsätze und Reden.* [Essays and speeches]. Stuttgart: Reclam.

Luhmann, N. (2002a). *Die Politik der Gesellschaft.* [The politics of society] (1st ed.). Frankfurt am Main: Suhrkamp.

Luhmann, N. (2002b). *Theories of distinction: Redescribing the descriptions of modernity.* (J. O'Neil, Trans.). Stanford: Stanford University Press.

Luhmann, N. (2003). *Social systems.* [Soziale Systeme] (J. J. Bednarz & D. Baecker, Trans. 2 ed.). Stanford, California: Stanford University Press.

Luhmann, N. (2006). *Organisation und Entscheidung.* [Organisation and decision] (2nd ed.). Wiesbaden: VS Verlag für Sozialwiss.

Luhmann, N. (2008a). The autopoiesis of social systems. *Journal of sociocybernetics, 6*(2), 84-95.

Luhmann, N. (2008b). *Einführung in die Systemtheorie.* [Introduction to the systems theory] (4th ed.). Heidelberg: Carl-Auer-Verlag.

Luhmann, N. (2009). *Soziologische Aufklärung: Konstruktivistische Perspektiven.* [Sociological enlightenment: Constructivist perspectives] (4th ed. Vol. 5). Wiesbaden: VS Verlag für Sozialwissenschaften.

Lupton, D. (1995). *The imperative of health: Public health and the regulated body.* London: Sage.

Lupton, D. (1999). *Risk.* London: Routledge.

Lüschen, G. (1976). Zur Strukturanalyse des Sports. [On the structure analysis of sport]. In G. Luschen & K. Weis (Eds.), *Die Soziologie des Sports* (pp. 52-69). Darmstadt: Luchterhand.

Lüschen, G., Abel, T., Cockerham, W., & Kunz, G. (1993). Kausalbeziehungen und sozio- kulturelle Kontexte zwischen Sport und Gesundheit. [Causal relationships and socio-cultural contexts between sport and health]. *Sportwissenschaft, 23*, 175-186.

Lüschen, G., Cockerham, W., & Kunz, G. (1996). The sociocultural context of sport and health: Problems of causal relations and structural interdependence. *Sociology of Sport Journal, 13*(2), 197-213.

Macionis, J. J. (2012). *Sociology.* Boston: Pearson.

Maguire, J. (1994). Sport, identity, politics and globalization: Diminishing contrasts and increasing varieties. *Sociology of Sport Journal, 11*(4), 398-427.

Mair, P. (1998). Comparative Politics. An Overview. In R. E. Goodin & H. D. Klingemann (Eds.), *A new handbook of political science* (pp. 309-372). Oxford: Oxford University Press.

Manzoni, A. (1985). *I Promessi Sposi.* Milano: Arnoldo Mondadori.

Marshall, A. L., Smith, B. J., Bauman, A., & Kaur, S. (2005). Reliability and validity of a brief physical activity assessment for use by family doctors. *British Journal of Sports Medicine, 39*(5), 294-297.

Marshall, C., & Rossman, G. B. (2010). *Designing qualitative research.* (5 ed.). Thousand Oaks, California: Sage Publications.

Martin, B. W., Beeler, I., Szucs, T., Smala, A. M., Brügger, O., Casparis, C., . . . Marti, B. (2001). Volkswirtschaftlicher Nutzen der Gesundheitseffekte der körperlichen Aktivität: erste Schätzungen für die Schweiz. [Economic benefits of the health effects of physical activity: first estimations for Switzerland]. *Schweizerische Zeitschrift für Sportmedizin und Sporttraumatologie, 49*(2), 84-86.

Martyn-St James, M., & Carroll, S. (2008). Meta-analysis of walking for preservation of bone mineral density in postmenopausal women. *Bone, 43*(3), 521-531. doi: 10.1016/j.bone.2008.05.012

Marzolini, S., Oh, P. I., & Brooks, D. (2012). Effect of combined aerobic and resistance training versus aerobic training alone in individuals with coronary artery disease: a meta-analysis. *Eur J Prev Cardiol, 19*(1), 81-94. doi: 10.1177/1741826710393197

Maturana, H. R. (2000). *Biologie der Realität.* [Biology of reality] (1th ed.). Frankfurt am Main: Suhrkamp.

Maturana, H. R., & Varela, F. J. (1980). *Autopoiesis and Cognition: The Realization of the Living.* Boston: Riedel.

Maturana, H. R., & Varela, F. J. (1987). *The Tree of Knowledge: The Biological Roots of Human Understanding.* Boston, MA: New Science Library/Shambhala Publications.

Maturana, H. R., & Varela, F. J. (1992). *L'albero della conoscenza.* [The Tree of Knowledge] (M. Ceruti, Trans.). Milano: Garzanti.

Mayer, J. (2009). *Verletzungsmanagement im Spitzensport : eine systemtheoretisch-konstruktivistische Analyse mit Fallstudien aus den Sportarten Leichtathletik und Handball.* (PhD), Eberhard Karls Universität Tübingen, Tübingen. Retrieved from http://nbn-resolving.de/urn:nbn:de:bsz:21-opus-42946 Bibliothekskatalog Tübingen database.

Mayntz, R. (1988). Funktionelle Teilsysteme in der Theorie sozialer Differenzierung. [Functional subsystems in the theory of social differentiation]. In R. Mayntz, B. Rosewitz, U. Schimank & R. Stichweh (Eds.), *Differenzierung und Verselbständigung. Zur Entwicklung gesellschaftlicher Teilsysteme* (pp. 11-44). Frankfut and New York: Campus.

Mayntz, R. (2003). New challenges to governance theory. In H. P. Bang (Ed.), *Governance as social and political communication* (pp. 27-40). Manchester: Manchester University Press.

Mayntz, R., Holm, K., & Hübner, P. (1974). *Einführung in die Methoden der empirischen Soziologie.* [Introduction to the methods of empirical sociology] (4th ed.). Opladen: Westdeutscher Verlag.

Mayntz, R., & Rosewitz, B. (1988). Ausdifferenzierung und Strukturwandel des deutschen Gesundheitssystems. [Differentiation and developement of the structure of the German health system]. In R. Mayntz, B. Rosewitz, U. Schimank & R. Stichweh (Eds.), *Differenzierung und Verselbständigung. Zur Entwicklung gesellschaftlicher Teilsysteme* (pp. 117-179). Frankfurt am Main: Campus-Verlag.

Mayntz, R., Rosewitz, B., Schimank, U., & Stichweh, R. (Eds.). (1988). *Differenzierung und Verselbständigung. Zur Entwicklung gesellschaftlicher Teilsysteme.* [Differentiation and independence. On the development of social sub-systems]. (Vol. 1). Frankfurt: Campus Verlag.

Mayntz, R., & Scharpf, F. W. (1995). *Gesellschaftliche Selbstregelung und politische Steuerung.* [Social self-steering and political steering]. Frankfurt: Campus Verlag.

Mayntz, R., & Streeck, W. (2003). *Die Reformierbarkeit der Demokratie: Innovationen und Blockaden.* [The reformability of democracy: Innovations and blockades] (Vol. 45). Frankfurt: Campus Verlag.

Mayring, P. (1995). Qualitative Inhaltsanalyse. [Qualitative content analysis]. In U. Flick (Ed.), *Handbuch qualitative Sozialforschung : Grundlagen, Konzepte, Methoden und Anwendungen* (2nd ed., pp. 209-213). Weinheim: Beltz, Psychologie-Verlag-Union.

Mayring, P. (2000). Qualitative Content Analysis. *Qualitative Social Research, 1*(2). Retrieved from http://nbn-resolving.de/urn:nbn:de:0114-fqs0002204

Mayring, P. (2001). Combination and Integration of Qualitative and Quantitative Analysis. *Forum: Qualitative Social Research, 2*(1). Retrieved from http://www.qualitative-research.net/index.php/fqs/article/viewArticle/967/2110

Mayring, P. (2002). *Einführung in die qualitative Sozialforschung : eine Anleitung zu qualitativem Denken.* [Introduction to Qualitative Research: a Guide to Qualitative Thinking] (5th ed.). Weinheim: Beltz.

Mayring, P. (2003). *Qualitative Inhaltsanalyse: Grundlagen und Techniken.* [Qualitative Content Analysis: Principles and Techniques] (8th ed.). Weinheim: Beltz.

Mayring, P. (Ed.). (2007). *Mixed Methodology in Psychological Research.* Rotterdam: Sense Publishers.

Mayring, P., & Brunner, E. (2009). Qualitative inhaltsanalyse. [Qualitative content analysis]. In R. Buber & H. H. Holzmüller (Eds.), *Qualitative Marktforschung: Konzepte – Methoden – Analysen* (2 ed., pp. 669-680). Wiesbaden: Gabler.

Mays, N., & Pope, C. (1995). Qualitative research: Rigour and qualitative research. *British Medical Journal, 311*(6997), 109-112.

McAuley, E., Konopack, J. F., Motl, R. W., Morris, K. S., Doerksen, S. E., & Rosengren, K. R. (2006). Physical activity and quality of life in older adults: Influence of health status and self-efficacy. *Annals of Behavioral Medicine, 31*(1), 99-103.

McDermott, L. (2007). A governmental analysis of children 'at risk' in a world of physical inactivity and obesity epidemics. *Sociology of Sport Journal, 24*, 302-324.

McDonald, M. G., & Birrell, S. (1999). Reading sport critically: A methodology for interrogating power. *Sociology of Sport Journal, 16*(4), 283-300.

McPherson, B. D., Curtis, J. E., & Loy, J. W. (1989). *The Social Significance of Sport: An Introduction to the Sociology of Sport.* (1st ed.). Champaign, Ill.: Human Kinetics Books.

Mead, G. E., Morley, W., Campbell, P., Greig, C. A., McMurdo, M., & Lawlor, D. A. (2009). Exercise for depression. *Cochrane Database of Systematic Reviews*(3). doi: 10.1002/14651858.CD004366.pub4

Michelini, E. (2011). Cooperation in the Promotion of Physical Activity. The Function of the WHO and the Role of Sports in the Global Strategy on Diet, Physical Activity and Health. In J. Schmid, K. Amos, J. Schrader & A. Thiel (Eds.), *Welten der Bildung? Vergleichende Analysen von Bildungspolitik und Bildungssystemen* (pp. 299-327). Baden-Baden: Nomos.

Michelini, E., & Thiel, A. (2013). The Acceptance of "Sport" in the Communication of the Health System. A Sociological Analysis. *European Journal for Sport and Society, 10*(4).

Minns Lowe, C. J., Barker, K. L., Dewey, M. E., & Sackley, C. M. (2009). Effectiveness of physiotherapy exercise following hip arthroplasty for osteoarthritis: A systematic review of clinical trials. *BMC Musculoskelet Disord, 10*, 98. doi: 10.1186/1471-2474-10-98

Mishra, S. I., Scherer, R. W., Snyder, C., Geigle, P. M., Berlanstein, D. R., & Topaloglu, O. (2012a). Can exercise interventions enhance health-related quality of life among people with cancer undergoing active treatment? *Cochrane Database of Systematic Reviews*(8). doi: 10.1002/14651858.CD008465.pub2

Mishra, S. I., Scherer, R. W., Snyder, C., Geigle, P. M., Berlanstein, D. R., & Topaloglu, O. (2012b). Exercise interventions on health-related quality of life for people with cancer during active treatment. *Cochrane Database of Systematic Reviews*(8), CD008465. doi: 10.1002/14651858.CD008465.pub2

Moeller, H. G. (2006). *Luhmann Explained: From Souls to Systems*. Chicago: Open Court.

Morey, M. C., Pieper, C. F., & Cornoni-Huntley, J. (1998). Physical fitness and functional limitations in community-dwelling older adults. *Medicine & Science in Sports & Exercise, 30*(5), 715-723.

Morgan, D. L. (1998). Practical strategies for combining qualitative and quantitative methods: Applications to health research. *Qualitative Health Research, 8*(3), 362-376.

Morison, S. E. (1951). Faith of a historian. *The American Historical Review, 56*(2), 261-275. doi: 10.2307/1840442

Morris, J. N., & Crawford, M. D. (1958). Coronary Heart Disease and Physical Activity of Work. *British Medical Journal, 2*, 1485-1496.

Morris, J. N., Everitt, M. G., Pollard, R., & Chave, S. P. W. (1980). Vigorous exercise in leisure-time: Protection against coronary heart disease. *The Lancet, 6*, 1207-1210.

Moseley, A. M., Stark, A., Cameron, I. D., & Pollock, A. (2005). Treadmill training and body weight support for walking after stroke. *Cochrane Database of Systematic Reviews*(4), CD002840. doi: 10.1002/14651858.CD002840.pub2

Müller, H., & Larson, P. (1994). Luhmann's systems theory as a theory of modernity. *New German Critique*(61), 39-54.

Murphy, M. H., Nevill, A. M., Murtagh, E. M., & Holder, R. L. (2007). The effect of walking on fitness, fatness and resting blood pressure: a meta-analysis of randomised, controlled trials. *Prev Med, 44*(5), 377-385. doi: 10.1016/j.ypmed.2006.12.008

Naidoo, J., & Wills, J. (2003). *Lehrbuch der Gesundheitsförderung*. [Textbook of health promotion]. Gamburg: Verlag für Gesundheitsförderung.

Netz, Y., Wu, M. J., Becker, B. J., & Tenenbaum, G. (2005). Physical activity and psychological well-being in advanced age: a meta-analysis of intervention studies. *Psychology and Aging, 20*(2), 272-284. doi: 10.1037/0882-7974.20.2.272

Nixon, H. L. (1994). Coaches' views of risk, pain, and injury in sport, with special reference to gender differences. *Sociology of Sport Journal, 11*(1), 79-87.

Offe, C. (2009). Governance: An "empty signifier"? *Constellations, 16*(4), 550-562. doi: 10.1111/j.1467-8675.2009.00570.x

Oja, P. (2004). Frequency, Duration Intensity and Total Volume of Physical Activity as Determinants of Health Outcomes. In P. Oja (Ed.), *Health enhancing physical activity* (Vol. 6, pp. 169-208). Adelaide: Meyer & Meyer Sport.

Opper, E., Woll, A., & Minnebeck, P. (1993). Sport und Bewegung in einem komplexen Gesundheitskonzept. [Sport and exercise in a complex health concept]. *Prävention, 2*, 52-57.

Osborne, T. (1997). Of health and statecraft. In A. Petersen & R. Bunton (Eds.), *Foucault, health and medicine* (pp. 173-188). London: Routledge.

Østerberg, D. (2000). Luhmann's general sociology. *Acta Sociologica, 43*(1), 15-25.

Owen, N., Humpel, N., Leslie, E., Bauman, A., & Sallis, J. F. (2004). Understanding environmental influences on walking; Review and research agenda. *Am J Prev Med, 27*(1), 67-76. doi: 10.1016/j.amepre.2004.03.006

Oxford Dictionaries. (2012). Health. Retrieved 2012-10-18. Retrieved from http://oxforddictionaries.com/definition/english/health?q=health

Øyen, E. (1990). *Comparative methodology: Theory and practice in international social research*. London: Sage.

Paffenbarger Jr, R. S., Hyde, R., Wing, A. L., & Hsieh, C.-c. (1986). Physical activity, all-cause mortality, and longevity of college alumni. *New England Journal of Medicine, 314*(10), 605-613.

Paffenbarger, R. S., & Hale, W. E. (1975). Work activity and coronary heart disease. *New England Journal of Medicine, 292*, 545-550.

Painter, P., Krasnoff, J., Paul, S. M., & Ascher, N. L. (2003). Physical activity and health-related quality of life in liver transplant recipients. *Liver transplantation, 7*(3), 213-219.

Palm, J. (1991). *Sport for all: Approaches from utopia to reality.* (1th ed.). Schorndorf: Hofmann.

Pang, M. Y., Eng, J. J., Dawson, A. S., & Gylfadottir, S. (2006). The use of aerobic exercise training in improving aerobic capacity in individuals with stroke: a meta-analysis. *Clin Rehabil, 20*(2), 97-111.

Parsons, T. (1939). The Professions and Social Structure. *Social Forces, 17*(4), 457-467.

Parsons, T. (1949). *The Structure of Social Action. A study in social theory with special reference to a group of recent European writers.* (2nd ed.). New York: Free Press.

Parsons, T. (1963). Social change and medical organization in the United States : A sociological perspective. *The ANNALS of the American Academy of Political and Social Science, 346*(1), 21-33. doi: 10.1177/000271626334600103

Parsons, T. (1989). *Sozialstruktur und Persönlichkeit.* [Social structure and personality]. Frankfurt: Europäische Verlagsanst.

Parsons, T. (2000). *The Social System.* London: Routledge & Kegan Paul.

Pate, R. R., Pratt, M., Blair, S. N., Haskell, W. L., Macera, C. A., Bouchard, C., . . . King, A. C. (1995). Physical activity and public health: A recommendation from the Centers for Disease Control and Prevention and the American College of Sports Medicine. *Journal of the American Medical Association, 273*(5), 402-407.

Peabody, J. W. (1996). Economic reform and health sector policy: Lessons from structural adjustment programs. *Social Science & Medicine, 43*(5), 823-835.

Pelikan, J. M. (1993). *Gesundheitsförderung durch Organisationsentwicklung : Konzepte, Strategien und Projekte für Betriebe, Krankenhäuser und Schulen.* [Health promotion through organizational development: Concepts, strategies and projects for businesses, hospitals and schools]. Weinheim: Juventa Verlag.

Pelikan, J. M. (2007). Understanding differentiation of health in late modernity by use of sociological systems theory. In D. V. McQueen, I. Kickbusch, L. Potvin, J. M. Pelikan, L. Balbo & T. Abel (Eds.), *The role of theory in health promotion* (pp. 74-102). New York: Springer.

Pelikan, J. M. (2009). Ausdifferenzierung von spezifischen Funktionssystemen für Krankenbehandlung und Gesundheitsförderung oder: Leben wir in der „Gesundheitsgesellschaft"? [Differentiation of specific function systems for medical treatment and health promotion or: Are we living in a "health society"?]. *Österreichische Zeitschrift für Soziologie, 34*(2), 28-47. doi: 10.1007/s11614-009-0011-x

Pelikan, J. M., & Halbmayer, E. (1999). Gesundheitswissenschaftliche Grundlagen zur Strategie des Gesundheitsfördernden Krankenhauses. [Health scientific bases for the strategy of Health Promoting Hospital]. In J. M. Pelikan & S. Wolff (Eds.), *Das gesundheitsfördernde Krankenhaus. Konzepte und Beispiele zur Entwicklung einer lernenden Organisation.* (pp. 13-36). Weinheim, München: Juventa.

Pelikan, J. M., Krajic, K., & Dietscher, C. (2001). The health promoting hospital (HPH): Concept and development. *Patient Education and Counseling, 45*(4), 239-243.

Pflanz, M. (1973). *Allgemeine Epidemiologie : Aufgaben, Technik, Methoden.* [General epidemiology: Tasks, technology, methods]. Stuttgart: Thieme.

Phillips, D. C. (1995). The good, the bad, and the ugly: The many faces of constructivism. *Educational researcher, 24*(7), 5-12.

Pietilä, A. M., Hentinen, M., & Myhrman, A. (1995). The health behaviour of northern Finnish men in adolescence and adulthood. *International journal of nursing studies, 32*(3), 325-338.

Plato. (1892a). Phaedrus (B. Jowett, Trans.). In B. Jowett (Ed.), *The Dialogues of Plato* (Vol. 1, pp. 391-490). Oxford: Oxford University Press.

Plato. (1892b). The Republic. (B. Jowett, Trans.). In B. Jowett (Ed.), *The Dialogues of Plato* (3 ed., Vol. 3). Oxford: Oxford University Press.

Plowman, S. A., & Smith, D. L. (2007). *Exercise Physiology for Health, Fitness, and Performance.* Philadelphia: Lippincott Williams & Wilkins.

Polidoulis, I., Beyene, J., & Cheung, A. M. (2012). The effect of exercise on pQCT parameters of bone structure and strength in postmenopausal women. A systematic review and meta-analysis of randomized controlled trials. *Osteoporos International, 23*(1), 39-51. doi: 10.1007/s00198-011-1734-7

Pöllmann, G. (2005). *Kooperativer Staat und Parteiendemokratie.* [Cooperative state and party's democracy] (Vol. 5). Berlin: Galda & Wilch.

Porro, N., Bizzaglia, G., & Conti, D. (2003). The sports system and sports organisations in Italy. In K. Heinemann & M. Friederici (Eds.), *Sport Clubs in Various European Countries* (Vol. 33, pp. 33-70). Berlin: Springer.

Porter, D. (1999). *Health, civilization and the state : A history of public health from ancient to modern times.* London: Routledge.

Powell, K. E., & Blair, S. N. (1994). The public health burdens of sedentary living habits: Theoretical but realistic estimates. *Medicine & Science in Sports & Exercise, 26*(7), 851.

Powell, K. E., Thompson, P. D., Caspersen, C. J., & Kendrick, J. S. (1987). Physical activity and the incidence of coronary heart disease. *Annual Review of Public Health, 8*, 253 - 287.

Preece, S. J., Goulermas, J. Y., Kenney, L. P. J., Howard, D., Meijer, K., & Crompton, R. (2009). Activity identification using body-mounted sensors - A review of classification techniques. *Physiological measurement, 30*, 1-33.

President's Council on Physical Fitness and Sports. (1965). *Exercise programs for adults.* Washington DC: US Government Printing Office.

President of the Italian Republic. (1992). *Legislative decree no. 502.* Rome: Gazzetta Ufficiale Retrieved from http://www.nursesarea.it/normativa/dec502/dlgs502.htm#art1

Pronger, B. (2002). *Body fascism: Salvation in the technology of physical fitness.* Toronto: University of Toronto Press.

Przeworski, A., & Teune, H. (1970). *The logic of comparative social inquiry.* New York: Wiley-Interscience.

Public Health Service. US office of the Surgeon General, & President's Council on Physical Fitness and Sports. (1998). *Physical activity and health: A report of the Surgeon General.* Toronto: Jones & Bartlett Publishers canada.

Puhl, R., & Brownell, K. D. (2012). Bias, discrimination, and obesity. *Obesity Research, 9*(12), 788-805.

Ragin, C. (1994). A quantitative comparative analysis of pension systems. In T. Janoski & A. M. Hicks (Eds.), *The comparative political economy of the welfare state* (pp. 320-345). New York: Cambridge University Press.

Rand, D., Miller, W. C., Yiu, J., & Eng, J. J. (2011). Interventions for addressing low balance confidence in older adults: a systematic review and meta-analysis. *Age Ageing, 40*(3), 297-306. doi: 10.1093/ageing/afr037

Reese-Schäfer, W. (1992). *Luhmann zur Einführung.* [Introduction to Niklas Luhmann]. Hamburg: Junius-Verlag.

Rejeski, W. J., Brawley, L. R., & Shumaker, S. A. (1996). Physical activity and health-related quality of life. *Exercise and sport sciences reviews, 24*(1), 71-108.

Rejeski, W. J., & Mihalko, S. L. (2001). Physical activity and quality of life in older adults. *The Journals of Gerontology Series A: Biological Sciences and Medical Sciences, 56*(suppl 2), 23-35.

Ricci, J. (2009). Global health governance and the state. *Global health governance, 1*(8), 85-89.

Rigauer, B. (1982). *Sportsoziologie : Grundlagen, Methoden, Analysen.* [Sociology of Sport: Principles, Methods, Analysis]. Reinbek bei Hamburg: Rowohlt.

Ritsert, J. (1972). *Inhaltsanalyse und Ideologiekritik : ein Versuch über kritische Sozialforschung.* [Content analysis and critique of ideology: An essay on critical social research]. Frankfurt am Main: Athenäum-Verlag.

Robertson, R. (1992). *Globalization : social theory and global culture.* (1 ed.). London: Sage.

Rose, N. (1999). *Powers of freedom: Reframing political thought.* Cambridge: Cambridge University Press.

Rosen, G. (1993). *A history of public health.* (Expanded ed.). Baltimore: Johns Hopkins University Press.

Rosenau, J. N. (1998). *Governance without government: Order and change in world politics.* (Repr. ed.). Cambridge: Cambridge University Press.

Ruger, J. P. (2005). Global tobacco control: an integrated approach to global health policy. *Development, 48*(2), 65-69. Retrieved from http://www.palgrave-journals.com/development/journal/v48/n2/abs/1100135a.html

Ruger, J. P., & Yach, D. (2005). Global functions at the World Health Organization. *British Medical Journal, 330*, 1099-1100. Retrieved from http://www.ncbi.nlm.nih.gov/pmc/articles/PMC557878/pdf/bmj33001099.pdf

Ruger, J. P., & Yach, D. (2008). The global role of the World Health Organization. *GLOBAL HEALTH, 2*(2), 1-11. Retrieved from http://www.ghgj.org/Ruger%20and%20Yach_The%20Global%20Role%20of%20WHO.pdf

Rutherford, G. W., & Schroeder, T. J. (1998). *Sports-related injuries to persons 65 years of age and older.* (Vol. 4). Washington, DC: US Consumer Products Safety Commission.

Rütten, A. (1993). Sport, Lebensstil und Gesundheitsförderung. [Sport, lifestyle and health promotion]. *Sportwissenschaft, 23*(4), 345-371.

Rütten, A., Abel, T., Kannas, L., von Lengerke, T., Lüschen, G., Diaz, J. A. R., . . . Bernasconi, P. Z. (2001). Gesundheitsförderung durch sport und körperliche aktivität: politik, verhalten und infrastrukturen im europäischen vergleich. *Sozial-und Präventivmedizin, 46*(1), 29-40.

Rütten, A., Abel, T., Kannas, L., Von Lengerke, T., Lüschen, G., Diaz, J. A. R., . . . Van der Zee, J. (2001). Self reported physical activity, public health, and perceived environment: Results from a comparative european study. *Journal of epidemiology and community health, 55*(2), 139-146.

Rütten, A., & Abu-Omar, K. (2004a). Perceptions of environmental opportunities for physical activity in the European Union. *Sozial-und Präventivmedizin, 49*(5), 310-317.

Rütten, A., & Abu-Omar, K. (2004b). Prevalence of physical activity in the European Union. *Sozial-und Präventivmedizin/Social and Preventive Medicine, 49*(4), 281-289.

Rütten, A., Frahsa, A., & Abu-Omar, K. (2010). Zur Entwicklung von politischen und infrastrukturellen Ansätzen in der Gesundheitsförderung durch Bewegung. Eine internationale Analyse. [The development of political and infrastructural approaches to health promotion through movement. An international analysis]. *Spectrum der Sportwissenschaften, 22*(2), 18-31.

Rütten, A., Lüschen, G., von Lengerke, T., Abel, T., Kannas, L., Rodriguez Diaz, J. A., . . . van der Zee, J. (2003). Determinants of health policy impact: Comparative results of a European policymaker study. *Social and Preventive Medicine, 48*(6), 379-391.

Rütten, A., Ziemainz, H., Schena, F., Stahl, T., Stiggelbout, M., Auweele, Y. V., . . . Welshman, J. (2003). Using different physical activity measurements in eight European countries. Results of the European Physical Activity Surveillance System (EUPASS) time series survey. *Public health nutrition, 6*(4), 371-376.

Sadoghi, P., von Keudell, A., & Vavken, P. (2012). Effectiveness of anterior cruciate ligament injury prevention training programs. *J Bone Joint Surg Am, 94*(9), 769-776. doi: 10.2106/jbjs.k.00467

Salisbury, J. (1955). *The Metalogicon.* (D. D. McGarry, Trans.). Berkeley: University of California Press.

Sallis, J. F., Bauman, A., & Pratt, M. (1998). Environmental and policy interventions to promote physical activity. *American journal of preventive medicine, 15*(4), 379-397.

Sallis, J. F., & McKenzie, T. L. (1991). Physical education's role in public health. *Res Q Exerc Sport, 62*(2), 124.

Sallis, J. F., McKenzie, T. L., Beets, M. W., Beighle, A., Erwin, H., & Lee, S. (2012). Physical education's role in public health: Steps forward and backward over 20 years and hope for the future. *Res Q Exerc Sport, 83*(2), 125-135.

Sartori, G. (1970). Concept misformation in comparative politics. *The American Political Science Review, 64*(4), 1033-1053.

Schafer, W. E. (1969). Participation in Interscholastic Athletics and Delinquency: A Preliminary Study. *Social Problems, 17*(1), 40-47. doi: 10.2307/799891

Scharpf, F. W. (2000). Economic changes, vulnerabilities, and institutional capabilities. In F. W. Scharpf & V. A. Schmidt (Eds.), *Welfare and work in the open economy* (Vol. 1, pp. 21-124). New York: Oxford University Press.

Schimank, U. (1988). Die Entwicklung des Sports zum gesellschaftlichen Teilsystem. [The Development of Sport as a Social System]. In R. Mayntz (Ed.), *Differenzierung und Verselbständigung: Zur Entwicklung gesellschaftlicher Teilsysteme* (pp. 181-232). Frankfurt am Main: Campus.

Schimank, U. (2000). Gesellschaftliche Integrationsprobleme im Spiegel soziologischer Gegenwartsdiagnosen. [Social integration problems in the mirror of sociological diagnoses of the present]. *Berliner Journal für Soziologie, 10*(4), 449-469. doi: 10.1007/bf03204366

Schimank, U. (2001). Die gesellschaftliche Entbehrlichkeit des Spitzensports und das Dopingproblem. [The social dispensability of elite sport and the problem of doping]. In H. Digel (Ed.), *Spitzensport – Chancen und Probleme* (pp. 12-25). Schorndorf: Hofmann.

Schimank, U. (2005). The autonomy of modern sport: Dangerous and endangered. *European Journal for Sport and Society, 2*(1), 25-33.

Schimank, U. (2008). Sport im Prozess gesellschaftlicher Differenzierung. [Sports in the Process of Social Differentiation]. In K. Weis & A. Abraham (Eds.), *Handbuch Sportsoziologie* (pp. 68-74). Schorndorf: Hofmann.

Schlicht, W. (1994). *Sport und Primärprävention.* [Sport and primary prevention]. Göttingen: Hogrefe.

Schlicht, W. (1995a). Gesundheitsverhalten und Bewegung : Grundlagen, Konzepte und empirische Befunde. [Health and exercise behavior: Foundations, concepts and empirical findings]. In W. Schlicht & P. Schwenkmezger (Eds.), *Gesundheitsverhalten und Bewegung : Grundlagen, Konzepte und empirische Befunde* (pp. 1-17). Schorndorf: Hofmann.

Schlicht, W. (1995b). *Wohlbefinden und Gesundheit durch Sport.* [Wellbeing and health through sport]. Schorndorf: Hofmann.

Schlicht, W., & Brand, R. (2007). *Körperliche Aktivität, Sport und Gesundheit : eine interdisziplinäre Einführung.* [Physical Activity, Sport and Health: An interdisciplinary introduction]. Weinheim: Juventa.

Schlicht, W., & Strauß, B. (2003). *Sozialpsychologie des Sports.* [Social psychology of sport]. Göttingen: Hogrefe.

Schmid, J., Amos, K., Schrader, J., & Thiel, A. (Eds.). (2011). *Welten der Bildung? Vergleichende Analysen von Bildungspolitik und Bildungssystemen.* [Worlds of education? Comparative analysis of educational policies and systems]. Baden-Baden: Nomos.

Schneider, C. H. (2009). *Legitimacy and global governance in managing global public health.* (PhD), Eberhard-Karls-Universität Tübingen, Tübingen. Retrieved from http://tobias-lib.uni-tuebingen.de/volltexte/2010/4526/pdf/HuckelSchneiderTobiasLib.pdf

Schneider, V. (1990). Gesundheit – Was ist das heute. [Health - What is it today?]. *Friedrich-Jahresheft, 8*, 8–9.

Schoenborn, C. A. (2004). Marital status and health, United States 1999-2002. *Advance Data from Vital and Health Statistics, 365*, 1-32.

Schulze, B. (2005). *Sportarten als soziale Systeme : Ansätze einer Systemtheorie der Sportarten am Beispiel des Fußballs.* [Sport disciplines as social systems: towards a systems theory of sport disciplines using the example of football]. Münster: Waxmann.

Seedhouse, D. (1986). *Health: The foundations for achievement.* Chichester: John Wiley & Sons Inc.

Seidl, D., & Schoeneborn, D. (2010). Niklas Luhmann's autopoietic theory of organisations: Contributions, limitations, and future prospects. *University of Zurich, Institute of Organization and Administrative Science*. Retrieved from http://papers.ssrn.com/sol3/papers.cfm?abstract_id=1552847#

Seven, A. (2008). *Zwischen Funktion und Leistung: zur systemtheoretischen Kritik des Sportbegriffs.* [Between function and performance: a system theoretical critique of the concept of sport]. Saarbrücken: Müller.

Sherrington, C., Tiedemann, A., Fairhall, N., Close, J. C., & Lord, S. R. (2011). Exercise to prevent falls in older adults: an updated meta-analysis and best practice recommendations. *N S W Public Health Bull, 22*(3-4), 78-83. doi: 10.1071/nb10056

Siddiqi, J. (1995). *World health and world politics: the World Health Organization and the UN system.* Columbia: University of South Carolina Press.

Siegrist, J. (2005). *Medizinische Soziologie.* [Sociology of medicine] (6th ed.). München: Elsevier, Urban & Fischer Verlag.

Silk, M. L., & Andrews, D. L. (2006). The fittest city in America. *Journal of Sport & Social Issues, 30*(3), 315-327.

Sjöström, M., Oja, P., Hagströmer, M., Smith, B. J., & Bauman, A. (2006). Health-enhancing physical activity across European Union countries: the Eurobarometer study. *Journal of Public Health, 14*(5), 291-300. doi: 10.1007/s10389-006-0031-y

Skolbekken, J.-A. (2008). Unlimited medicalization? Risk and the pathologization of normality. In A. R. Petersen & I. Wilkinson (Eds.), *Health, risk and vulnerability* (pp. 16-29). New York: Taylor & Francis.

Skrabanek, P. (1994). *The Death of Humane Medicine and the Rise of Coercive Healthism.* London: Crowley Esmonde Ltd.

Smith, A., & Jacobson, B. (1988). *The nation's health: A strategy for the 1990s.* London: King Edward's Hospital Fund.

Snook, E. M., & Motl, R. W. (2009). Effect of exercise training on walking mobility in multiple sclerosis: a meta-analysis. *Neurorehabil Neural Repair, 23*(2), 108-116. doi: 10.1177/1545968308320641

Spencer-Brown, G. (1979). *Laws of form.* New York: Dutton.

Sridhar, D., & Gostin, L. (2009). Introduction. *Global health governance, 3*(1), 1-4. Retrieved from http://www.ghgj.org/Sridhar%20and%20Gostin_Introduction.pdf

Ståhl, T., Nutbeam, D., Kannas, L., & Rütten, A. (2002). The importance of policy orientation and environment on physical activity participation - A comparative analysis between Eastern Germany, Western Germany and Finland. *HEALTH PROMOTION INTERNATIONAL, 17*(3), 235-346.

Stamatakis, E. (2006). Obesity, eating and physical activity. In M. Bajekal, V. Osborne, M. Yar & H. Meltzer (Eds.), *Focus on health* (pp. 47–61). London: Palgrave Macmillan.

Steinkamp, E. (1983). *Was ist eigentlich Sport? Ein Konzept zu seinem Verständnis.* [What is sport? An approach to its understanding]: Wuppertal: Hans Putty.

Stichweh, R. (1990). Sport-Ausdifferenzierung, Funktion, Code. [Sport Differentiation, Function, Code]. *Sportwissenschaft, 20*(4), 373-389.

Strasser, B., Siebert, U., & Schobersberger, W. (2010). Resistance training in the treatment of the metabolic syndrome: a systematic review and meta-analysis of the effect of resistance training on metabolic clustering in patients with abnormal glucose metabolism. *Sports Medicine, 40*(5), 397-415. doi: 10.2165/11531380-000000000-00000

Stygermeer, M. (1999). *Der Sport und seine Ethik : zur Grundlegung einer Dogmatik des Sports.* [The sport and its ethics: The foundation of a doctrine of sport]. Berlin: TENEA.

Suits, B. (2007). The elements of sport. In W. J. Morgan (Ed.), *Ethics in sport* (2 ed., pp. 9-19). Champaign; IL: Human Kinetics.

Tacke, V. (2000). Netzwerk und Adresse. [Network and address]. *Soziale Systeme : Zeitschrift für soziologische Theorie, 6*(2), 291-320.

Tashakkori, A., & Creswell, J. W. (2007). Editorial: The new era of mixed methods. *Journal of Mixed Methods Research, 1*(1), 3.

Thiel, A. (1997). *Steuerung im organisierten Sport : Ansätze und Perspektiven.* [Control in organized sport: Approaches and perspectives]. Stuttgart: Naglschmid.

Thiel, A. (2003). *Soziale Konflikte.* [Social Conflicts]. Bielefeld: Transcript.

Thiel, A., Alizadeh, M., Giel, K., & Zipfel, S. (2008). Stigmatisierung von adipösen Kindern und Jugendlichen durch ihre Altersgenossen. [Stigmatization of obese children and adolescents by their peers]. *Psychotherapy, psychosomatic medicine, medical psychology, 58* (12), 462-270.

Thiel, A., & Braun, S. (2009). Steuerung im Sportsystem. [Steering in the sport system]. In E. Balz & D. Kuhlmann (Eds.), *Sportentwicklung: Grundlagen und Facetten* (Vol. 21, pp. 77 - 88). Aachen: Meyer & Meyer.

Thiel, A., & Cachay, K. (2004). *Vom Sportstudium zum Beruf. Eine Absolventenstudie zum Bielefelder Diplomstudiengang "Prävention/Rehabilitation".* [From Sport Student to Professional in Sport. A Survey on the Graduates of Bielefeld's Diploma Course "Prevention / Rehabilitation".]. Hohengehren: Schneider Verlag.

Thiel, A., & Meier, H. (2004). Überleben durch Abwehr–Zur Lernfähigkeit des Sportvereins. [Surviving through defense. On the learning skills of sport clubs]. *Sport und Gesellschaft, 1*(2), 103-124.

Thiel, A., Seiberth, K., & Mayer, J. (2013). *Sportsoziologie. Ein Lehrbuch in 13 Lektionen.* [Sociology of Sport. A Textbook in 13 Lessons]. Aachen: Meyer & Meyer.

Thomas, C., & Weber, M. (2004). The politics of global health governance: Whatever happened to "Health for All by the Year 2000?". *Global Governance, 10* (2), 187-205.

Timpka, T., & Lindqvist, K. (2001). Evidence based prevention of acute injuries during physical exercise in a WHO safe community. *British Journal of Sports Medicine, 35*(1), 20-27.

Tokarski, W., & Steinbach, D. (2001). *Spuren - Sportpolitik und Sportstrukturen in der Europäischen Union.* [Traces - Sport policy and sport structures in the European Union]. Aachen: Meyer und Meyer.

Trost, S. G., & van der Mars, H. (2010). Why we should not cut physical activity education. *Educational Leadership, 67*(4), 60-65.

Trudeau, F., Laurencelle, L., Tremblay, J., Rajic, M., & Shephard, R. (1999). Daily primary school physical education: effects on physical activity during adult life. *Medicine and science in sports and exercise, 31*(1), 111-117.

Unknown. (1872). De excusacione in extremis non habenda. In H. Oesterley (Ed.), *Gesta Romanorum* (pp. 378-380). Berlin: Weidmannsche Buchandlung.

Üstün, B., & Jakob, R. (2005). Re-defining 'Health'. *Bulletin of the World Health Organization, 83*. Retrieved from http://cdrwww.who.int/bulletin/bulletin_board/83/ustun11051/en/

van Poppel, M. N. M., Chinapaw, M. J. M., Mokkink, L. B., van Mechelen, W., & Terwee, C. B. (2010). Physical activity questionnaires for adults: a systematic review of measurement properties. *Sports Medicine, 40*(7), 565-600.

Vansteenkiste, M., & Sheldon, K. M. (2006). There's nothing more practical than a good theory: Integrating motivational interviewing and self-determination theory. *British Journal of Clinical Psychology, 45*(1), 63-82. doi: 10.1348/014466505x34192

Varela, F. J. (1997). Autopoiese, strukturelle Kopplung und Therapie. Fragen an Francisco Varela. [Autopoiesis, structural coupling and therapy]. In F. B. Simon (Ed.), *Lebende Systeme: Wirklichkeitskonstruktionen in der systemischen Therapie* (pp. 148-164). Frankfurt am Main: Suhrkamp.

Varela, F. J. (1999). *Ethical know-how.* [Un know-how per l'etica] (1 ed.). Stanford: Stanford University Press.

Vogd, W. (2005a). Medizinsystem und Gesundheitswissenschaften – Rekonstruktion einer schwierigen Beziehung. [Medicine System and Health Sciences - Reconstruction of a Difficult Relationship]. *Soziale Systeme, 11*(2), 236-270.

Vogd, W. (2005b). *Systemtheorie und rekonstruktive Sozialforschung : eine empirische Versöhnung unterschiedlicher theoretischer Perspektiven.* [Systems theory and reconstructive social research:Aan empirical reconciliation of different theoretical perspectives]. Opladen: Budrich.

Vogd, W. (2007). Empirie oder Theorie? Systemtheoretische Forschung jenseits einer vermeintlichen Alternative. [Empirical or theoretical? System theoretical research beyond a putative alternative]. *Soziale Welt, 58*(3), 295-321.

Von Foerster, H. (1993). *Wissen und Gewissen.* [Knowledge and belief] (1 ed.). Frankfurt am Main: Suhrkamp.

Vuillemin, A., Boini, S., Bertrais, S., Tessier, S., Oppert, J. M., Hercberg, S., . . . Briançon, S. (2005). Leisure time physical activity and health-related quality of life. *Prev Med, 41*(2), 562-569.

Waddington, I. (1996). The Development of Sports Medicine. *Sociology of Sport Journal, 13*, 176-196.

Waddington, I., Malcolm, D., & Green, K. (1997). Sport, health and physical education: A reconsideration. *European Physical Education Review, 3*(2), 165-182.

Wagner, P., Singer, R., Woll, A., Tittlbach, S., & Bös, K. (2004). Der Zusammenhang von habitueller körperlicher Aktivität und Gesundheit. [The relationship between habitual physical activity and health]. *Zeitschrift für Gesundheitspsychologie, 12*(4), 139-147.

Waller, H. (2006). *Gesundheitswissenschaft: Eine Einführung in Grundlagen und Praxis.* [Health science: An introduction to principles and practice] (4th ed.). Stuttgart: Kohlhammer.

Wang, C., Bannuru, R., Ramel, J., Kupelnick, B., Scott, T., & Schmid, C. H. (2010). Tai Chi on psychological well-being: systematic review and meta-analysis. *BMC Complement Altern Med, 10*, 23. doi: 10.1186/1472-6882-10-23

Weber, M. (1978). The foundations of social theory. (E. Matthews, Trans.). In W. G. Runciman (Ed.), *Weber: Selections in translation* (pp. 1-64). Cambridge: Cambridge University Press.

Weber, R. P. (1983). Measurement models for content analysis. *Quality and Quantity, 17*(2), 127-149. doi: 10.1007/BF00143616

Weiss, O. (2000). *Sport und Gesundheit: Die Auswirkung des Sports auf die Gesundheit – eine sozioökonomische Analyse.* Wien: Bundesministerium für Soziale Sicherheit und Generationen

Wendel-Vos, G., Schuit, A., Tijhuis, M., & Kromhout, D. (2004). Leisure time physical activity and health-related quality of life: cross-sectional and longitudinal associations. *Quality of Life Research, 13*(3), 667-677.

Westle, B. (Ed.). (2009). *Methoden der Politikwissenschaft.* [Methodology of politics]. (1st ed.). Baden-Baden: Nomos.

Wheatley, E. E. (2005). Disciplining bodies at risk: Cardiac rehabilitation and the medicalization of fitness. *Journal of Sport & Social Issues, 29*(2), 198-221.

White, M. D., & Marsh, E. E. (2006). Content analysis: A flexible methodology. *Library Trends, 55*(1), 22-45.

WHO. (1946). Constitution of the World Health Organization. *Official Records of the WHO, 2*, 16-28.

WHO. (1978). *Declaration of Alma Ata.* Paper presented at the International Conference on Primary Health Care, Alma-Ata.

WHO. (1986). *Ottawa Charter for Health Promotion.* Geneva: WHO Retrieved from http://www.who.int/healthpromotion/conferences/previous/ottawa/en/index.html

WHO. (1997). *Jakarta Declaration on Leading Health Promotion into the 21st Century.* Paper presented at the 4th International Conference on Health Promotion, Jakarta.

WHO. (2000). *Prevention and control of noncommunicable diseases.* Paper presented at the WHA53.17, Geneva.

WHO. (2002). *"Move for Health".* Paper presented at the World Health Day 2002, Copenhagen.

WHO. (2004). Global Strategy on Diet, Physical Activity and Health. *WHA57.17.*

WHO. (2006). Addressing the Socioeconomic Determinants of Healthy Eating Habits and Physical Activity Levels Among Adolescents. In A. Mathieson & T. Koller (Eds.), *WHO/HBSC Forum 2006.* Geneva: WHO.

WHO. (2010). *Global recommendations on physical activity for health.* Geneva: WHO

WHO. (2011a). 2002: Move for Health. Retrieved 31.01.2014. Retrieved from http://www.who.int/moveforhealth/about/en/index.html

WHO. (2011b). Governance. Retrieved 2011.02.15. Retrieved from http://www.who.int/governance/en/index.html

WHO. (2011c). Jakarta Statement on Active Living. Retrieved 2011.02.15. Retrieved from http://www.who.int/healthpromotion/conferences/previous/jakarta/statements/active_living/en/

WHO. (2011d). Process for developing the Global Strategy. Retrieved 2011.02.15. Retrieved from http://www.who.int/dietphysicalactivity/strategy/en/index.html

WHO. (2011e). School and Youth Health. Retrieved 2011.02.15. Retrieved from http://www.who.int/school_youth_health/gshi/hps/en/index.html

WHO. (2011f). WHO European database on nutrition, obesity and physical activity (NOPA). Retrieved 2013.03.15. Retrieved from http://data.euro.who.int/nopa/

WHO. (2012). Countries. Retrieved 2012.11.09. Retrieved from http://www.who.int/countries/en/index.html

WHO. (2013). International inventory of documents on physical activity promotion. Retrieved 2013.03.15. Retrieved from http://data.euro.who.int/PhysicalActivity/

Wiesenthal, H. (2006). *Gesellschaftssteuerung und gesellschaftliche Selbststeuerung : eine Einführung.* [Social control and social self-control: An introduction]. Wiesbaden: VS Verlag.

Wikipedia. (2011). Physical Activity. Retrieved 2013.03.05. Retrieved from http://en.wikipedia.org/wiki/Physical_activity

Willis, E. (1996). *The sociological quest: An introduction to the study of social life.* New Jersey: Rutgers University Press.

Willke, H. (1990). Political intervention - Operetional precondition for generalized political exchange. In B. Marin (Ed.), *Governance and Generalized Exchange. Self-Organizing Policy Networks in Action* (pp. 235-254). Frankfurt/New York: Campus Verlag.

Willke, H. (1994). Staat und Gesellschaft. [State and society]. In K. Damman, D. Gunov & P. Japp (Eds.), *Die Verwaltung des politischen Systems. Neuere systemtheoretische Zugriffe auf ein altes Thema* (pp. 13-26). Opladen: Westdeutscher Verlag.

Willke, H. (2001a). *Atopia : Studien zur atopischen Gesellschaft.* [Atopia: Studies on atopic society] (1 ed.). Frankfurt am Main: Suhrkamp.

Willke, H. (2001b). *Systemtheorie : Steuerungstheorie, Grundzüge einer Theorie der Steuerung komplexer Sozialsysteme.* [Systems Theory: Control Theory, Basic Principles of a Theory of Steering Complex Social Systems] (3rd ed.). Stuttgart: Lucius & Lucius.

Willke, H. (2005). *Systemtheorie : Interventionstheorie, Grundzüge einer Theorie der Intervention in komplexe Systeme.* [Systems theory: Intervention theory, basic principles of a theory of intervention in complex systems] (4th ed.). Stuttgart: Lucius & Lucius.

Willke, H. (2006a). *Global Governance.* Bielefeld: Transcript.

Willke, H. (2006b). *Systemtheorie : Grundlagen : eine Einführung in die Grundprobleme der Theorie sozialer Systeme.* [Systems theory: Foundations: An introduction to the basic problems of the theory of social systems] (7th ed.). Stuttgart: Lucius & Lucius.

Willke, H. (2007a). Politische Strukturbildung der Weltgesellschaft. Symbolordnung und Eigenlogik lateraler Weltsysteme. [Political structure formation of world society. Symbology and internal logic of lateral world systems]. In M. Albert & R. Stichweh (Eds.), *Weltstaat und Weltstaatlichkeit* (pp. 133-156). Wiesbaden: VS Verlag.

Willke, H. (2007b). *Smart Governance: Governing the Global Knowledge Society.* Frankfurt: Campus.

Witte, E. (1973). *Organisation für Innovationsentscheidungen: Das Promotoren-Modell.* [Organisation for innovative decisions: The promoters model]. Göttingen: Schwartz & Co.

Woll, A., & Bös, K. (2004). Wirkungen von Gesundheitssport. [Effects of health sport]. *B & G Bewegungstherapie und Gesundheitssport, 20*(3), 97-106.

Woll, A., Tittlbach, S., Bös, K., & Opper, E. (2003). FINGER: Finnisch-deutsche Längsschnittstudie zum Zusammenhang von sportlicher Aktivität, Fitness und Gesundheit im kommunalen Rahmen. [FINGER: Finnish-German longitudinal study on the relationship between physical activity, fitness and health in the local context.]. In K. Eisfeld (Ed.), *Gesund und bewegt im Alter. Interdisziplinäre Ansätze für eine Community Medicine* (pp. 38-57). Butzbach-Griedel: Afra-Verlag.

Yach, D., Hawkes, C., Gould, L. C., & Hofman, K. J. (2004). The global Burden of Chronic Diseases: Overcoming Impediments to Prevention and Control. *Journal of the American Medical Association, 291*(21), 2616-2622. doi: 10.1001/jama.291.21.2616

Yach, D., Wipfli, H., Hammond, R., & Glantz, S. (2007). Globalization and tobacco. *Globalization and health, 48*, 39-67.

Zainuldin, R., Mackey, M. G., & Alison, J. A. (2011). Optimal intensity and type of leg exercise training for people with chronic obstructive pulmonary disease. *Cochrane Database Syst Rev*(11), CD008008. doi: 10.1002/14651858.CD008008.pub2

Zheng, H., Ehrlich, F., & Amin, J. (2010). Economic evaluation of the direct healthcare cost savings resulting from the use of walking interventions to prevent coronary heart disease in

Australia. *Int J Health Care Finance Econ, 10*(2), 187-201. doi: 10.1007/s10754-009-9074-2

Zheng, H., Orsini, N., Amin, J., Wolk, A., Nguyen, V. T., & Ehrlich, F. (2009). Quantifying the dose-response of walking in reducing coronary heart disease risk: meta-analysis. *Eur J Epidemiol, 24*(4), 181-192. doi: 10.1007/s10654-009-9328-9

Zola, I. K. (1983). *Socio-Medical Inquiries*. Philadelphia: Temple University Press.

Zola, I. K. (1991). Bringing our Bodies and Ourselves Back in: Reflections on a Past, Present, and Future "Medical Sociology". *Journal of Health and Social Behavior, 32*(1), 1-16.

Druck: KN Digital Printforce GmbH · Schockenriedstraße 37 · 70565 Stuttgart